The
Christian
Dad's

ANSWER BOOK

The
Christian
Dad's
ANSWER BOOK

Mike Yorkey

Cook Communications

Faith Parenting is an imprint of
Cook Communications Ministries, Colorado Springs, Colorado 80918
Cook Communications, Paris, Ontario
Kingsway Communications, Eastbourne, England

Editors: Jerry Yamamoto, Barbara Williams
Designer: Bill Gray
Cover Photo: Image Bank

First paperback edition © 2000
Paperback ISBN: 0-78143-364-9

CONTENTS

4—DADS AND THEIR WIVES

5—DADS AND THEIR GOD

6—DADS AND THEIR FINANCES

9—DADS AND DIFFICULT PROBLEMS

FOREWORD

by Steven Curtis Chapman

I'm not looking for sympathy, but life can get pretty hectic when you're on tour.

As a Christian music artist, I'm asked to meet a lot of people, take innumerable interview requests, and make umpteen appearances at music stores. But let me tell you about one particularly hectic day not long ago.

The morning after a concert date in Wichita, Kansas, I hopped on a plane and flew to Denver, where a car was waiting to drive me seventy-five miles south to Colorado Springs. I had an appointment with Dr. James Dobson, president of the Focus on the Family ministry, and his wife, Shirley.

I spent an enjoyable two hours conversing with the Dobsons, and then I had to scoot back to Denver for a sound check at McNichol's Arena. It was all I could do to grab a bite to eat before a "Meet and Greet" session one hour ahead of the concert.

One of the persons I recognized that evening was Mike Yorkey. Mike is the editor of *Focus on the Family* magazine, and he's interviewed me several times over the years. Mike understands what busy families—and dads—are up against these days, and I've appreciated his work.

That's why the book you're holding, *The Christian Dad's Answer Book*, will be very helpful for you. The seventy-two chapters are presented in a highly readable format that will keep you turning pages. You should have no problem reading one or two chapters at the beginning of the day or just before turning the lights out.

I'm proud to say that I'm even mentioned in the book. You'll find me in Section 8—Dads and Their World—in a chapter by Amy Stephens called "A Culture That's In Our Face." (It's the part where Amy talks about plugging your teenagers into Christian music.)

But that's not why you should read this book. Instead, you should look at *The Christian Dad's Answer Book* as a resource you can pick up time and time again.

INTRODUCTION

A friend of mine, David Smallbone, called one day and said I had to read the interview of evangelist Billy Graham in the political magazine *George*, published by John F. Kennedy, Jr., the slain President's son.

The question-and-answer session between JFK, Jr., and Mr. Graham was engaging and thoughtful. The evangelist, who has preached to more individuals—210 million in person and billions more on TV—than anyone in history, talked about being scared each time he mounted the platform. Why? Because Billy Graham knew that tens of thousands of people were waiting to hear him proclaim that their only hope was in Jesus Christ, and the way they received that message had eternal ramifications.

The long interview ended with a question you'd expect to be asked of a seventy-eight-year-old man battling Parkinson's disease and knowing that his time on earth could be short.

"Do you have any regrets?" asked Kennedy. "Do you wish that you had done something differently?"

I can imagine Billy Graham looking off into the distance and thinking a minute before answering. But his response stunned me.

"I wish I'd watched less television," said the most famous evangelist of the twentieth century.

Watched less television? When did Billy Graham even have time to flip on the tube?

His answer got me to thinking about how much television I watch, and of the times I'd been glued to Wimbledon or the U.S. Open (tennis is my passion) or even the Masters (I'm warming up to golf).

What I think Billy Graham was saying was that he regretted letting the TV take precious hours—time that could never be regained—away from his family life.

That's welcome advice I will take to heart, and I hope you will too. In fact, *The Christian Dad's Answer Book* is filled with similar wisdom. I've divided this book into nine different topical areas. Please note that the questions are designed to move you along in a breezy, fast-paced style that works for busy dads.

You're going to find a lot of practical information and solid encouragement in the pages of *The Christian Dad's Answer Book*. So turn off that TV and start reading!

1

Dads and Their Kids

Four Things Every Father Should Know

■ When I'm driving along the freeway, my thoughts often turn to my three children, all under the age of fourteen. I wonder if I'm doing the right job as a father. I wonder if I have the kids traveling the right path. What's some good, simple parenting advice that I can keep coming back to time and time again?

We're not going to mince any words at the start of this book: There are two things you have to give your children in order for them to make it, and two things your children will have a hard time forgiving you for. Those may seem like bold statements, but John Croyle, the founder of Big Oak Ranch (a Christian home in Alabama for abused, orphaned, and neglected children), has worked with more than 1,300 children since 1974. He says some people in this world may be able to take these concepts apart, but he assures us they are true.

■ What are the four concepts?

If you want your children to make it, you have to let them know that:

1. You love them unconditionally, no matter what.
2. You believe in them, no matter what. (Notice we didn't say *believe* them, but believe *in* them. There's a difference.)

As for the two things your children will have a hard time forgiving you for, they are:

1. Not disciplining them—or waiting too late to discipline them.
2. Not trying.

■ Not trying? What do you mean by that?

That means giving up on them. But let's talk about the first item—unconditional love. Here's a story that illustrates this point well.

One day, a father took his two elementary school-age children for a ride in a pontoon boat. They were traveling down the river when suddenly the motor stopped. When the father looked behind him, he noticed something familiar about the red sweater tangled up in the propeller. Then his young son yelled, "Missy fell in!"

In horror, the father saw his little girl entwined in the propeller of the boat. She was submerged just beneath the surface of the water, looking straight into the eyes of her father and holding her breath.

He jumped into the water and tried to pull the motor up, but the heavy engine wouldn't budge. Time was running out. Desperately, the father filled his own lungs with air and dipped below the surface, blowing air into his daughter's lungs.

After giving her air three times, the father took a filet knife from his shocked son's hand. He quickly cut the red sweater from the propeller and lifted his daughter into the boat. Although she had survived, her deep cuts and bruises needed medical attention. So they rushed her to the hospital.

When the crisis was over, the doctors and nurses asked the girl,

"How come you didn't panic?"

"Well, we've been raised on the river, and my dad always taught us that if you panic, you die. Besides, I knew my daddy would come and get me."

Do your children know beyond the shadow of a doubt that you would come and get them, no matter what? If your son was busted in a drug raid, would you go and get him? If your daughter got caught being a prostitute, would you get your little girl? If your son was drunk on skid row, would you disown him?

■ **No, I wouldn't, but shouldn't my children face the consequences of their actions?**

Of course, they should, but you should still believe in them and love them unconditionally. Many of the abused children at the Big Oak Ranch come from homes where they know without a shadow of a doubt their dads and moms wouldn't come to get them. The Bible says that children are a blessing from the Lord. Do your children know that they are blessings, or do they think they are burdens—financially and emotionally?

■ **I know my children are blessings, and I try to be a good father. What I can't understand is reading in the newspaper about parents who lock up their children in closets or treat them no better than dogs. How does this stuff really happen?**

Who can read the minds of evil people, but unfortunately abuse happens in this day and age. A lot of people think that children will never forgive their parents for abusing them, but John Croyle says he had one little boy whose mother dipped his legs in hot grease and burned him horribly. During the seven years the little boy lived at Big Oak Ranch, however, all he could talk about was how much he loved his momma.

Remember: Children *want* to love their parents. Children want discipline from their parents. John had one small boy, Michael, who stood in front of him one day and stomped on his flowers.

"Michael, if you stomp on those flowers one more time, I'm going to spank you," John warned.

Michael looked up at John—he must have seemed like a giant to him because John's six-feet-six—and looked back down at the flower bed. Then he raised his foot and smashed the flowers into the ground.

"Okay, come on inside," John said. He took a Ping-Pong paddle and gave him three licks, but when he got through, Michael wasn't crying.

"You done?" he asked.

"Yeah, but why did you deliberately stomp on those flowers?"

"Because I didn't think you'd spank me."

"Really?"

The answer was in Michael's eyes. They were saying, *No one's loved me enough to discipline me and keep their word.*

■ But aren't some parents afraid to discipline because they fear their children won't love them afterward?

Yes, and it's like when you go into a grocery store, and you hear a mother say, "Josh, if you touch that cereal box again, I'm going to punish you." When the youngster continues to pull cereal boxes off the shelves, the mom threatens him—again and again. You feel like saying, "Hey, lady, will you just go ahead and do it?"

You see, a broken promise is a lie to a child, and if you promise him that you're going to do something, he'll test you to see if you're going to keep your word.

■ Why will children have such a hard time forgiving parents for not trying?

That's a great question. John Croyle has known fathers who've had fourteen-year-old rebels, and they've thrown up their hands and said, "I don't know what to do."

And when these children arrive at the Big Oak Ranch, some of them ask, "Why did my parents give up? I know I was being a real jerk, but did they have to get rid of me?"

If you're in a situation where you and your spouse are considering divorce or separation (and every child has said that he blames himself for the breakup), know that sooner or later your child is going to say, "You didn't try. You didn't care enough about me to work through your problems."

At Big Oak Ranch, they've had children dumped in their driveway in the middle of the night. These kids are looking for an explanation. "Well, your mother thought it would be best if you live with us," John will say.

■ **I would never abandon my child in that way. Are you kidding?**

But you can emotionally abandon your child. One of the girls at Big Oak Ranch hates golf because her dad loved hitting balls at the driving range more than he loved her. The average father spends about four minutes a week in conversation with a child, and if you divide that time in half, figuring the child is saying something, most dads are using their time to lecture and not to listen. That's a killer.

When John played football at the University of Alabama, the star running back was Johnny Musso. After Johnny's playing days were over, he had a big party at his house with a lot of guests. During the middle of the party, Johnny's little son came down the stairs, calling for his dad. Johnny excused himself, and right there in the middle of the living room, he knelt down in front of his little boy and asked, "What is it, buddy?"

What impressed the guests was that Johnny was six inches from his son's face, and it didn't matter that his house was filled with sports celebrities—his

> **QUESTIONS TO ASK**
>
> Is your parenting life in balance? If you're not sure, ask yourself:
> ► Who taught my son how to walk?
> ► Who taught my daughter how to tie her shoes?
> ► Who taught my son how to pitch?
> ► Who took my daughter to buy her first tennis racket?
> ► Who taught my son how to keep his eye on the ball when he's swinging the bat?
> ► Who taught my daughter that she's a princess?
> ► Who taught my son how to make pancakes?
> ► Who taught my daughter how to pray?
> ► Who taught my son how to drive a hammer and nail?
> ► Who taught my daughter how to drive?
> ► Who taught my son how to have a daily devotion?

boy needed to talk to him. Seeing that can remind us to be good listeners.

Children *want* to be listened to. Children want structure and order. The Big Oak Ranch has had children go there who are *totally* undisciplined. They think God has a last name and that church is a building you drive by. On the other hand, they've received children from half-million dollar homes who would give anything in the world for Daddy to say, "Honey, I want you in at 10 P.M." They were never given a curfew.

■ Are we talking about "tough love" here?

It's more than that. When children arrive at the Big Oak Ranch, John tells them four things:

(1) I love you;

(2) I'll never lie to you;

(3) I'll stick with you through thick and thin; and

(4) if you ever do me wrong, I'll get you.

■ That last one sounds pretty harsh.

But what has John given those children with his four statements? He's given them:

(1) emotional support;

(2) honesty;

(3) endurance; and

(4) the knowledge that there are boundaries.

Those are four things abused children desperately want, and so do your children.

This material is adapted from writings by John Croyle, author of Bringing Out the Winner in Your Child *(Cumberland House). If you would like to contact John Croyle about possible speaking engagements or to learn more about Big Oak Ranch, write: Big Oak Ranch, 250 Jake Mintz Rd., Gadsden, AL 35905, or call (205) 892-0773.*

2

"You Decide"

. . . .

■ **How can I handle face-offs and showdowns with my children? There has to be a calmer approach than the one I've been taking.**

Rich Wilkerson, who's one of America's better youth speakers, wrote a book a few years ago with a totally illogical title. It sums up the crazy, contradictory, push-pull job of parenting: *Hold Me While You Let Me Go.*

■ **That's pretty much the story with my two teenagers. Well, which is it? Hold them or let go?**

Every one of us knows that the task of raising kids entails *controlling* them, keeping the lid on, preventing harm, restraining goofiness, running the show, and calling the shots. If we leave children unsupervised, they'll kill themselves within twenty minutes, we think.

That's the *Hold Me . . .* part.

On the other hand, we don't want to do this forever; we want to launch our offspring, over an eighteen-year period, into responsible independence. We want to get them to the point where they are self-controlled, able to run their own show.

That's the . . . *While You Let Me Go* part.

■ **I'm tracking with you. So what's the trick?**

You have to stay current with the adjustments along the way. You've kept a firm hand with your kindergartner—but now, what is a first-grader capable of doing alone? How about a fifth-grader? What can you expect of a teenager?

Each child is a moving project, learning new skills on almost a weekly basis, becoming just a little more competent with every turn of the calendar page. We parents have to keep up or risk a battle every time we say, "No, you're not ready for that yet."

■ **What are some benchmarks for where children should be at a certain age?**

Two Ph.D.s in the area of child development, Gerald D. Alpern of Indiana University and Thomas J. Boll of the University of Virginia, have published a set of touchstones for kids, a definition of "normal," if you will.

Toddlers age two-and-a-half to three ought to be able to work a pair of scissors, for example. A five-year-old should be able to open the refrigerator and come up with an acceptable sandwich. An eight-year-old should have figured out that Santa Claus and the Easter Bunny aren't real. A twelve-year-old should be able to read and understand a front-page newspaper story (not just the sports or fashion section). Drs. Alpern and Boll's standards go on for pages and pages.

As you think about their work, the thought should come to you that in the area of granting permission, most parents *assume a little less maturity than is in fact the case.* In other words, the child is slightly ahead of what we think is "safe." (We like to worry!) And even if we force ourselves to catch up to reality, the son or daughter keeps growing and stretching, so that three months down the road we're behind the curve again.

■ Can you give me an example?

Dean Merrill will never forget the Thanksgiving Day when an older cousin introduced his innocent seventh-grade son, Nathan, to contemporary Christian music at a family gathering. Suddenly—overnight!—Nathan wasn't satisfied with the children's tunes he'd grown up with and even performed in church. Things had to be louder, more rhythmic, more intense.

Dean and his wife, Grace, were irked. How dare this outsider pollute their home and drag their son away from the "cultured" musical taste that the Merrill parents had carefully instilled! (Nathan's cousin is now an upstanding seminary graduate and associate pastor, by the way.)

It took a week of teeth-grinding and late-night debate before they finally admitted that their son was once again growing up. He'd stumbled into one of the Big Four Issues that almost all teenagers use to express their individuality and rattle their parents' cages: Music, Clothing, Hair, and Jargon. (Any one of those is good for a rousing argument almost every day of the week, you've probably noticed.)

Dean and Grace reluctantly decided to judge Nathan's songs by their lyrics rather than their strangeness, and as the teenage years went along, music turned out to be a blessing in their home rather than a curse.

Kids *are* going to grow up on us, like it or not. In fact, they'd *better!* We certainly don't want them frozen in time.

■ What are some ways to let them know that we understand this concept?

By adding the Two Magic Words of Parenting to your vocabulary: "You decide."

■ Really? Just abdicate my God-given role as a father?

Not at all. What you're going to say is something like this:
Guess what, Ross. I'm not going to dictate the outcome this time. I think you can handle this one. You weigh the pros and cons, the dangers

and opportunities, and then YOU make the decision.

Wow! What a surprise for your son. He'll think that Dad isn't a total dictator after all. Amazing.

Not every decision can be handed over to a young person, however. You would never say "You decide" about whether to drop out of school, for example, or whether to drink.

But in hundreds of other matters, where in fact you can live with either option, parents can avoid tumultuous battles and teach responsibility for the future by handing over the power of choice. Granted, your adult wisdom says one option is better than the other, but neither one is disastrous. So why not let the child learn something along the way?

■ **I think I follow what you mean. Can you give me another illustration?**

Let's say you arrive home from a business trip late one Friday afternoon, only to find that your two high school-age daughters are fervently lobbying their mother for permission to go to a birthday party that will run till midnight. While the party would be properly supervised, the problem lays with what follows immediately afterward on Saturday: an all-day music competition, with a crack-of-dawn departure.

"Can we go? Can we go?" they plead. "We'll be fine tomorrow; don't worry about it. We won't be tired at all."

This may be the time that your wife gives you the look that says, *Your turn, big fella. Glad you're home to handle this.*

You hardly may be in the mood to play Solomon after a three-hour plane flight. But giving them the brush-off with an "I dunno. We'll talk in the morning" won't do it, either.

Of course, you could bring down the hammer and deny the Friday night event so as to safeguard Saturday's performance—and take the heat that would surely erupt. But wait a minute. . . . Could the girls comprehend the issue here? You can always give it a try.

"Okay," you announce, "you can go to the party tonight. I'll even drive you and pick you up. But you might want to think about how hard you've worked the past three months getting ready for this competition. Do you want to jeopardize it? How late would you choose to stay?"

"How late *can* we stay?" one of your daughters will ask, putting the onus back on you.

"You tell me," you reply, refusing to take her bait. "If you were on your own, and I were out of the picture, when would you leave the party in order not to be dog-tired for Saturday?"

Don't be surprised if your daughters look at each other, figuring out what to say. One girl may say 9:30. The other may say 10:00. When they do, suppress the urge to smile, but suddenly this won't be a case of what Dad will allow, but rather what is in their own self-interest. They may even decide not to go to the party. Problem solved—and no fight!

■ **I'm not sure this approach would work in my home. Why should it?**

The trendy adult word for this is *empowerment*—giving the steering wheel temporarily to the weaker, younger, less experienced person so he or she can get a feel for making choices and see what causes what.

Ed Bissonnette, a member of the Focus on the Family public affairs department, was formerly associate dean of students at Southern California College, a Christian campus. He says with a smile, "I used to tell kids who got summoned to my office for this or that,

WHAT'S SAFE?

Young people of every age can grow through hearing "You decide." Examples:

Preschool Years

► which of two (preselected) shirts to wear
► which stuffed animal to take to bed
► which breakfast cereal to eat

Elementary Grades

► which game to play with a friend or parent
► whom to invite to a birthday party
► which musical instrument to study

Middle School Years

► which sport (if any) to pursue
► how to decorate their bedrooms
► which Christian music to listen to

High School Years

► what electives to take in school
► what summer job to seek (unless it's dangerous)
► what ministry options to pursue through church or youth group

'You know, we have padded walls around here. We give you a certain amount of latitude so you can bounce around, find out the consequences, and still not get terribly hurt. It's learning time for you. The point is to figure out what behavior works and doesn't work . . . before you get outside in the bigger world, where the walls are made of concrete and brick.' "

If children don't get to make independent decisions until they leave home, the result is likely to be bloody. Far better for them to hear the words "You decide" from a loving and wise dad all along the way.

This article is adapted from writings by Dean Merrill, who has an editorial consulting firm called Colorado Wordmaster based in Colorado Springs, Colorado.

3

From Your Faith
to Theirs

■ One Sunday morning in church, I watched a father struggle to quiet his toddler. The little girl kicked and screamed
when her toy fell under the pew. Hurriedly, the embarrassed
father grabbed the toy, picked up the child, and headed for
the exit. As he stumbled past me, I flashed an understanding
smile. *Boy, have I been there,* I thought.

My toddlers have become teens, and my challenge is not
picking up Cheerios off the church carpet but keeping them
on the right spiritual track. How can I keep them growing
with Jesus?

Many Christian dads agree with those who say spiritual development is the most difficult area in which to parent. We can easily
measure our children's physical growth with a yardstick, judge
their social development by how they relate to others, and evaluate
emotional advances by how they handle disappointments. But
spiritual growth doesn't fit into a neat package, and it's hard to
gauge the extent to which our children are growing with God.

If you are like other dads, you may have used the difficulty of
assessing your children's growth as an excuse for not nurturing
their spiritual lives. Or, if that excuse doesn't fit, maybe you'll

recognize one of these:

► "I'm not a theologian. My child is asking the same questions I'm asking. I can't help him come to terms with issues like, 'Why does God let people suffer?' "

► "I don't know if I can do enough. I wonder how my feeble attempts at passing on the faith can equip my child to deal with life in the twenty-first century."

► "My faith is personal. It's embarrassing to talk about it with my child."

As dads, we play a critical role as spiritual educators in our children's lives. In Matthew 19:14, Jesus tells us to make ourselves approachable to our kids: "Let the little children come to me, and do not hinder them, for the kingdom of heaven belongs to such as these." Each time we let the little children come to us, He will bless our efforts.

■ **Finding a supportive church can sometimes be a problem. We've been church shopping for nearly two years.**

Don't stop going to church no matter how frustrating your search is. Even if the church you're attending isn't the one you plan to join, worshiping with fellow believers and with our children is a responsibility God has given us: "Observe the Sabbath day by keeping it holy, as the Lord your God has commanded you. Six days you shall labor and do all your work, but the seventh day is a Sabbath to the Lord your God" (Deut. 5:12-14).

■ **Yes, but getting everyone ready for church on Sunday morning creates stress on my wife, and I get the brunt of it.**

Preparing on Saturday night for church Sunday morning can help a great deal—setting out cereal boxes, filling the offering envelope, having your children lay out the clothes they plan to wear.

You might even agree on an "order of service" for Sunday-morning bathroom use. Other parents have their children put their Bibles and other belongings in the car the night before. All these things will give you a head start.

Before your family pulls out of the driveway, pray the traveler's prayer from Psalm 121:1-2: "I lift up my eyes to the hills—where does my help come from? My help comes from the Lord, the Maker of heaven and earth." Talking to our Father can become as natural as talking to each other across the kitchen table.

■ **Before the birth of my first child, I visualized our family living out the scene on Sunday School leaflets—everyone sitting around the kitchen table listening attentively to me reading from the Bible. How quickly dreams die.**

When I announced that we would begin regular family devotions, my daughter Christy responded with a four-letter word—"yuck."

I never understood how Christy, at the age of five, had learned devotions would be yucky, but I knew I had to do something. Any ideas?

Relevance is the key to meaningful devotions. Search for everyday events that will motivate your children to talk about their faith experiences.

When they are young, bring up topics like "losing a tooth" and "fear of the dark." When they go to grade school, look for phrases like "being left out of the group on the playground" and "when your teacher yells." When they become teens, you can encourage them to choose their own material.

Here are two other ideas that could work for you:

► **Begin a family prayer journal.** Buy another spiral notebook and pen during a back-to-school sale. Then discuss what will be recorded: blessings, sorrows, troubles, joys. Young children can draw pictures. Leave the notebook open on the kitchen table while dinner is being cooked each night. Occasionally, talk about what's been written, or use the entries as the basis for your mealtime prayers. This is a great way to encourage talking with God and to each other.

► **Buy your child a Bible.** Many stores have occasional sales on Bibles and an array of devotional books. Encourage your children to begin a Bible reading plan, and you might read with them before they go to bed at night.

■ **What if I feel like my efforts to raise spiritually minded kids aren't going so well?**

Keep in mind that your child's spiritual development will not follow a straight line. You will see peaks and valleys as your child alternately accepts and then questions God's love. Don't get discouraged: Just keep plugging away and work on *your* spiritual life too.

By doing this, you will convey to your child that spiritual development is a lifelong process, and your house chooses to participate.

This material is adapted from writings by Dr. Mary Manz Simon, author of How to Parent Your "Tweenager" *(Thomas Nelson Publishers). She lives with her family in Belleville, Illinois. Charles White lives in Topeka, Kansas.*

SOME MINIMUM DAILY REQUIREMENTS

Your child's journey from four to fourteen is very short. Christian parents need to put God into each day during this impressionable time.

The following ideas will help your children hold onto God during the difficult adolescent period:

1. Hang a picture of Christ in each child's bedroom. Children are often quicker to respond to pictures than to words.

2. Teach your child how to pray. By the time a child is five, he should be able to speak one-sentence prayers with a parent. By the time he's six, he should be looking for answers to his prayers. But avoid correcting his prayers. They are between him and God.

3. Bless your children each morning. If you want to see dramatic improvement in your family and young children, try this: Place one hand on your child's shoulder or head and repeat a blessing from Scripture, such as "May the Lord bless you and shine upon you and give you peace" (Num. 6:24-26) or "May God strengthen you with power through his Spirit in your inner being, so that Christ may dwell in your heart through faith" (Eph. 3:16). You can also choose your own words.

4. Take short walks. Get outside to God's world as much as possible. You can identify trees, capture bugs, and look at scenery. Let creation declare the glory of God.

5. Purchase Scripture cards from your Christian bookstore and leave them on the kitchen table. Reading from God's Word as part of the mealtime prayer is a great way to remind the family of God's presence.

6. Display your child's Sunday School lesson. Letting a youngster's efforts die a painful death on the car floor can leave hurt feelings.

Of course, none of these efforts is a guarantee that your son or daughter will know God. But incorporating some of these ideas will be a daily reminder of His presence and love.

—Charles White

4

The Art of the Handoff

. . . .

■ **Our oldest child, Will, just turned ten years old, and while we've talked a little bit about girls and the opposite sex, I want to be sure that he will understand what it means to be a teenager when he reaches adolescence. What can I do about that?**

Bart Starr, quarterback of the Green Bay Packer football dynasty of the sixties, believed that one of his most important responsibilities was the handoff, an aspect of football few fans notice.

What Will needs is for you to hand him the ball. Like Bart Starr, you should determine that Will will never wonder if he is going to get the ball when and where he should.

■ **But how do I accomplish this handoff?**

Dr. James Dobson's book *Preparing for Adolescence* will help you begin this handoff. You should read it cover to cover, and then buy another copy for Will and read along with him.

That's what Fred Stoeker did in Iowa. With some trepidation, he walked into his eleven-year-old son's room one night and handed him *Preparing for Adolescence*, expecting a deep, resigned sigh from

Jasen when he realized that Dad was enacting another "plan."

"Jasen, I know this might feel a little uncomfortable, but you will soon be entering a very interesting period of development," said Fred.

"Oh, yeah?" he responded. "I've heard of that. It's called *perverty*, right?"

Fred suppressed a laugh. "Well, it's something like that, but you're soon going to be experiencing more peer pressure, and you might care more about your friends' opinions than mine for a while. But you're also going to be facing embarrassments and hurts, and I want to prepare you for them."

Fred paused and waited for the dreaded sigh.

"Dad, I really think it's good that we're going to read this book, especially right now," he said. "I've been kind of scared—it's been harder for me to stand up to my friends lately."

■ I see the direction Fred is heading. To get Will the ball, what do I need to do?

The mechanics are simple, and no preparation is necessary. Two or three nights a week, read four to eight pages out loud together. You might try reading on the bedroom floor face-to-face. Facing each other is important, since it ensures you two will be listening to each other.

When Fred Stoeker started their little discussions, he asked personal questions like, "Has anyone made fun of you on the school bus?"

Fred fully expected Jasen to say no since he was so perfect to him. Instead, he responded, "Almost every day. The kids call me hickey face."

Fred was angered, remembering the birthmark on Jasen's right cheek. "When I was your age, kids made fun of my bowlegs, and that hurt," he said.

"I don't really mind, Dad," Jasen said. "We all have things that could be made fun of. I know I'm okay."

■ How did Fred handle the issue of conformity?

When Fred came to a section on conformity, Jasen declared that both he and his father were nonconformists, which Fred found interesting since that wasn't always true of him. To prove it, one night they skipped the reading and headed for the storage room, where Fred found a picture of himself wearing some once-stylish blue-suede shoes. Regardless of fashion trends, blue-suede shoes on size 13 feet never look cool! They spent the next hour laughing at old pictures of Fred trying to look hip—with widely varying degrees of success.

The father and son had two important moments in the conformity section. Fred told Jasen, "If someone I know had conformed one Friday night long ago, neither you nor I would exist today." Jasen's eyes got big as he wondered what was coming next.

When Fred's dad was a teen, four friends pulled into his driveway to pick him up. Getting into the car he noticed some beer in the back seat. So he told his friends that he was going to take a pass. His friends roared away, spitting gravel and jeering that they didn't want to be friends with a sissy anyway. A couple of hours later all four teens were killed in a grinding wreck.

"Dad's strength not to conform saved his life . . . and mine . . . and yours," said Fred. "Sometimes we will never know what harm we save ourselves from by not conforming. We must simply do the right thing."

■ I imagine any discussion about adolescence won't be complete without talking about girls. What do I do here?

Although your son, Will, may think girls are kind of dumb or weird, you need to point out that if God hadn't given us the appetites that puberty brings, none of us would ever choose to live with someone as weird as a girl. Ask your son, "How many marriages would happen if all of us guys felt like you feel toward Jennifer or Mary?" You can watch your son nod his head, and then you will know that he's beginning to understand.

■ **But sex. I know he's expecting me to talk about that.**

If you don't bring up the subject, then Dr. Dobson will for you on the dreaded page 78—the one in which Dr. Dobson describes sexual intercourse. Fred Stoeker asked his wife, Brenda, to read it beforehand and to let him know if he should skip the section. She read it, emitting laughter, interspersed with ominous mutterings. In the end, regardless of how unsettling the description was to them, Fred decided to proceed. He headed for Jasen's room with these final instructions from Brenda: "Honey, just save us some self-respect."

He strapped himself in and hung on. As Jasen and he read each sentence, the father was peppered with questions.

When they came to the description of intercourse, Jasen blurted, "You and Mom do *this?*"

For the first time in his life, Fred felt shame about it and sheepishly answered, "Well . . . yes, Son."

"Oh, *yuck!*" Jasen cried out.

They spent a few more nights on this section, of course, discussing babies, purity, and the importance of "saying no."

■ **When will I know that I've successfully handed the ball to my son? I don't want him to fumble.**

Perhaps when you come to the end of *Preparing for Adolescence*, you'll know that the ball has been handed off. And in the years to come, you'll watch your son start running for daylight, and when he does, a lump will come to your throat. You'll pray and whisper: "Godspeed, dear runner. Carry it home!"

This material is adapted from writings by Fred Stoeker, a father of four who lives in Johnston, Iowa.

5

Your Child's Most Important Teacher . . . Is You!

. . . .

■ **My son is heading into fourth grade and starting to become his own little man. Although I expect others in his life to gain influence, such as schoolteachers, coaches, and Sunday School teachers, I still want to be the "go-to" guy for Max. How can I be sure that happens?**

Author and speaker John Maxwell can remember the time when he was ten years old and was going over his multiplication tables in Mrs. Tacy's class. That's when he looked up and saw his dad walk into the classroom. John could feel his face turn red and his heart pound as he tried to think of what he might have done wrong to bring his dad to school.

"Mrs. Tacy," he heard his dad say, "I'm going out of town tomorrow, and I'm going to take John with me for a few days and teach him." John couldn't believe it. He was going to get to miss school *and* spend time with Dad! He about jumped out of his chair.

His dad continued, "You've been doing a real good job teaching him, but it's my turn for a while." Then his father turned to him and said, "I'll see you at home tonight, John."

In all his life, John couldn't ever remember the clock moving as slowly as it did that afternoon. When three o'clock finally came, he was out the door, running for home before the bell finished ringing. When his father got home from work, John found out that the two of them were going to Pennsylvania, and Mom had already packed their bags. Young John didn't fall asleep for a long time that night.

What John remembers most about that trip in Dad's Ford Fairlane was talking for hours about everything: baseball, basketball, current events, music, church, school, and his friends. It was the first time he had Dad all to himself.

■ **So is John Maxwell saying that dads should take their kids out of school and go on spontaneous trips?**

Not really, but a once-in-elementary-school-trip will certainly make your grade school children feel important and grown up. Getting involved with your children one-on-one will also set the tone for how you take charge of their educations.

Of course, you should value the teaching they are receiving in school, but your children should learn the difference between schooling (acquiring knowledge) and life learning (developing wisdom).

■ **Ah, I get it. John's father wasn't taking him to Pennsylvania to work on contractions, but to help him learn about life.**

That's right. Education is so misunderstood. The word *education* has a Latin root meaning "to draw out." Rather than pushing facts in, a true education uses experiences to draw a person out. That's what those trips with his father did for John. He mentored him, imparted new experiences and ideas, and helped him find talents within himself.

His parents knew that an important part of a good education involved the discipline of daily learning. They had family devotions every morning to aid them in their spiritual growth. But that wasn't all. Every evening from 5:00 to 6:30 was set aside as family time where they ate dinner and talked.

Having dinner together created strong emotional bonds between the Maxwells. But those were also times of great learning about their world, their relationships, and their responses to life.

But the most important education John received from his parents was their modeling. They lived what they taught every day of their lives. And modeling is the most lasting way of teaching. As Abraham Lincoln said, "There is just one way to bring up a child in the way he should go, and that is to travel that way yourself."

■ **If I want to live out what I'm teaching my kids, what principles should I be sure to instill?**

If you grew up in a solid Christian home, then you know you wouldn't be where you are today if it weren't for the love, encouragement, and teaching of your parents. John Maxwell feels just as fortunate. Here are the Top 10 principles that John's parents used to teach his brother, sister, and him as they were growing up. They are described in John's own words:

1. Responsibility

As early as I can remember, we were taught to be responsible. For example, as soon as I learned to walk, my mother required that I pick up my own toys and put them away.

My dad's system of chores also helped us. Every Sunday, he let each of us know what our duties would be for the week. Some tasks were daily responsibilities to be done by the same person. Washing the dishes, for example, was my job. Other assigned jobs were to be completed by noon on Saturday. As our reward, we got to participate in a fun family activity. But anyone who didn't do his chores had to stay home to finish them. It was a good system that helped us learn to make good choices and manage our time well.

2. Stewardship

Mom and Dad taught us early the promise in Malachi 3:10, that we were to "bring the whole tithe into the storehouse" and that God would throw "open the floodgates of heaven and pour out so much blessing that you will not have room enough for it." We were told as children that everything we had belonged to God and that our job was to faithfully take care of what He gave us—to be good stewards. And part of that meant giving back to God at least 10 percent of what He gave us.

3. Determination

Another of my dad's favorite sayings was from Lincoln: "Always bear in mind that your own resolution to succeed is more important than any one thing." Dad's determination helped him maintain a positive attitude despite some negative circumstances.

That same sense of determination has served me well in adulthood. It helped me keep going when my responsibilities sometimes seemed overwhelming.

4. Potential

My parents practiced Colossians 3:21 which says, "Parents, don't come down too hard on your children or you'll crush their spirits" (TM). They constantly built us up, encouraging us and instilling in us a desire to reach our potential. To this day that desire continues to be a driving force in our lives.

5. Relationships

I attended Circleville Bible College, the school where my father was president. One day I met him at the library, and we walked across campus together to his office. We weren't 10 feet outside the library door when Dad stopped to say hello to a student. He gave him a warm handshake and pat on the back, asked how his parents were doing, discussed his studies, and encouraged him to persevere. As he finished talking to that student and we began walking again, he saw another student and talked with her. This continued until we were in his office. What should have been a five-minute walk had taken more than thirty minutes.

My parents put relationships at the top of their list of priorities. They modeled a good relationship with each other and with the other people around them. Mom and Dad stressed the importance of our relationship with Christ and our marriages. I accepted Jesus as my personal Savior when I was three years old, and my parents helped me develop and strengthen that relationship until I married and left home.

6. Work ethic

My dad grew up during the Great Depression. At a time when huge numbers of people couldn't find work, he sometimes held down two and three jobs at once. Here's how he did it. He would go to a business where he wanted to get a job, and he would meet with the owner and make him an offer.

"I'd like to work for you today for free," he'd say. "Put me working on anything you need done, even the worst job in the place. At the end of the day, if you want to hire me, great. If not, then I'll be on my way, and you'll have gotten a good day's work for nothing."

Dad said he worked a lot of free days, but he also got jobs when he needed them. He's always said that there's work to be had by anyone who wants it bad enough.

Dad and Mom's example was good for us, but they also taught us to work. We were required to do our homework before we played. They also taught us that as we got older, we were to work more and play less. So it never came as a surprise when we got additional duties to perform as we got older.

7. Attitude

I learned the importance of a positive attitude from my dad, and he continues to model positive thinking and living to me. A few years ago, when he was seventy, Dad was visiting, and I noticed that he was reading *The Power of Positive Thinking* by Norman Vincent Peale.

"What are you doing reading that book, Pop?" I asked. "You're already positive."

"Well, John, I don't want to slip up and fall into negative thinking—especially at my age," he said. "So I read good books like this every now and then. It keeps me positive."

8. Honesty

Thomas Jefferson called honesty "the first chapter in the book of wisdom," and I'm sure my parents would agree. I count both of them wise; there was always a consistency between their words and actions, and I could count on them to be honest with me about anything.

9. Generosity

I grew up in a pastor's household, which meant that we weren't rich. But I never knew that. Because of my parents' generosity, I thought we were the richest people in town. They were always giving and expecting nothing in return. And at home we certainly had everything we needed.

10. Dependence on God

The final—and most important—principle taught to me by my parents was dependence on God. "Cast your cares on the Lord," my mother used to say, "and he will sustain you; he will never let the righteous fall" (Ps. 55:22).

One of my father's favorite phrases while I was growing up was, "Without us, God will not; without God, we cannot." And he used to love to quote John 15:5, which says "apart from me [Jesus] you can do nothing."

As you begin thinking about taking charge of your children's educations, know that at different ages, your children need different things from you. Just remember—your goal is to prepare them all during their lives for the time when they will be making their own choices. That's the real value of education, and you are their most important teacher.

This material is adapted from Breakthrough Parenting *by John Maxwell and published by Focus on the Family. Copyright © 1996, John Maxwell. Used by permission.*

6

Always Daddy's Girl

- -

■ **I'll admit it: I'm the proud dad of a wonderful little girl, and one of her first words was "Dada"—not "Mama." Can you tell me what Brittany sees in me as her father?**

A father enters a little girl's world wearing several hats. She often perceives you as the director of her life, her mentor, and her guide. She may see you as her provider and the source of her security. Many young girls grow up hearing the comforting words, "When Daddy gets home, he'll fix it." Perhaps you grew up with a father who solved every problem and unscrambled even the worst messes.

Perhaps you also grew up in a fairly traditional home where your father was the primary source of income. He paid the bills and awarded allowances on payday. He took the family on vacations, and when you went to a restaurant, he ordered for everybody. In your youthful innocence, you saw your father as all-powerful. Daughters like the feeling of safety and strength this image conveys.

Your image of your father may include the scriptural characteristics of a family leader, such as the description of a godly man in 1 Timothy 3:4: "He must manage his own family well and see that his children obey him with proper respect." Perhaps he was a good example of such biblical guidelines for fathering as: "Fathers, do not exasperate your children; instead, bring them up in the training and instruction of the Lord" (Eph. 6:4).

■ How do fathers influence their daughters' lives?

Adult women have told researchers that they see father-daughter parallels in their marriages and love relationships, and they also said their fathers cast a long shadow over their sexuality, work, and recreation.

A father is the vehicle for introducing his daughters to the opposite sex. How carefully you teach her about masculinity—both directly and indirectly—will be evident in her interaction with the men in her personal and business life. You can color her perception of men and shape her expectations of how men will or should behave toward her.

■ Do mothers and fathers express love for their daughters in different ways?

Yes. A mother's love tends to be unconditional, providing a general sense of security. But a father's love is often given as a reward for his daughter's performance, causing a daughter to assume that your love must be earned.

The expression of a father's love is further complicated by the fact that many fathers are unable to offer spontaneous, direct affection to their daughters. They tend to hide their emotions. Mothers often must translate for their daughters the unexpressed love of fathers. "Your father really loves you," a mother will console her daughter, "but he just doesn't show it openly."

A daughter who is fortunate enough to have a father capable of expressing his deepest feeling has been given a precious gift that will enrich her life.

The validation and approval you give your daughter in her early years is also different from a mother's. Since moms are usually around much more than fathers, your comments and responses often have more impact.

■ **Why is that?**

Because they are expressed differently and less frequently. Your positive involvement can help keep your daughter from becoming overly dependent on her mother. Your confidence in your daughter and her capabilities will instill in her the confidence to survive on her own.

It is important that you respect, admire and, above all, take seriously the fact that your little girl will become a woman. If you do not let go of your "little girl" at some point, an unhealthy psychological dependence may develop.

When an overdependency persists after the daughter reaches adulthood, the two of you will continue to respond to each other as parent and child, instead of moving to the level of relating to each other as adults.

■ **Since my daughter was very young, I sat her on my knee and told her there wasn't anything she couldn't do. What will this do for her?**

So much that you won't believe it! You gave your daughter a belief in herself and her abilities. Fathers play a crucial role in their daughters' perception of ambition, achievement, and competence. A wise father will convey that none of these characteristics are incompatible with femininity.

■ **I've read that a daughter's perception of God the Father is largely determined by her perception of her earthly father. Can you explain that one to me?**

An integral element in your daughter's self-image is her perception of God. Ideally, her overall response to God, based on a proper perception of Him, will be one of trust. But many women struggle with accepting the fact that God loves them and that He is trustworthy.

Imagine a seven-year-old girl who has known only rejection and abuse from a father whom she loves dearly. At Sunday School, she is taught that God is her Heavenly Father. What is her perception of Him going to be? Based on her experience with her natural father, she will see God as an unstable, rejecting, abusing person she cannot trust.

As a result, she feels unworthy of God's intervention in her life. She finds it difficult to draw close to Him because she sees God as uninterested in her needs and wants.

Show her the following Scriptures:

► He is a loving, concerned Father, who is interested in the intimate details of her life (Matt. 6:25-34).

► He is the Father who will never give up on her (Luke 15:3-32).

► He is the God who sent His Son to die for her, though we are undeserving (Rom. 5:8).

► He stands with her in good and bad circumstances (Heb. 13:5).

► He is available to her through prayer (John 14:13-14), is aware of her needs (Isa. 65:24), and values her (Luke 7:28).

► God comforts her (2 Cor. 1:3-5), strengthens her through His Spirit (Eph. 3:16), and cleanses her from sin (Heb. 10:17-22).

► He is for her (Rom. 8:31) and at work in her (Phil. 2:13).

► He helps her to resist temptation (Heb. 2:17-18) and provides a way to escape temptation (1 Cor. 10:13).

► He is a God of hope (Rom. 15:13) and wants her to be free (Gal. 5:1).

► He created her for an eternal relationship with Him (John 3:16).

■ **I always try to say positive things to my daughter, but sometimes her classmates jibe, "Big nose, big nose!" Or her teachers say, "You're just one of those slow learners." I fear Misty is growing up believing she is a sloppy, homely, stupid girl. Why does she listen to them?**

Unfortunately, she has given those people tremendous power and control over her life. Are there other people who can give her a more accurate picture of who she really is?

Most of us have critics residing within that significantly influence what we believe about ourselves and how we respond to others. Her internal critic is like a condemning conscience, and her internal critic is quick to point out that she doesn't measure up to those standards.

What your daughter needs to do is clean house and redecorate. Tell her she can clean house by getting rid of some of her old beliefs about herself. They do nothing but limit her.

To redecorate, she will have to replace some of her deeply entrenched beliefs and replace them with new, accurate, and positive beliefs about herself.

Remind her that she can build a new self-concept based on the unconditional love and acceptance of God. To do so, she needs to decide what she values more: her old, false identity or her true, God-given identity. Once she decides which one is of greater value (is there any question?), then she needs to let go of one and grab the other.

Overcoming negative feelings will take time and effort, but *change is possible.* Christian psychologist Dr. Dick Dickerson has written a beautiful summary of how God looks at her. Read this passage aloud to her and see if it doesn't make a difference:

Because God loves me, He is slow to lose patience with me.

Because God loves me, He takes the circumstances of my life and uses them in a constructive way for my growth.

Because God loves me, He does not treat me as an object to be possessed and manipulated.

Because God loves me, He does not need to impress me with how great and powerful He is because He is God. Nor does He belittle me as His child in order to show me how important He is.

Because God loves me, He is for me. He wants to see me mature and develop in His love.

Because God loves me, He does not send down His wrath on every little mistake I make, of which there are many.

Because God loves me, He does not keep score of all my sins and then beat me over the head with them whenever He gets a chance.

Because God loves me, He is deeply grieved when I do not walk in the ways that please Him because He sees this as evidence that I don't trust Him and love Him as I should.

Because God loves me, He keeps working patiently with me even when I feel like giving up.

Because God loves me, He keeps on trusting me when at times I don't even trust myself.

Because God loves me, He never says there is no hope for me. Rather, He patiently works with me, loves me, and disciplines me in such a way that it is hard for me to understand the depth of His concern for me.

This material is adapted from writings by author Norm Wright of Christian Marriage Enrichment in Tustin, California.

7

Just Keep Talking

· ·

■ **The last chapter talked about the influence a father carries over his daughter as she becomes a young woman. I know I have a lot of influence, but I also want to develop a great relationship with my daughter. Where do I start?**

Fathers and daughters who converse together stay together. Properly teaching conversation skills is one of the most critical things a dad can do. The ability of you and your daughter to effectively exchange words—and the feelings they're usually connected to—will build a bridge between the two of you that will last the rest of your life.

From the time she's small, you must also teach your girl to respect conversation—words connecting two human beings. This lesson is usually taught when she interrupts you as you're talking to your wife or another person.

The first time, and every time, this happens, you must stop talking. Then look at your daughter and say, "Honey, I'm talking. Just as soon as we're finished, you and I can talk. I promise. Do you understand?"

Then, when you're done, go to your daughter and ask what she has to say. She may have forgotten. If she has, start a conversation.

As you're talking to your girl, make sure your eyes connect. Don't let your mind wander, either. Pay attention as long as you possibly can.

By listening carefully while she's speaking, you are telling your daughter nonverbally that conversation is very important. You are also communicating your love for her.

■ What can we talk about? After all, our worlds are so different.

When your girl is small, there aren't many interesting things you can talk about. You live in a world that's foreign to her. You've got pressure at work and are struggling to make ends meet. She's got a dolly who scraped her knee. How can you find things to discuss and time to talk about them?

Here's a good fathering lesson you can take to heart: On weekends, never go anywhere alone. Simple advice with wonderful consequences. As you drive to Home Depot, you can ask your daughter questions, like: "Look over there. Have you ever seen so many cows? I wonder how many there are?" Your daughter might start counting.

Or you could say, "Between here and the store, let's count how many trucks we pass." Or you could ask, "If you were an animal, which one would you like to be?"

■ I grew up in a home where children were seen, not heard. At big family gatherings like Thanksgiving, my wife wants to make a "kids' table," while I want everyone at the same table. How can I win this argument?

We can't tell you how to convince your wife that the holidays are great times for family conversation, especially around the dinner table. If you don't have room, then set up a card table or two next to the dining room table, extending it well into the living room.

The card tables may be a different height from the formal table, but don't let that be a problem. Since you're a family, you're going to all eat together. All ages at the big table. No *kids' table* in the other room.

Your children will learn the importance of conversation. They will be taught that the dinner table isn't a conveyor belt covered with food. One day, they'll be grateful for that.

■ **Well, I have two sons. Isn't it important to teach a boy how to converse too?**

Yes, it is, and boys are famous for grunting replies just like their dads. Don't forget, however, that girls become adept at conversation at an earlier age than boys. If you are a good conversation instructor for her, she will "teach" others, especially boys, what she learns from you.

When she becomes a teenager and starts conversing with boys, she'll find out what they're like and what's important to them. She will less likely be surprised by a boy's errant belief system or broken moral compass if she has talked to him regularly.

Because your daughter has learned the art of good conversation, she will also be less likely to get caught in compromising physical situations. One reason is that she'll know how to openly express her commitment to purity. Also, young lovebirds usually choose between talking and touching. They don't do both simultaneously. Your preference is for your daughter to talk!

■ **If I can give my kids the gift of conversational skills, what will our relationship be like in the future?**

The best it can be, and they will return the gift many times in the years to come. Let Robert Wolgemuth illustrate.

On his forty-fourth birthday, he got the phone call every entrepreneur dreads. The man on the other end had a brief message: "Robert, we have to call the note on your business loan. I know what this means, and I'm sorry. I have to do what I have to do."

After they hung up, he sat there stunned. He took a deep breath, walked into his business partner's office, and gave him the news. Their eyes welled up as they realized the impact of that phone call.

A few minutes later, they gathered their whole staff together. Robert and his partner had done their best to protect them from the rough seas their business had encountered, but now they had to tell them they were out of work and should start looking for other jobs.

Robert went back to his office, closed the door, and called his wife, Bobbie. When he heard her voice, he broke down, sobbing uncontrollably. Once he gathered his composure, he told her what had happened. "We've lost everything, Honey," he said. "I can't believe it."

Over the next few weeks, he had to make many painful calls. One of the most difficult was to his oldest daughter, Missy, then a college sophomore. After telling her about closing his business, Robert let her know that they wouldn't be able to continue paying for her private college education after the current semester.

Her response was quick and full of grown-up resolve. "That's okay, Daddy," she said. "I love this school, but if I need to work for a year to help us make ends meet, I'll do it."

The rest of the conversation was filled with tenderness and affirmation. As they hung up, Robert thanked Missy for her encouragement. He told her how grateful he was that she still believed in him and how much he loved her.

For those moments, their

BUILDER'S CHECKLIST

Conversation is absolutely foundational in your relationship with your children. But it won't happen automatically. Here are several reminders:

1. Show your children that words are wonderful. Read to your children even before you think they can understand a word. It will create in them a love for words.

2. Look for places to call your own. It can be an old diner or a city park. It doesn't have to be fancy or expensive; it just needs to be a place where the two of you can enjoy talking.

3. Apologize for words poorly chosen. Because you're normal, you're going to say the wrong thing at the wrong time. You're going to hurt people's feelings, including your child's. Let him or her hear Dad correct his words and, if necessary, ask forgiveness.

4. Realize that all this will take time and patience. But the rewards of having your child grow up to be one of your best friends are incredible. And conversation is how your relationship will grow.

roles had reversed. Robert had needed his daughter more than she needed him. And because he had taught her the art of listening and conversing when she was small, she could now return the gift to him.

Give your children that same gift.

This material is adapted from She Calls Me Daddy *by Robert Wolgemuth and published by Focus on the Family. Copyright © 1996, Robert Wolgemuth. Used by permission.*

"To talk to a child, to fascinate her, is much more difficult than to win an electoral victory. But it is also more rewarding."

—*Colette*
French poet and novelist

8

Tough Parental Questions

· ·

■ **The saddest thing happened recently. Some friends of ours confided that their adult son had been arrested for committing armed robbery. They were beside themselves with guilt, thinking they had "blown it" somewhere, and they sobbed uncontrollably in our home. Who was to blame for this family tragedy? The devil?**

After the death of his son Absalom, David lamented, "O my son Absalom! My son, my son Absalom!" The grief and pain that pour from the broken hearts of broken parents can be stunning, but the fact remains that children can "go wrong" regardless of a parent's education or intent.

Most people probably agree that a child's temperament and environment determine much of his development. But as Christians, we believe it all begins with a much more important factor: God's sovereignty. Psalm 139:13-16 indicates that God weaved that child according to His own design while the child was being carried in the womb. Even at that fragile state of growth, the child's days were "numbered."

God is in charge. He is sovereign in choosing our children's genetic characteristics. For example, you have no control over your child's temperament. The environmental factor, on the other hand, is the only one you can control to some degree. The decisions you make daily as a parent do leave indelible impressions with your children.

■ **So much of society thinks corporal punishment is "barbaric," but I want to discipline my child. What does that really mean?**

Discipline is the means by which we modify the child's will. God knows that the will must be prepared before the child will listen to teaching. This is the most crucial part of child rearing. We don't spank our children to take out our own frustrations and unresolved problems on them. The purpose of corporal punishment is to modify the will so that the child can learn discipline. If the will is not bent, the child could be fighting with a spouse later in life or arguing constantly with coworkers.

■ **I see where my goal is to modify my child's will when I spank him, not vent my anger. Can you give me an example on how this is done?**

Let's say four-year-old Billy has pulled all the mixing bowls from the kitchen cupboard. You discover the mess and say angrily, "How many times have I told you to stay out of there? You deserve a spanking!" With that, you give Billy a few good swats on his bottom and send him off to his room. Head down and teary-eyed, Billy walks slowly away. You have successfully punished him for his actions.

Contrast this with the way you *should* have handled the situation. You discover Billy on the kitchen floor with all the mixing bowls. In a firm voice, you say, "Billy, Dad has told you not to put the bowls on the floor. Dad will spank you so you will remember not to do it again." With that, you give Billy a few swats on the bottom.

But here's where things are different. Instead of sending Billy on to his room, you say lovingly, "Now, let's help Dad pick these bowls up. There's a good boy." Using this approach, you are successfully disciplining your child.

■ **What about parents who spank too much?**

Figuring that we're talking about parents who are overdisciplining without being abusive, overdiscipline can be counterproductive. A disobedient youngster knows inherently—though perhaps subconsciously—that he has done wrong and deserves a punishment. But you don't take a belt and put welts on his back for sneaking a cookie. Overdiscipline does not *modify* the will; it *reinforces* the will. The overdisciplined child is ready to fight back, and he will look for any means available to hurt you. The will must be modified in love and self-control. Then, in time, the child will learn to put his body—his old nature—in subjection to the will of God.

■ **To keep from overdisciplining, what are some alternatives to spanking?**

Be creative! If your son is allowed to watch a certain show every Friday night on TV, make it clear in advance that disobedience will mean he can't see that show. Take away dessert. Don't allow him to see a popular video.

But discipline can be thought of in a positive manner. You can also help your children reach goals and keep out of trouble by:

1. Offering rewards. If you punish bad behavior, you can reward good behavior. If your child receives a string of good citizenship marks at school, take her out to her favorite fast-food restaurant. Used properly, rewards can be incentives toward growth and development.

2. Giving explanations and praise. All of us respond to warmth. It's easy for a busy dad to grunt and keep reading his newspaper when his son asks, "Dad, do you like my picture?" Take time to comment favorably on questions like that, which will serve as positive reinforcement and thus discipline him.

■ **We have an unruly child in the neighborhood who never follows instructions. But I know I've heard his father say, "If I've told you once, I've told you a hundred times. . . ." This kid will not listen!**

That's because he has a little button behind his right ear that gets turned off after he hears his mom say, "If I've told you once. . . ." Your children must realize that when you say something, you mean it.

■ **When I say something, I do mean it, but when my wife says something to the kids, she doesn't stick to her word, and the kids know it.**

If the parents aren't on the same page, the kids will use that information to their advantage. Your children will also discover that they can pit Dad against Mom to their advantage. For instance, the kids may ask your wife if they can go down to TCBY's and buy a frozen yogurt, and she said no because it's too close to dinnertime. When they come to you and ask, your response should be, "Did you ask your mother?"

If they say yes, then you should ask, "And what did she say?"

"She said no," they say.

"Then why are you asking me?"

End of discussion. But if your children say, "She said to ask you," then your wife is asking you to make the decision.

■ **How do you modify the will of a teenager?**

By negotiating. Let's say your son is enthralled by his new computer game, and he neglects a chore. You say, "David, you haven't fed the dog yet." The onus is on David to respond.

"Dad, I'll do it as soon as I die in this game," he says from the basement.

David, in essence, has agreed that feeding the dog is his responsibility. As long as he responds in a timely manner, his will has been modified. Your negotiation was successful because of your ability to give and take. As long as he responds in a timely manner, he is exercising discipline.

■ **Let's say David decides he'd rather try for Level 7 on his Specter Challenger computer game instead of feeding the dog. What do I do then?**

There are three levels of alternatives, which depend on whether he is a "repeat offender" or not. Here they are:

1. He decides; he chooses. This is for the first offense. Your teenager has stayed out late or has not done a specific chore. You are aware that he needs to be confronted. At this level, you ask him, "What do you think would be fair punishment?" Remember, whatever he decides—within reason—you are buying. He wants to be treated as a young adult, and you are doing that by letting him be involved in the decision-making process.

2. You decide; he chooses. This is for the second offense. "Son, I told you that if you came in late again, I was going to make the decision. I want to be fair with you, so I will give you three options. You may choose one."

You are still treating him as an adult. But you end the conversation by saying, "Next time, I will choose."

3. You decide; you choose. This is for the third offense—kind of like "three strikes and you're out." Your teen knows he has crossed the line, and in this case, the power rests with the parents. The punishment should fit the crime.

This material is adapted from Raising Your Child, Not Your Voice *(Victor) by Dr. Duane Cuthbertson.*

> ### WHAT THE BIBLE SAYS ON DISCIPLINE
>
> "He who scorns discipline will pay for it, but he who respects a command is rewarded" (Prov. 13:24).
>
> "Discipline your son, for in that there is hope; do not be a willing party to his death" (19:18).
>
> "Folly is bound up in the heart of a child, but the rod of discipline will drive it far from him" (22:15).
>
> "Do not withhold discipline from a child; if you punish him with the rod, he will not die. Punish him with the rod and save his soul from death" (23:13).
>
> "The rod of correction imparts wisdom, but a child left to himself disgraces his mother" (29:15).

9

Raising
No-Compromise Kids

■ **I want to raise kids who are rock-solid in their faith for Christ, who won't be pushovers when it comes to dealing with the world. Where do I begin?**

Consider this story about Charity Allen. While a student at the Los Angeles High School for the Performing Arts, Charity was offered a plum role in NBC's "Another World," a daytime soap opera. She was promised the world: a townhome in New York City for her and her family, chauffeured limos, private tutoring, and a Hollywood salary—up to $20,000 a week!

There was a little problem, however: Charity's teen character was scripted to have an affair with an older, married man. After *that* bedroom romp, she'd fall for the lead singer of a rock band and eventually become pregnant.

When Charity protested to the producers, they asked, "Do you need some time to think about it?"

"I don't need *any* time to think!" Charity replied. "There's no way I can *ever* be a part of that. That's betraying everything I believe in. I want God's absolute best for my life."

When Charity's story appeared in *Brio*, Focus on the Family's magazine for teen girls, the Allen family received thousands of letters from across the United States and around the world. Many came from parents, pastors, and youth workers asking Bill and Cynthia Allen how they raised a child who would take such a stand.

■ **What did the Allens say?**

After some thought, they arrived at some simple pointers:

1. Dedicate each of your children to the Lord. Not only at their births, but also on every day of their lives. Begin each morning on your knees. Bringing each child before the Lord helps you stay focused as they grow older.

2. Teach them the Word. This is the "reap what you sow" principle. If you don't put it in, you won't get it back out. God's Word forms the standards that govern our lives as Christians. Children must know how to live a life pleasing to the Lord.

Insist that your family members play by God's rules. This includes not allowing sons or daughters to play the world's games. Protect their innocent, impressionable consciences. And *dare to discipline.* You may have once read about this somewhere!

3. Communicate. Ephesians 6:4 tells us to "bring them up in the nurture and admonition of the Lord." *Admonish* means to warn and caution; to reprove mildly; to advise; to inform or remind, by way of a warning. When a loving parent admonishes in a nurturing way, the lasting effect is positive.

Psychologists state that during all our adult lives, our parents' opinions circulate like tape recordings in our minds. Most often the "experts" mean that this is the cause of many of our dysfunctions. But why can't these "parental recordings" be a constructive thing?

Repeat verbal blessings and scriptural warnings until they become indelible absolutes in your children's lives.

4. Listen to them. Be available for your children so they can bounce things off of you that are happening at school. This is a perfect time to share your values—values often in opposition to the world's.

5. Support them. Kids will look for support somewhere. The ideal is that they experience affirmation from their parents and family. The Allen kids have told their parents, "It helps, when we make fools of ourselves for Christ, that we are able to come home and feel loved and accepted."

Once, Charity Allen stood up for her Christian beliefs in her freshman class, and her schoolmates and teacher ridiculed her. When she came home crying, they all talked it out.

The next day, Cynthia wrote her an encouraging note and mailed it to her at school. That made a lasting impression on Charity.

6. Instill a sense of importance in each of your children. Their easiest choice will be to follow the crowd, but God has a special purpose for each of them. As they strive to pursue His plan in an excellent way, the approval they receive from Him and from us, their parents, will far outweigh the applause of the crowd.

7. Make knowing Jesus Christ and developing His character your family's goal. Driving home from a meeting at NBC's television casting studio, Charity and Cynthia were discussing the glittering offer from "Another World."

"Charity," her mom said, "I'd prefer you to be poor and unknown as a missionary in Africa, if that is God's purpose for your life, rather than rich and famous in New York but out of His perfect will.

"Besides," she added, "it's not so important where you are, but *who* you are while you're there."

8. Pray, pray, pray! Prayer releases the presence and power of God in the life of your child. When you come to God on behalf of your children, something supernatural happens. In addition, you are acknowledging your own dependence on Him.

The Allens, who are parents of five children, say that raising an uncompromising child can be the most challenging thing you ever do, but you'll never regret it.

■ **With all those children, what did the Allens do about overcoming sibling rivalry?**

Sibling rivalry has been around since Cain and Abel, and competition among brothers and sisters is so universal that comedians often use it to create their funniest jokes. In the seventies everyone laughed at the Smothers Brothers, when Tommy whined, "Mother always loved you best!"

Since Cynthia Allen grew up among eight brothers and sisters, Tommy's fear was no laughing matter in her family. All the children competed for attention. Which one of them could race to the car fast enough to sit in the honored front seat? Who could tell the funniest joke or be the most clever or wise? Who would be the favorite of the day?

■ **So things must have gotten pretty bad for Cynthia, right?**

Thankfully, she grew to love her brothers and sisters very much, but she has used those experiences to raise her five children without sibling rivalry getting out of hand. Here are some tips that she keeps in mind when sibs quibble:

► **Be fair and don't compare.** God's Word warns us not to measure ourselves against anyone. We shouldn't do this to our children. The Creator has made each individual unique. The damage is great when siblings are compared.

► **Don't play favorites.** Jacob was the father of twelve sons and several daughters. Yet he favored Joseph, praising him above the others and spoiling the boy with personal gifts.

Resentment and bitterness can arise easily in such situations. The writer of Genesis 37:4 says, "When his brothers saw that their father loved him more than any of them, they hated [Joseph] and could not speak a kind word to him."

► **Develop a team spirit.** Jacob would have been wiser to encourage his family to work together, and he should've treated each child as special. Differences shouldn't be a source of division; there should be a blending of different positions on the same team.

Allowing one child to regularly tattle on the others, as Joseph appears to do in Genesis 37:2, further disrupts family unity.

► **Teach respect for others and their property.** Children must get permission before using each other's possessions.

Establish a line that members of your family can't cross when teasing and quarreling. Insist on a family rule of kindness, such as "Do unto others as you would have them do unto you."

► **Praise and correct privately.** For some reason, human nature gloats when another is finally "getting his." Sibs are no exception. As much as possible, discipline one-on-one behind closed doors.

► **Find each child's gift and develop it.** In the Allen family, they have a singer, an artist, a dancer, an athlete, and a . . . well, a four-year-old! Early on, Bill and Cynthia eagerly watched to see which of God's special gifts each of these tiny individuals would have. Once their talents were determined, they've done everything possible to fine-tune them. It promotes congeniality when family members encourage each other along the path God is leading them.

► **Assure each child of his or her worth to God, to you, and to the world.** Every child is unique. God's plan includes a role for each of us in advancing His kingdom in the world.

Verbally remind your children of their distinct positions in the family. Physically demonstrate your love with hugs, kisses, and gestures of esteem. When you pray as a family, audibly thank God for each of your youngsters and his special gifts.

Hold celebration days for individual family members, perhaps after success on a difficult exam or some other noteworthy accomplishment. Breakfast in bed amounts to a nice treat, or you can set a special red plate at the star's place at the dinner table. These celebrations will add a holiday spirit to any routine day!

Brothers and sisters can learn to love each other. When they do, friendships often flower and last a lifetime.

This material is adapted from writings by Cynthia Allen, who lives with her family in Corning, California. Since Charity turned down NBC's "Another World," she has been speaking around the country to young people and has recorded her first album. The Allens can be reached by writing P.O. Box 214, Corning, CA 96021.

10

Teaching Your Children
the Value of Money

. . . .

■ **I'm looking for some old-fashioned, biblically based advice for helping my four children handle their money. Where do I get a good start?**

It's the responsibility of parents to teach their children God's principles, and that includes principles of managing money.

When armed with God's truth, our children will be able to detect the lies that society throws at them, lies such as:

▶ "Go ahead and buy it, you owe it to yourself."
▶ "You need to stretch yourself financially."
▶ "Interest is a good tax shelter."

■ **How old should my child be before I begin training him to handle money?**

The younger the better. In the very early ages (before elementary school), teach your children through fair but consistent financial discipline around the home. Have some jobs the children do without pay, such as cleaning their rooms and picking up their toys.

As they grow, establish some elective jobs they can do *for* pay.

This might include cleaning the garage, washing cars, mowing lawns, cleaning the bathrooms, and vacuuming. This teaches both the value of money and the ethics of doing a job well. The earlier you begin to do this, the better off your children will be.

Two principles should guide you as you begin to teach your children about finances. First, whatever you do, be fair. Don't overpay, but don't underpay.

Second, be consistent. If you have announced that you won't pay until a job is done to your satisfaction, then stick to it. If you have promised to pay on completion, pay promptly. Don't promise what you can't or won't do.

One way to teach young children the value of money is to help them establish a goal. This can be as simple as earning 50 cents to buy ice cream, or to save enough to buy a new Steven Curtis Chapman CD.

Associating work with reward is an important concept. As the writer of Proverbs 16:26 says, "The laborer's appetite works for him; his hunger drives him on."

■ At what age should children open savings accounts?

Encourage your children to do this at the earliest possible age, but help them understand that a bank is not a place where they put money and never see it again. It's a place where money is saved for future use. Young children especially should be encouraged to save for short-term projects, such as a trip, a bike, or a skateboard. This lets them associate saving with a reward. You could add to or match their money. This "bonus" may be the key to start them saving regularly.

Saving money is a short-term sacrifice to achieve a long-term goal. As children get older, help them begin saving for longer-term goals: clothing, an automobile, and eventually college. Saving money is good discipline. As the writer of Proverbs 21:21 says, "He who pursues righteousness and love finds life, prosperity and honor."

■ **How can a father teach his children the value of money if their mother spends it foolishly and spoils them continually with new clothes and toys? Won't the children learn to imitate the parent who is the least disciplined?**

Sometimes children will imitate the least-disciplined parent because children are enthralled with spending, particularly when they are younger. Many times, however, children migrate toward the disciplined parent, because that person represents security. A permissive parent or grandparent could lose the children's respect if he or she gives too freely.

You and your wife should sit down together and discuss this, clearly and objectively, from God's Word. Help your spouse understand that love doesn't mean giving children all they desire. Scripture says that a person whom God loves, He disciplines, and the same is true of parents. A parent who really loves a child will establish boundaries for giving, not to restrict the child's freedom, but to teach the concept of stewardship.

■ **Do you think it's a good idea for children to work their way through college, or to pay at least part of their own college costs?**

Since all children are different, the same advice can't apply to everyone, but in principle, children should work, not only while they are in college, but also in high school, at least during the summers. Many students go to college only because their parents are footing the bill. If these students had to work to pay tuition, most would probably drop out, and many should.

You will probably find that your children will not regret the work experiences at all. It will also help them appreciate their educations, and upon graduating, they should have many job opportunities, simply because of their work experiences.

Each family must decide what's best for them. Once you and your wife decide together, share the decision with your children. Give them plenty of time to financially prepare for their college education.

■ **We have grown children living at home who refuse to take our advice. One can't hold down a job. He refuses to contribute to the family finances. I believe that, as a parent, I have the responsibility to ask him to leave, but my wife won't do that. What should we do?**

Weakness is not a substitute for love. As Dr. Dobson says in one of his books, *Love Must Be Tough*, tough love means that you do what is right, not what is easy. If you really love that child, then make the decision that's best long-term for him, even though it may not be easy for either of you. "Discipline your son, and he will give you peace; he will bring delight to your soul" (Prov. 29:17).

Allowing a child to be slothful, disobedient, and disrespectful is not going to help him or her in the long run. Take upon yourself the role that God has often taken with His own people. He would exile them for a period of time to help them understand their responsibilities.

■ **What do you mean?**

Christian financial counselor Larry Burkett once counseled a woman whose daughter was a nurse. She lived at home but refused to help in any way and spent her money frivolously. In an effort to help discipline her daughter, the mother asked her to pay for room and board. She refused, saying, "You don't need the money. I'm not going to help you. This is as much my house as it is yours."

The mother asked her daughter to leave. When the daughter refused, the mother had some friends from church help her pack up the daughter's things and move her out.

For almost a year, the daughter was alienated from her mother, although the mother wrote regularly and told her how much she loved the daughter and that she was welcome to come back any-time she was willing to conform to the rules.

The daughter got married and ended up in great marital difficul-ty because she adopted the same attitude toward her husband. She refused to share the money she earned or help maintain the house. She wanted to live the life of a single person while she was married.

When her husband left and filed for divorce, she "woke up" and went to her mother for help. Her mother began to counsel her, and she was finally wise enough to listen. As a result, she is now a happily married mother of three.

This material is adapted from Answers to Your Family's Financial Questions *by Larry Burkett and published by Focus on the Family. Copyright © 1987, Larry Burkett. Used by permission.*

How Much Time Does a Child Need?

. . . .

■ **I've read all the books and glanced at all the magazine articles on being a good dad. I know kids need my time. I know there are a limited number of hours in the day. So how much time do my children need?**

A child needs "enough" of your time.

■ **What kind of answer is that?**

Not the best one, but there is no single answer. The question is like asking, "How much sleep does a person need?"

"Enough" is the right answer, and when it comes to being a good father, the amount of time will vary from father to father, depending on your age, work load, stress level, and general health.

In the father-child relationship, similar variables exist—the child's age, stage of emotional development, and the stability of the marriage and home. Each is a factor that affects how much of a dad's time a child needs at any given moment.

■ **I've also read that fathers spend something like three minutes a day talking with their children on the average. Is this really true?**

To some degree, yes. You would be surprised how little verbal interaction goes on between fathers and children, especially if Dad gets home late from work or the kids have baseball practice and dinner is a catch-can thing.

A couple of generations ago, in the 1930s, children typically spent a couple of hours a day involved with various family members. Of course, the TV had yet to be invented. But today, that interaction has been slashed to less than fifteen minutes, and a lot of it is negative, one-way communication: Dad bellowing commands or reproving kids for something done wrong.

■ **I've been really busy at work the last six months. What could happen by not spending enough time with the kids?**

In view of your reduced time with your children, you should know that social research is showing that young people who are the highest risks for drug and alcohol abuse, teen pregnancy, delinquency, underachievement, crime, and vandalism are those who have not spent enough time with their parents learning values and living skills critical to being a godly person.

The fact that you are asking the question—"How much of a dad's time does a child need?"—suggests that you instinctively know that you are shortchanging your kids.

■ **If I can't spend a lot of time with my kids due to my job, then I should strive to spend "quality time" with them.**

Yes, you'll hear some parenting experts emphasize that "quality time" is essential, but it realistically cannot be achieved without a corresponding quantity of time. Think about it: Could you go to your boss and tell him that you've decided to work less hours, but those will be "quality" hours? Of course not. You need to put in quantity hours, as well.

But another thing to think about is that when you schedule time to do something with your child under the guise of "quality time," he or she may not be prepared to respond to your schedule at a moment's notice.

With children and with fathers, a "warm-up" period is needed to change frequencies from peers or other concerns to the relationship at hand. Spontaneous conversation, mutual learning, and personal sharing occur more often and with greater meaning in an unrushed atmosphere, where children have become confident they will be heard and understood. Kids especially need time to formulate what they're feeling and what they really want to say.

■ **How will I know that I've been spending the right amount of time with my children?**

To determine how much time is "enough" for a *locking together* of your interests, attention, and heart with those of your child's, answer thoughtfully these questions about the significant times you've recently spent together:

1. Were both of you fully present emotionally, as evidenced by active listening?

2. Did you both get to say what you each genuinely wanted to? Or did you dominate the conversation?

3. Was there a one-on-one opportunity to express private thoughts where a sibling or

---

CAN YOU ANSWER THESE QUESTIONS?

You're spending enough time with your children if you know the answers to these questions:

► Can you name your children's best friends?

►Within three pounds, how much do your children weigh?

► What is their greatest disappointments or unfulfilled desires?

► If your children could change one personal physical characteristic, what would it be?

► What chores do your children hate the most?

► If your children could visit anywhere in the world, where would it be?

► What qualities do their friends most admire about your children?

► What do your children enjoy doing with you? Have you done them recently?

► What are their favorite and worst subjects in school?

► What are their teachers' names?

► What books are they reading now?

others couldn't overhear?

4. Were these interruptions stopping your son or daughter from opening up to you?

5. Did you or your child have to always jump in and keep lulls in the conversation from feeling awkward?

6. Did you come away confident that you "know" what's really going on in your child's mind—the dreams as well as disappointments and confusions?

7. Did you praise and affirm your child enough to counterbalance whatever disappointment, critique, or requirements you may have expressed?

8. Were you appropriately open and vulnerable to your children?

9. Was there a good mix of work and play in the times you've recently spent together?

Finally, keep this thought in mind. If your child is feeling a need for more of your time, one interesting validation is to watch his or her response when you announce a reward of "special time with Dad" for something well done or a good report card.

And finally, there's one other reliable way a father can discover whether he's spending enough quantity and quality time with his children—ask your wife! Her answer is often more accurate and objective than most men would care to admit.

This material is adapted from writings by Paul Lewis from the book Parents and Children *(Victor), and* FaithTraining *by Joe White and published by Focus on the Family. Copyright © 1995, Joe White. Used by permission. Joe White is president of Kanakuk-Kanakomo Kamps in Branson, Missouri, which are Christian sports camps.*

TWENTY WAYS TO TELL YOUR CHILD "I LOVE YOU" (WITHOUT SAYING THE WORDS)

by Joe White

1. Snuggle in bed together as you tell a good-night story.

2. The next time you take a child to an athletic practice, stay and watch from a distance.

3. Have a family worship time after a meal by singing together, praying together, and reading Scripture together.

4. Write a crazy poem by taking turns writing the next line (make sure it rhymes!).

5. At the beach or in a park sandbox, play ticktacktoe in the sand.

6. Plant trees in your yard in honor of your kids (one for each child).

7. On a hot day, hook up a water hose and sprinkler in the backyard and run through the water together.

8. Roast marshmallows over the barbecue.

9. Show your child where you've kept for a long time a special card or picture he or she has given you.

10. Honor your child with a "just because" party ("just because I love you") and invite his or her friends.

11. Make a photo gallery somewhere in your home, and display your children's school pictures from each year.

12. Play hide-and-seek with your children (don't find them too quickly).

13. Talk with your child about what you're learning personally about Jesus Christ.

14. Start praying now for the spouses your children will have someday. Pray that their marriages will be strong and Christ-centered.

15. Have lunch together in the school cafeteria before the school year ends.

16. When your child talks to you, put down what you're doing and look into his or her eyes. Maintain an encouraging expression, and when you speak, make your comments positive.

17. At your very next opportunity, give your child a hug. If your child is young, pick up and hold him or her.

18. When your child says, "Watch me!"—watch. Clap and cheer, "Great job!"

19. Make a special effort to get a good view of your city's Fourth of July fireworks display.

20. Take advantage of the long days and go on an evening walk together.

Put Me in, Coach!

. . . .

■ **I have an eight-year-old son who's going to play his first season of baseball this spring. When I signed him up at registration, I was asked if I could coach. I told the other coaches that I would think about it. When I drove home and did think about it, I felt guilty that I hadn't said yes. What should I do?**

By all means, volunteer to coach your child's baseball team. You'll never regret it, although it may mean going to work a little early or giving up weekends for practice and games.

When you make that commitment to coach, it forces you to spend time with your children. That's the way Jeffrey, a Dallas father, slices out hours with his four children, ranging in age from three to fifteen. He's coached baseball for eight years, from Little League to Pony League.

"Baseball is real competitive in Texas, and with a lot of competition comes a lot of pressure," said Jeffrey. "There's a struggle to keep sports in the right perspective. I tell my boys to use the talents the Lord gives them—but to have fun too. I think the lessons sports teach are good for kids because they learn about life's ups and downs."

■ **I agree with all those sentiments, but I'm an attorney, and I just can't commit to getting away from the office or courtroom by 4:30 P.M.**

If you can't be a coach, then cheer from the grandstand. Even if your sons or daughters say it doesn't matter if you are there, they really want you at the game. In fact, they know if you are watching.

If there are occasions that you can't make the game until the second inning, make sure your son is aware that you've arrived by yelling, "Let's go, Jeremy!" when he runs to his position. Your presence will give him a boost of encouragement.

■ **I'm in my first year of coaching Little League baseball, and like every team, we have a player who is terrible—Ryan. League rules state that he has to play at least two innings, but my players constantly plead with me to take him out when his two innings are up. Sometimes I want to leave him in right field to build his confidence. How should I handle this sticky situation?**

Tell your youngsters that no one player wins or loses a game. Remind them that you're a team, and everyone is going to get a turn to play. Then reiterate your confidence in Ryan's ability. Sure, Ryan doesn't have much athletic talent—everyone on the team knows that—but he deserves a shot.

David Peterson, a Southern California Little League coach, had a "Ryan" on his team. But David insisted on sticking with the gangly lad in the last inning. With two outs, a routine fly ball was hit to Ryan in right field, and David and everyone on the bench held their breath. But his heart-stopping catch ended the game, and Ryan became a momentary hero, earning respect from his teammates and giving him a huge jolt of confidence.

That's what youth sports is all about. If you're coaching a team this spring, be prepared for some challenges. Here are some ideas that will help you be the best coach you can be:

▶ **Build relationships.** Game scores and win-loss records will fade away, but friendships and fun will be remembered long after the last out. Teaching your players to care about one another promotes camaraderie.

► **Earn their respect.** Kids appreciate knowledgeable coaches who admit mistakes and don't act like they know it all. Before each season, study videos and books to learn age-appropriate drills and coaching tips. You can attend clinics and recruit other coaches to lend you a hand. You can also follow a plan for practices, which keeps you on track.

► **Set rules and standards of behavior.** Peter was a skilled player with a bad temper. After striking out one game, he tossed his bat and let out a stream of expletives.

"Peter, you're benched for the rest of this game!" David Peterson admonished, realizing this would penalize his team.

THE NITTY DETAILS

If you're coaching this season, think about sending a "welcome letter" to the parents. Be sure to tell parents and players about:

► **The coach.** Give a brief introduction of who you are and where you can be contacted. State your goals and priorities for the season. Also ask parents for help with coaching, scorekeeping, team parents, or carpooling.

► **Uniform and equipment.** What is needed for practice and for games? Give specifics on type of ball, type of cleats, weight of bat, etc. You might also want to recommend a sporting goods store where these items can be purchased.

► **Practice and game schedule.** Outline dates, locations, maps, snack assignments, rainy-day plans, and procedures for make-up games. Be sure to ask the parents for a phone call if their son or daughter can't make the game.

► **Team roster.** List the names, addresses, and phone numbers, plus the names of the parents, on a separate sheet of paper. Don't forget to name the "team parents" and assistant coaches.

► **Miscellaneous.** As needed, include a copy of game rules, maps of how to find the local ball fields, and information on preseason or postseason clinics and camps. You can also describe ways the young player can practice at home.

"Please, Coach, give me another chance," he begged. "I won't do it again."

David held firm, and they lost the game. But Peter's conduct improved, and his parents thanked David in the end.

Rules need to be spelled out from the start, then reinforced consistently. Good sportsmanship and appropriate behavior have to be expected from players and coaches.

► **Even if you're not coaching material, you can still be involved.** Can you learn how to keep score? Can you be the "stat man" or hold the first down marker? Coaches always need a parent to do the little things, like phone other parents when there's a make-up game, bring snacks, or just warm up a relief pitcher.

► **Motivate, encourage, and have fun!** Enthusiasm is contagious. Kids like coming to practice and playing games when the parents are fun to be around. Laugh with them. Surprise them. Some coaches will hand out bubble gum during practice or organize a parent/player pizza night after a game.

Look for something to praise about each child. If one of your players strikes out every other time, praise him for a ground out just the same as if he had bounced a ball off the wall.

► **Set an example.** It's difficult keeping spirits up when a team loses game after game. But this is a good chance to build character, develop proper attitudes, and teach lessons about life.

But then come the blessings, both on and off the field. One Sunday morning, David Peterson ran into one of his players, Robert, and his mother in front of his church.

"Coach Peterson, what are you doing here?" Robert asked, his cheeks fighting a grin. "It's our first time at this church, and we don't know anybody. I thought this'd be boring, but it'll be cool with your sons here."

Not only did David introduce them to his church, but his wife, Kris, shared her faith and love for Christ with Robert's mom, and they began a friendship.

In our position as coaches, we must realize the Lord pencils us into His game plan to demonstrate His rules, score His points, and love His participants. Playing joyfully for Him and for His glory is the way to be a winner and have a ball!

This material is adapted from writings by David and Kristan Peterson of La Jolla, California, and Daddy's Home *by Greg Johnson and Mike Yorkey, Copyright © 1992. Used by permission of Tyndale House Publishers, Inc. All rights reserved.*

2

. . . .

Dads and Their Families

Making Your Family Number One

■ One Saturday morning, my five-year-old son went out to play with his two friends across the street, just as he does most Saturday mornings. On this day, however, his friends couldn't play. They had left with their mother for the weekend so their father could pack his belongings and move out of the house. The parents were getting divorced.

"Why is their dad leaving?" my son asked me.

I could tell the situation bothered my son, but I didn't know what to say. How should I have replied to my son?

According to the secular sociologists and psychologists, you were supposed to tell him that the American family is simply changing with the times, taking new forms, seeking new solutions. People expect too much from marriage. Breakups are inevitable. And with a little counseling, his friends would survive the transition as if it were little more than a rearrangement of their family's living room furniture.

■ Let's get serious here. It was gut-wrenching to watch their father throw his suitcases and a few cardboard boxes into the

Honda sedan and drive away. Don't parents think about the human cost when they split up?

We don't, because collectively the United States has the highest divorce rate in the world. At the current rate, stepfamilies will outnumber biological families early in the twenty-first century. More than half of all marriage partners commit adultery. And more than *six times* as many unmarried Americans were living together in the 1990s as were cohabiting in 1970.

Beyond that, thousands of families that have avoided such statistical snares find themselves comatose—clinically alive but showing no signs of the abundant life God intended for them. Though, plainly, many families are thriving, it seems many more are either losing the battle—or are too busy to fight.

■ **Given such realities, isn't it time we recommitted ourselves to our own families? Isn't it time we concerned ourselves less with fatter paychecks and thinner thighs—and more with those people who share our lives?**

By all means, the answer is yes, and please start with your own family. Don't make this like some New Year resolution in which you boldly resolve to lose ten pounds, clean the attic, write Aunt Edna, grow a beard, drink decaf coffee, break ninety on the golf course, or scrub the grout in the shower.

Instead, ignore the trivial resolutions and decide you're going to listen more to your teenage children. Decide you're going to spend less time at the office and more time with your wife. Decide you're going to turn off the TV one night a week and explore the ancient art of conversation with your family.

■ **I recently saw a story in the newspaper about two parents who, combined, made $190,000 a year, lived in a plush suburban home, but raised two teens who dealt cocaine. Then I've seen stories about welfare moms who watch MTV all day, letting their children run free outside. Are families going down the drain or what?**

Those stories making the headlines reflect a more subtle trend that marks many of our faltering families. Living in a world that often rationalizes wrongs into rights, we find ourselves becoming anesthetized to the chaotic changes that have rocked the American family these past three decades.

Thus, instead of raging against such changes, we begin accepting them—and settling for less ourselves. Subconsciously, we find ourselves agreeing that all is well. But, clearly, all is not well—it's just that the standards have been lowered and the rules changed to make it seem that way.

■ What could the Creator of the family be thinking about all this?

Would God settle for the handsome, middle-aged businessman who makes six-figures a year, drives a $60,000 Porsche, but didn't know the name of the high school his son attended? Would He settle for a teen suicide rate that has nearly tripled in the last twenty years? A teen drug problem that's reaching epidemic stages? A teen pregnancy rate that shows 40 percent of today's fourteen-year-old girls will be pregnant at least once by the age of twenty?

Sociologists and psychologists are right—the American family is changing. But the statistics above reflect a quiet desperation in the American family, suggesting we dare not accept those changes as nonchalantly as we accept the change from winter to spring.

In a sense, society's continual devaluation of the family is analogous to the way making toys has changed. Long ago, toy makers intricately handcrafted their wooden toys with time and care. As a result, they were functional, creative, and sturdy. Today, plastic toys are punched off assembly lines with little thought given to their quality. As a result, they rarely last more than a week.

But as long as we, the consumers, accept low-quality toys, they will continue to be produced as cheaply as the market will bear. And so it is with our families: As long as we, as a society, accept low-quality families, they will continue to be produced as cheaply as the market will bear.

■ **What should I do to commit myself to making my family number one?**

Commitment, of course, is easier said than done. It's interesting to note that in a recent national poll, 86 percent of the respondents felt extramarital affairs were wrong under any circumstances, yet more than half had them. What does that tell you about commitment?

Talk to any divorced father, and they will wax poetic about how much they love their children. But two-thirds of ex-husbands renege on their child-support payments. What does that tell you about commitment?

If you choose to recommit yourself to your family, don't casually decide during halftime of the Super Bowl. Pray about it. See what the Bible has to say about commitment and families. Gather information on specific changes you need to make. Sketch out a plan of action. And act on that plan.

It might mean giving some things up, which won't be easy. Everywhere we look, we're told we can "have it our way." Right now. We are an on-the-go society, perhaps because if we're always running we won't have to stop and look at ourselves in the mirror.

We are spoiled with the swift efficiency of convection ovens, keyless entries, and 200 megahertz PCs. We want quick fixes to problems—get on the Internet and log on for an answer. We want our Big Macs ready when we arrive at the drive-up window. We want our dreams to develop as if life were a speedy print photo lab.

But strong families don't work that way. They take patience and perseverance to develop. They take energy and enthusiasm, sacrifice and spontaneity. They take loving someone who's not always lovable, listening when you'd rather talk, and caring enough to see boundaries. They take living our lives in a way that often goes against the grain of our looking-out-for-Number-One society. What's more, the payback isn't immediate, nor is it even guaranteed.

■ **If it's not guaranteed, why should I make all these changes?**

Because plenty of people in their twilight years have wished they could wind back the hands of time and wrestle on the rug with their three-year-old or take an evening walk with their spouse. But nobody, while lying on his deathbed, has ever said, "I wish I spent more time at the office."

This material is adapted from writings by Bob Welch, features editor of the Register-Guard *newspaper in Eugene, Oregon, and by Dean A. Ohlman of Jenison, Michigan.*

THE IDEAL MAN

by Dean A. Ohlman

Madison Avenue, Hollywood, and the National Football League have given us the image of what the Ideal Man should be. He is the living Ken to every blue-eyed, Barbie doll woman. With a fur-lined leather jacket slung casually over his shoulder, he alights from his helicopter and gallops around the lower forty of his dude ranch. He dominates the corporate boardroom.

We've all seen the ads. We know that the Ideal Man begins his day in the bathroom with shaving cream in one hand and a beautiful female in the other. After a hard day's work, he sprints to the local health spa, where he lifts weights in front of mural-size mirrors. Towel around his neck, his sweat shines and his hair holds.

He smiles at a dazzling and trim woman who bounces during an aerobic exercise. Her Danskins shine and her moussed hair holds. After smooth and confident introductions, the radiant couple slips off to the clubhouse bar. The evening ends with Ken and Barbie sharing a nightcap, a roaring fire, and his pajamas.

But what about the Average Guy? Joe Average also begins his day in the bathroom. Since he doesn't have much of a beard, one quick lick with the old Norelco is all it takes. He ignores the few blond whiskers lodged in the cleft of his double chin.

After a quick gargle with medicinal mouthwash, he dons dark wool pants and a starched white shirt. His breast pocket holds an assortment of colored pens and pencils. For breakfast, he gulps down some Cheerios with the family, than dashes off to the office in his aging Plymouth Reliant, dropping the kids off at school on the way.

After another day of punching computer keys, Joe hurries to his son's Little League game. Afterward, he treats the little benchwarmer to McDonald's before rushing off to a church deacons' meeting. Weight lifting was a passing

continued next page

fancy for this average guy, whose idea of "pumping iron" now amounts to stepping in and ironing his work shirts when his wife is tired.

Mr. and Mrs. Average end their evening by tucking the kids in after a bedtime prayer. Don't tell anyone, but he also cries with his wife when they watch "Little House on the Prairie" reruns on the Family Channel. He also wears pajama tops.

I know them both—the Ideal Man and Joe Average. I've spent hours golfing with the Ideal Man, watching Monday Night football games with him, and fixing his Corvette. The last time we got together, I tried to talk him out of leaving his wife and kids for Barbie and her Porsche. I told him it would devastate his family. He didn't care.

I've also spent hours with Joe Average. Actually, he's spent hours with me. He sat with me in the emergency room while my son was being stitched up. He encouraged me during a midlife crisis. He labored with me as we tore out my old kitchen sink. He cried with me when my father died.

I did Joe's tax returns last year, and when I tallied his deductions, I learned why he has polyester pants and a rusty car. During the year, he contributed $4,000 to his church, donated fifty hours of work to the Little League snack bar, went door-to-door for the American Cancer Society, and gave his old personal computer to a halfway house for runaway teens.

Joe Average may not be able to keep up with the Ideal Man on the indoor track, but if you ask me, Joe's got the Ideal Man beat by a country mile.

2

How to Be a Cool Dad

■ We have all seen them at the mall. A guy will be walking quickly down the aisle next to his preteen son. He's got an earring and a rat tail down his back—just like junior. They're probably headed to the record store to pick up the new Pearl Jam CD.

Or there's the guy at the Little League baseball game. He's more well-built now than I was in high school. When his kid hits a homer, he's the first one off the sidelines to give him a double high-five.

I don't feel with it when I'm around guys like these. Why don't I feel cool?

It's obvious that for many dads, being buds with their kids is just another way to extend their own adolescence. After all, don't most men feel as if they're just big kids wrapped in a body that refuses to age? Or if they know they can't delay the inevitable or admit to the physically obvious, a few will try to stay young by their behavior. Having a child somehow gives them permission to act their shoe size, not their age.

Is this what your child wants? More important, is this what your child needs?

■ **Uh, I guess not, but I still want to be halfway cool with my kids. I don't want to be the neighborhood dork.**

Well, if you're determined to be cool, you should know that there are two types of cool: short-term and long-term.

■ **What's the difference?**

The "short-term cool dad" does what he can to relate to his child the way a buddy would—and not just occasionally. He believes that to win his child, he must look the part. That means his clothes, hair, jewelry, music, and movie tastes must match his younger charge.

(We need a quick time-out. The point here isn't to lump the dad who really *does* like long hair or loud music. Obviously, this stuff isn't a sin. But every dad is occasionally tempted to try a little too hard in relating to his child.)

A "long-term cool dad" has the bigger picture in mind. He realizes that having his kids and their friends think he's cool is a pretty weak goal. He'd much rather settle for that special moment off in the future when he overhears his son or daughter telling their spouse something like this: "My dad was cool; he was fair. He listened, too. Yeah, he was kind of a nerd sometimes, but I didn't need another buddy. I needed someone to help keep me in line. For the most part, he was cool."

■ **Can you tell more about becoming a long-term cool dad?**

Long-term cool dads have six attitudes:

1. A cool dad understands his child's embarrassment.

Greg Johnson remembers dropping off his son, Troy, for his first day of school in fourth grade. After meeting the teacher, he went back outside to the playground to say good-bye. All of Troy's buddies were around, but it didn't even hit Greg that his son didn't want to give his ol' dad a hug.

About twenty feet away, Troy gave Greg a weak wave and turned toward his friends. Dad was still clueless. Calling his name, he kept walking toward him until Troy turned around. Troy knew what was coming. His eyes pleaded for him not to touch him, but Greg was on a "hug mission" and wouldn't be deterred.

Later that evening Greg's wife, Elaine, took him aside. "Troy told me you hugged and kissed him on top of the head today at school in front of his friends. Now, don't take this wrong, but that really embarrassed him."

He's growing up, Greg thought. *I can't give him any more affection in public until he's twenty-five and doesn't care about the crowd anymore.*

After apologizing and telling Troy he would try not to embarrass him again, Greg hugged him. "Hugging at home is still okay, isn't it?" he asked.

"For a little while longer, but no kissing."

Respecting your child's space and his wishes isn't easy. But a cool dad makes sure he knows in what ways he can embarrass his child . . . and doesn't do it! Troy's fourteen now and girls are calling. So far, Dad has fought the urge to tease.

2. A cool dad listens first.

There will always be words to say; every dad has a sermon ready to preach when his kid steps out of line. The "right and wrong" stuff is easy to dish out. And we need to dish it out. But as they say in comedy: "Timing is everything."

A junior high son came home one semester with an "unacceptable grade." He had a "D" on a report card otherwise filled with A's and B's. The father's first inclination was not call him on the carpet, revoke privileges, make him quit basketball, or cut his pizza allowance in half. When the two sat on opposing couches that night, the son was ready for the worst.

"Tell me about that D," the dad said calmly.

"Huh?" came the dumbfounded response.

"Your side, I want to hear your side."

After a few stammers, the son talked about the teacher not liking athletes ("The kid knew that would push my button," the father told friends later, "but I let him get away with it"), his desire to do well in more important classes, how everyone hated that particular teacher . . . and the fact he'd chosen to goof around a bit more than usual.

"What do you think I can do to encourage you to take each of your classes a bit more seriously?" Dad queried.

Again, stunned into silence by this low-key blow, his son searched for words. "Well, I guess you could get me talking a little more specifically about each of my classes during the term and remind me to work hard in them all."

"That's fair. I can do that. Now what should we do about this D?"

"Well, two weeks without watching sports on TV would probably get my attention."

Though the dad couldn't believe his son had just chosen his own punishment, he fought the urge to grin. The issue was settled, and he didn't have to moralize once. All he did was ask questions . . . and listen.

No, not every issue can be handled this way—or this easily—but most can. Listening first, asking a few questions, and letting your child talk will communicate respect quicker than any logical fatherly counsel. And it usually accomplishes your goal of changed behavior.

3. A cool dad uses his weaknesses as strengths.

When Greg Johnson was in full-time youth ministry, several members of his group felt it was their mission to let him know the state of his retreating hairline. Since he was only in his late twenties, their gentle jabs were a continual reminder that he was getting old—and therefore, a little less attractive.

Did Greg get defensive or quietly let them know he didn't like it? Nope. Instead, he used it. By pointing out—and making a joke of—a visible "imperfection," he somehow got a little closer to their level. Greg wasn't "Joe Perfect, Youth Leader" who pontificated from on high. He was a normal guy with weaknesses. He could be trusted; listened to.

Are you short? Is your hairline in full-blown retreat? Do your ears stick out, or is your nose a little big? Are there a few too many pounds around the middle?

For those who endured ridicule about physical imperfections during their own growing-up years, letting others make a joke might resurrect bad memories. But if you are secure enough in who God made you to be, then minor imperfections like thinned-out hair can win you the right to be heard with your kids.

Philippians 2:5-9 illustrates what Jesus did to show us what God was like. He left heaven and became one of us. He laid aside His kingly robes and took the form of a man, became a servant, and even died on a cross. His weakness became our strength.

Just as physical imperfections can somehow bring us down to their level, so can admitting our failures. When your son or daughter hit the teen years, they'll need to hear less sermons and more revelations from you. "Failure" stories have the potential to teach more than "you should have seen me that time" stories.

You don't have to tell them all of your deep, dark secrets—just some of them. If they see you as a fallible human—like them—they'll be more likely to talk to you when they blow it. Which is what you want anyway.

4. A cool dad isn't embarrassed about his relationship with God.

A sixth-grade Sunday School teacher asked the boys in his class what they noticed about their dad. Listen to these three responses:

- ► "My dad has to wait for me at baseball practices a lot. Instead of sitting in the car like most parents, he comes up on the bleachers and brings his Bible. He even reads it when he's not watching me."
- ► "My dad can pray out loud anywhere."
- ► "While we were out doing yard work one day, I heard my dad talk to the guy next door about our church."

Hmmm. Is more being caught than taught in these homes?

5. A cool dad admits his mistakes.

It finally happened. Greg Johnson, sitting with his son in a restaurant, ogled a shapely female who happened to be walking by. Greg had vowed to himself that this would never occur; that he'd always be a good example and keep his eyes focused straight ahead. Actually, he wasn't really looking. She happened to stroll into the area where his eyes were scanning the room.

"Ooooh, Dad, you looked at her. I saw you."

"Looked at who?" he innocently replied.

"You know, that lady in the tight dress."

"Son, your dad is married. He doesn't need to look at women in skimpy, low-cut dresses."

"What does low-cut mean?"

Gotcha!

Greg now has a new general rule: *Whenever I start talking about myself in the third person, I'm trying to hide something.*

Fortunately, Troy didn't press it any further. But Greg really blew an opportunity. He should have said, "You're right, Son, I did look at her. Men have a tough time not looking at women just for their bodies, even old married guys like your dad. But it's not right. God didn't create women just to be looked at, did He?"

Next time.

6. A cool dad acts like an adult, but understands what it's like to be a kid.

Some moms can have a tough time understanding boys. She doesn't get how boys can become hysterical over whoopee cushions for hours on end, or why shoot-em-up action movies are so . . . engaging.

They're boys! And dads like us have been given an awesome task in assisting their safe navigation toward becoming men. Sometimes that means remembering the days when life was simple: childhood.

As much as we'd sometimes like to return to those carefree days, we can't. Though we can (and do) live a little through our kids' lives, we have to be selective. They need us to stay as adults. We're their visible lighthouse, pointing out the rocks and guiding them to safe harbors. If we acted like a flashlight in the fog, the consequences could be disastrous.

It's often easier to be a flashlight, but we've got to take the challenge (most of the time) to be an immovable lighthouse. It's what they need, it's what they want.

No matter how much we want to be cool.

This material is adapted from writings by Greg Johnson, an accomplished author of nearly two dozen books and former editor of Breakaway, *Focus on the Family's teen magazine for boys.*

3

The Two Swords of Power

. . . .

■ My friend Ty and I were talking over coffee at our twentieth high school reunion. "You just can't imagine the feeling,"
Ty said. "Flying an F-16 is the closest thing you can get to
being strapped onto a guided missile."

Ty was the flight leader of an Air Force quick-deployment
fighter group. Now a veteran pilot and a still-youthful Air
Force major, he was respected by those ranking above him,
saluted by everyone under him, and counted on by those who
flew with him.

He was also losing his family. Why would that happen
when he had so much going for him?

Ty was the type of guy who openly resented being at home
instead of hanging out at the air base. He broke dozens of promises
of weekend trips and romantic dinners. All that potential for good,
for love, for memories that could have warmed the hearts of his
children over the years. Instead, he'll be left with cold memories. If
only he knew that he had lived half a life.

All of Ty's training as an elite Air Force officer never prepared
him for the quiet warfare on the home front. Perhaps you saw his
eyes reflect pain and helpless frustration. The same power that

helped him in the Gulf War had destroyed his family.

■ **What power are you talking about?**

We're talking about a power deep and wide and high enough to influence and change human lives.

It's the power to send strong sons and clear-eyed, confident daughters into the world to right wrongs, fight worthy battles, and build strong families of their own.

It's a power that can change a family tree forever. In time, it can move a nation.

That's what it *could* do. But for so many men ruling their homes with an iron fist, that's not what's happening. Yes, the power is there. And yes, it's changing lives and affecting generations to come. But in many families, it's a power that destroys. And most men don't even realize that such power covers them.

Men, whether you realize it or not, you own two "swords" that are actually two forms of power. The handle of one gleams silver-blue, as though chiseled from a block of ice. You acquired the silver-handled sword early in your manhood, and you have continued to use it down through the years. You obtained it through sweat and grit and long, weary hours of labor. It's the sword you use most often in your job, and it remains your constant sense of protection, an equalizer in a rough-and-tumble world.

But you have a second sword as well.

Its handle is burnished gold. This sword has been yours since birth, part of your inheritance, your birthright. You often leave it where it has been as long as you can remember—mounted over the fireplace. Something you may hardly notice. Something to dust twice a year.

■ **Can you tell me more about the differences between silver and gold swords?**

Most of the men you know in the work-a-day world want to wield the *silver*-handled sword. So do you. From the moment you completed your training in its use, it has been your deepest, most fervent desire to brandish that sword with all the strength, cunning, and endurance you can pull out of yourself.

Yet, it's curious. The sword that looks so impressive in the marketplace seems a heavy, awkward thing when you walk through your front door in the evening. It can catch on the screen door or even knock over the umbrella stand and a vase or two.

For that matter, you've found it extremely difficult to use the thing at home. You've tried to swing it around according to your training, but it causes your sons to wince and drives your daughters away.

You stand by the hearth and contemplate these strange things when suddenly, you find yourself gazing at a reflection of firelight in the molten gold of the "ornamental sword" hanging over the mantle. How it catches and holds the light!

Your own father rarely used it, just like his father before him. It may have been months since you've seen one brandished. In your corner of the world, few of the sword handlers in the marketplace even speak of it.

But how beautiful it is! On a whim, you unhook it from its mountings and draw the sword from its finely tooled scabbard. Catching and holding the red flames of a cherry wood fire, it seems to glow with a life of its own.

What if there was a tool, you wonder, *that could draw my sons and daughters to me rather than thrust them away? What if it could bring gladness and laughter? What if that tool also served as a weapon strong enough to drive back the darkness, banish loneliness from beneath this roof, overwhelm harsh words, force back the fears of childhood, overcome bitterness, slay the insecurities of adolescence, and kindle courage and hope whenever it was raised?*

You do hold such a tool. And you do have a chance to use it, as well as your silver sword, for either tremendous good or great evil.

■ What are the strengths of the silver-handled sword?

The silver-handled sword is a man's *positional* power. That's the clout, control, prestige, and authority that come to you because of where you work or what you do. It's your job title, whether you work on the line or supervise from the catwalk. It's the number of academic degrees you have earned or the way other men respect the clear mark of a craftsman when you finish a job.

Personal power, on the other hand—the gold-handled sword— may or may not be accompanied by an impressive title, an American Express gold card, or a Ph.D. It has more to do with *who you are* rather than with where you work or what you do.

When you speak of a man's personal power, you immediately think of words reflecting character, such as warmth, sensitivity, dependability, determination, genuine compassion, and caring. It's what you are (for good or ill) on your day off in your blue jeans and stocking feet. It's who you are when no one else is looking.

■ Is it a matter of choosing between the two swords? Does it have to be one or the other?

Not at all. What we're talking about is a working knowledge of *both* positional and personal power. There are times when you'll have to be skillful with the silver sword in your work-a-day, competitive, difficult world. There were times when Jesus picked up the silver sword of His positional power: stilling the storm, casting out demons, and raising the dead.

But more often than not, you saw Jesus choosing the gold sword, as when He expressed His personal power in touching a leper, calling Zaccheus to come down from a tree, or weeping unashamedly at the death of a friend.

There's great benefit in having two swords. But many men have focused for so long on the silver-handled sword that they've neglected the deeper, stronger, longer-lasting power of the gold sword. We're calling men to pick up both weapons of warfare, for we're in a raging battle for the hearts of our families.

■ But can I really learn to be an expert with two weapons at once?

The truth is, *you have to.* You have no choice, that is, if you want to win the love of your children, the genuine affection of a wife, and a "Well done" from your God.

You can learn the fine art of mastering your gold sword—and

seeing your relationships improve greatly as a result.

■ **What happens when I do make the extra effort to pick up a sword that may not be natural for me?**

Whenever you choose to let the warmth of your gold sword radiate through your home, *it triples in power.* It opens eyes. Pulls back shades. Causes a stir. In some instances, it will be virtually unforgettable.

John Trent remembers playing his heart out for a high school football coach who rarely (he actually thought never!) used his gold sword to encourage or praise. It was late in a game his team was supposed to win, but they were losing. And while John thought he had played a good game, in the fourth quarter he was pulled out after making a tackle.

Here it comes! John thought as he jogged up to the coach and waited for his words. As the captain of the defense, he was going to get blasted for losing the game. But that's not what happened.

"John," he said, "I just want you to know that I wish I had ten more of you out on the field. I'm proud of how you're playing today. Now get back in the game!"

It has been more than twenty-five years since John nearly fell down after hearing those words. He remembers floating back onto the field and playing even harder than before.

■ **Did John's team come back to win the game?**

No, they lost the game, but John won something that never showed up on the scoreboard—a crystal-clear picture in his mind. He has the memory of a silver sword expert who picked up the gold sword one time—and made four years of effort seem worthwhile.

Men tend to remember for decades specific words of encouragement their fathers spoke to them. When a man makes an effort to pick up the gold sword and use it under God's control, the world takes note. And the more we pick it up, the more we will shape those who love us and look to us to help define their lives.

Scripture encourages us to be strategic in the use of our words. When we speak, let's make our words count for something! Let's use

THE SILVER SWORD: CUTTING INTO A CHILD'S HEART

A child's heart is easily bruised. Easily broken. And once seriously damaged, no surgeon can repair it. Only the Almighty Himself has the skill to restore its original balance, potential, and capacities.

Recently, a forty-year-old man described a Saturday morning twenty-eight years before that nearly stopped his heart—and is still affecting him today!

"I was just twelve when my Boy Scout troop planned a father-son camp-out," he said. "I was thrilled and could hardly wait to rush home and give my dad all the information. I wanted so much to show him all I'd learned in scouting, and I was so proud when he said he'd go with me.

"The Friday of the camp-out finally came, and I had all my gear out on the porch, ready to stuff it in his car the moment he arrived. We were to meet at the local school at five o'clock and carpool to the campground. But Dad didn't get home until 7 P.M.

"I was frantic, but he explained how things had gone wrong at work and told me not to worry. We could still get up first thing in the morning and join the others. After all, we had a map. I was disappointed, of course, but I decided to make the best of it.

"First thing in the morning, I was up and had everything in his car while it was still getting light, all ready for us to catch up with my friends and their fathers at the campground. He had said we'd leave around 7 A.M., but he didn't get up until 9:30.

"When he saw me standing out front with the camping gear, he finally explained that he had a bad back and couldn't sleep on the ground. He hoped I'd understand and that I'd be a 'big boy' about it . . . but could I please get my things out of his car? He had several commitments he had to keep.

"Just about the hardest thing I've ever done was to go to the car and take out my sleeping bag, cooking stove, pup tent, and supplies. And then—while I was putting my stuff away and he thought I was out of sight—I watched my father walk out to the garage, sling his golf clubs over his shoulder, throw them into the trunk, and drive away to keep his 'commitment.'

"That's when I realized my dad never meant to go with me to the camp-out. He just didn't have the guts to tell me."

How do you recalibrate a child's heart after a dad's broken promise has damaged it?

words that build and encourage, rather than tear down or demean. As the Apostle Paul said in Ephesians 4:29: "Do not let any unwholesome talk come out of your mouths, but only what is helpful for building others up according to their needs, that it may benefit those who listen."

■ **I need some tools to forge my own gold sword. How do I go about it?**

After you've taken inventory of where you are, what negative effects you may have had on your spouse, children, and friends, look carefully at the future you want. Here are several steps to help you achieve a brighter one:

▶ **Honor your loved ones.** The most important ingredient in a successful family is placing high value on one another. When you decide someone is valuable, that's a major step in acting out your love for the person.

Honoring those in your home means making a decision that they're heavyweights, worthy of great importance and appreciation.

▶ **Develop meaningful communication.** If you talk to successful families across the country, most will say they need about an hour of real conversation sprinkled throughout each day. Perhaps it's five minutes in the morning, a ten-minute phone call from work, twenty minutes at dinner, and another twenty-five minutes carved out of the evening to provide this much-needed aspect of intimacy.

▶ **Deal with anger in a timely, healthy way.** In close-knit

HOW TO MAKE YOUR WORDS COUNT

How can your words be like gold? Here are some suggestions:

▶ A timely compliment to a discouraged mate.

▶ A firm but loving word of warning to a wandering adolescent.

▶ A big heaping of praise to a child who is trying very hard to please you.

▶ An upbeat, confident appraisal of a situation when "the facts" are sending another message.

▶ Words of trust in the Lord God.

▶ The words "I love you" anytime.

relationships, friction is inevitable. Often, that anger comes out of a blocked goal, an unmet expectation, or as a fear-based response. Other times, it comes out of a rightful sense of reaction to wrong.

Usually, by genuinely seeking to understand what happened, admitting when we're wrong, and specifically asking for forgiveness, we can see anger drain away. But if anger continues to reside in your heart or that of your loved one, don't assume it will simply get better over time. Talk it through.

► **Exhibit meaningful touching.** Meaningful, nonsexual touching is an important way of expressing warmth and security to a loved one. It puts actions to our words of affection and both physically and emotionally blesses those who are touched.

► **Provide regular emotional bonding experiences.** Genuine friendship comes from doing something more than just sitting around talking about friendship. Emotional bonding comes in the hundreds of "little" things we do with another person and usually become the biggest factors in building a satisfying relationship.

Yes, it takes effort to carve out time to play together, exercise together, enjoy each other, and laugh with each other. But the closeness that results is worth it.

This material is adapted from The Two Swords of Love *by Gary Smalley and John Trent, Ph.D., and published by Focus on the Family. Copyright © 1990, 1992, Gary Smalley and John Trent, Ph.D. Used by permission.*

4

Finding Some Time for Ourselves

. . . .

■ **Earlier in this book, I read that all-too-familiar refrain: "You have to spend 'enough' time with your wife and kids." I've been pouring any spare time I come across into my family, but what about personal time for myself? A guy has to putter around the garage some time, you know.**

Among us fathers, we can agree that "time for ourselves" is a pretty hilarious topic. We're always last in line . . . but that's okay. It's like being captain of a passenger ship; we're always the last to leave a sinking liner. It comes with the territory.

At a men's retreat, a survey asked the fathers what activities they would drop if life got too hectic. The top three were:

1. Reading the newspaper
2. Exercise
3. Hobbies

While we can accept those responses, we also know men aren't happy campers when we have little time to goof off. When life gets too busy (and when kids enter the picture, it usually does), we're left with three choices:

► Play the martyr and pretend we don't really need time for ourselves.

▶ Say "heck with this" and go do our own thing, no matter how it affects the family.

▶ Find ways to include much-needed personal time in our overscheduled lives.

The best alternative, of course, is the third one. While many men find themselves playing the martyr or doing their own thing, both have negative long-term results.

■ Yes, but I spent ten hours at the office today, plus another forty-five minutes fighting traffic, heat, and smog. When I eased my car into the driveway, the kids came running out. They had been waiting three hours for me to get home to play with them, and they were wired to blow. I was so tired that I mumbled, "Hi, kids," and worked my way past them. I know I should have stopped and played some, but what could I do?

If you work in a stressful environment, you need some time to air out. But if you play the martyr, don't expect the family to read your mind. When Marty arrives home, his wife tries to sense what type of day he's had at the office. "She acts as a buffer between me and the kids," he says. "After our twins were born, we put this into practice. It gives me extra time to collect my thoughts and get ready to be a constructive part of the family."

Another father, Skip, said, "Sometimes you go home, and all you want to do is sit down, kick up your feet, and read the newspaper. I try not to do that. I listen to my six-year-old babble on for fifteen minutes. She can talk the arms off a brass monkey."

Other men say that they have a "ten-minute time-out" rule after they walk in the front door. Dad's given a few minutes to change his clothes, check the mail, and talk to Mom before it's open season for the kids.

That's a good idea—as long as you don't make it a "ten-hour" rule. But several fathers said the key was showing some flexibility so the wife and kids don't get their feelings hurt by a stressed-out grump.

■ **My ideal "Honey, I'm home" routine would be to kiss my wife, say hi to the boys, get out of my suit and tie, scan the mail, turn on the nightly news, and read the paper—thirty minutes to do what I want. Real personal time. Too bad this happens about once every six months—and only on the days Elaine and the kids aren't home!**

Who wouldn't love an hour of racquetball before dinner, or a chance to tinker in the garage, or curl up with a new Tom Clancy novel? Perhaps you can pull it off, but for the rest of us mortals, we have to strong-arm our schedule to pick up a free hour here and there.

When I (Mike Yorkey) once surveyed fathers on how many hours a week they read for pleasure, the results were:

► none—1 percent
► one to two hours—37 percent
► three to five hours—50 percent
► six to ten hours—12 percent

The best—and usually only—time to read is after the kids are in bed. Leave the TV off. Reading also promotes communication with your wife. I (Mike) always find it easier to put my book down when my wife, Nicole, talks to me (since I can come right back to my place) than to turn my eyes away from the TV set.

■ **What about flex time in the workplace? Is that catching on?**

It is, especially for a lot of white-collar workers. Starting work at 7 or 7:30 A.M. may mean a *whole* different commute since you're beating the main dose of traffic. And when you leave work at 4 or 4:30, you can save dozens of minutes, if not an hour, by getting a jump on the commute home.

Pulling into your driveway a few minutes before five o'clock may give you enough time to go on a bike ride with the kids, hit tennis balls with them, or see a soccer game.

When I (Mike) moved to Los Angeles to work for Focus on the Family, we settled in a neighborhood about eight blocks from the main headquarters. I could literally walk to my office, which I did a couple of times. Living close to work goes against the grain of most Southern Californians, who wear their two-hour commutes like a red badge of courage.

Well, I didn't want a stinking badge. And you know what? I actually *liked* Los Angeles during my five years there. I always told my friends, "If you can beat the freeways, L.A. is a lot better place to live." You'll feel a lot better about the city you're living in if you live within a reasonable distance from work.

■ **What are some good ideas for spending time with my kids?**

Here are a few examples:
► stamp collecting
► gardening
► woodworking
► collecting sports cards
► setting up electric train sets
► computer games
► reading
► working on the car
► participating in sports the entire family can do (basketball shooting, skiing, ice skating, softball, etc.)
► attending ball games as a family instead of with the guys

■ **Does watching sports on TV with the kids count as a hobby? Please answer affirmatively.**

Sorry, that doesn't count, Dad. While sharing a seventh game of a World Series or a Super Bowl matchup certainly qualifies as family time, letting an ESPN college basketball tripleheader drone on and on is not.

Some dads are obsessed by sports. We find it awfully easy to get glued to the tube. So choose your viewing wisely. You can't follow every sport, every league, every game. Pro and college sports are all over the tube, and there's a game on every night. You'll live if you don't see every touchdown or every home run.

■ **But what if there's a big NBA playoff game on a Sunday afternoon. Do you mean I'm stuck?**

Here's what I (Mike) do if there's a great game on during the weekend: I tape the event on my VCR. Then, a few hours later, I'll rewind the tape and fast-forward through the event. NBA basketball games are a joke. Nothing happens until the fourth quarter, a time when the players turn up the intensity level. Same goes for NFL football. Then it takes a half hour to play the final two minutes.

With a VCR, you can zip your way through all the timeouts and zillions of commercials. You can watch a Cowboys game in thirty minutes, forty-five max if it's really close.

The only drawback to taping sports happens when you run into a friend before you've seen the event. "Did you see that catch Deion Sanders made to beat the Redskins in the last minute?" your buddy exclaims.

"No, I didn't," you'll have to reply through clenched teeth. At times like that, resist the urge to deck your close friend.

■ **I just turned the big four-oh, and look at my belly! But I never find any time to exercise. What can I do to get into some semblance of shape?**

For some men, exercise was something you did in gym class twenty years and fifty pounds ago. If that's you, you may think that since you don't belong to a health club, you're off the hook, right?

Well, don't think so. Exercise is a great way to relieve stress and beat the Battle of the Bulge. You don't have to keep the body toned up, but you'll feel a lot better if you do. Working out and staying in shape will give you a good feeling. You'll enjoy the competition and the challenge of pushing your body to the limit.

■ **If I join a health club, what are some do's and don'ts?**

► **Pick one close to home.** If you have to drive twenty minutes or more one-way to exercise, the time cost will be too high.

► **Purchase a family membership.** That way, you can take

the kids too. Many clubs have a children's play area that
they can use while you make the rounds of the Nautilus
machines.

▶ **Make sure the club has a swimming pool.** Children
love the water, and there's nothing better than having the
whole family around the pool on a hot summer's day. In
Southern California, I (Mike) used to pack a picnic dinner
and go for a twilight swim with the kids—a great way to
cool them off.

▶ **Ask other members if the club is "kid friendly."** Some
clubs are havens for the social set who believe kids should
be seen and not heard. You want to join a club where kids
are welcomed.

▶ **Finally, if a club is beyond your budget, use municipal
facilities.** Many towns and cities have a public pool and
parks with fantastic facilities. Use them—after all, you're
paying for their upkeep too!

■ **Okay, I'm resolved to getting back in some sort of fighting
shape. The dilemma, as usual, is to find time to exercise
without leaving the family in the dust. What are some ways I
can incorporate exercise into my daily routine?**

At work . . .

▶ If your office building has a shower, go jogging or run the
stairs at noon. Eat a light lunch afterward.

▶ If you can't change out of your work clothes, bring soft
shoes and go for a brisk walk.

▶ Play tennis, basketball, or racquetball before work.

▶ Take stairs instead of elevators. Climbing steps is a great
aerobic activity.

▶ Keep moving during the workday. Don't be desk bound.

With the family . . .

▶ Biking. Many towns have constructed bike paths. Be sure
to wear helmets.

▶ Hiking. We're not talking about shimmying up a sheer
cliff. No, we're talking about going for a walk in the woods
or a scenic spot near town.

▶ Shoot baskets, flip the Frisbee, hit tennis balls, or play catch with the kids.

▶ Take on outdoor projects, such as yard work or big chores around the house. Mowing grass and hauling tree limbs will increase your heart rate too.

▶ Pop an exercise video in the VCR and do aerobics together. The kids will be entertained, and you and your spouse will get a workout.

It's hard to keep the big picture in mind when you exercise. But remember this: By exercising now, you'll increase your chances of being around when the grandkids arrive and grow up. By eating right and staying in shape (especially if you're a desk jockey with a silk rope and a leather lunch bucket), you should be around to influence two generations of your family.

Who knows? The time you spend with your children's children could make the difference whether they come to know Christ.

THE TOP 10 REASONS NOT TO JOIN A HEALTH CLUB

10. On your first no-cost visit to Biff's Body Bar, you were caught leaving the club with a twenty-five-pound barbell in your gym bag because you didn't know what "free-weight" meant.

9. To pay someone just so you can exercise is definitely not good stewardship.

8. Locker-room talk with a bunch of overweight men isn't half as interesting as it was in high school.

7. Like most health club members, since you'd probably work out only five or six times a year, why not just skip it and pocket the cash?

6. If you join a health club, you'll discover just how out of shape you really are (talk about depressing).

5. People will see your legs.

4. If you try pumping iron with the big boys, you'll only bruise your ego . . . and pull every muscle in your body!

3. You don't have the right shoes, and your wife would never let you take out a loan to buy a pair.

2. The girls in the skimpy aerobics outfits could be hazardous to your health—especially if your wife ever caught you looking at them.

1. You're too old to be healthy.

5

Pizza for Breakfast?

. . . .

■ I teach Spanish in a suburban Chicago high school, and my
first period starts at 7:45 A.M. I usually start off by reviewing
vocabulary words like *queso* (cheese), *huevos* (eggs), *frijoles
refritos* (refried beans), and *arroz con pollo* (chicken with rice).

In recent years, I've noticed more and more students are
not tracking with me. Then I overheard one student say to
the other, "Man, I'm starving." Like many teenagers today,
he had shown up at school without breakfast. Then his friend
had a solution. "Hey, why didn't you grab a piece of cold
pizza like I did? It works great."

Welcome to nutrition in the nineties. So much for antiques like
oatmeal or grapefruit. Family mealtimes in North America are on
a skid, according to nearly every poll. Three-fourths of families
now eat together only half the time. Some of these separations are
necessary, of course, due to work and school. But a lot more are
lifestyle choices: Sitting down in the kitchen can't compete with
working out at the gym, staying late at the office, or simply not
wanting to wait on someone else.

As for your Spanish class, probably half of the parents work
downtown, which means dads and moms are up very early to catch

the train or hit the expressway. Kids get themselves off to school, and that usually means without eating breakfast.

■ **Yes, but since our cafeteria opens shortly after 7 A.M., why aren't the kids eating there? At least they can eat some cold cereal or a warm bagel.**

Do you want to know what your school's biggest breakfast seller is? *Doughnuts.* That means some of your students are already on a sugar high before the first bell rings. You should be able to tell the hyper kids who've been to the cafeteria, and the sluggish kids who haven't eaten a thing and are still waking up.

■ **How did this "not eating right" business all start?**

Nobody decided over the last thirty years to slack off on eating together as families. It just sort of happened, due to a number of factors. Employment is certainly one. It takes longer to get to and from work in today's traffic, and modern bosses want more time once we're there. The steady rise in the number of employed women—the traditional cooks in most families—has had its effect. Wives' time and energy for fussing in the kitchen is greatly curtailed; simply getting the weekly *shopping* done is an achievement.

Meanwhile, modern technology—most notably the microwave—has made every family member his own cook . . . sort of. When each person can pop in a Ravioli Lunch Bucket or a Lean Cuisine, why "bother" trying to eat together? In fact, things go smoother if you don't; microwaves are one-at-a-time machines. So wait your turn! Hopefully, you'll find some fresh lettuce or an apple in the fridge to fill in missing nutrients.

If zap-cooking takes too much effort, a battery of fast-food chains waits at every stoplight—another invention of the late-twentieth century. Speedy and cheap (but it adds up), propelled by razzle-dazzle advertising, they provide exactly what millions are looking for. The notion of roast beef, mashed potatoes, and five-cup fruit salad grows dimmer by the month.

■ **What do families miss by not eating together and talking to each other over a plate of food?**

Hearing what went well—or badly—during the day. Enjoying a joke together. Debating an issue. Looking forward to a challenge—a report to give at school, an important sales call, a special song to perform at church. To one busy, breathless parent, Dr. Dobson wrote the following comments: "It takes time to be an effective parent. . . . It takes time to listen, once more, to the skinned-knee episode and talk about the bird with a broken wing. These are the building blocks of esteem, held together with the mortar of love. But they seldom materialize amidst busy timetables. . . .

"The great value of traditions is that they give a family a sense of identity and belonging. All of us desperately need to feel that we're not just part of a busy cluster of people living together in a house, but we're a living, breathing family that's conscious of our uniqueness, our character, and our heritage."

■ **I didn't realize how much cultural shift had taken place until a recent evening when our two teenage daughters reported, "Our friends at school think we're totally weird that we eat breakfast and dinner together as a family. They're just astounded—like, 'You must be the Waltons or something.'" I got the feeling _weird_ was actually more of a compliment (in a weird sort of way).**

It was a compliment. You and your wife have juggled a lot of balls to adjust your schedules to accommodate the family mealtime. Over the years, you'll see that it was worth the effort. The rhythm of regular family meals will prove its worth.

Here are three reasons to eat together as a family:

> ► **Overall nutrition.** The easiest things to pop in our mouths are not always the best. High-fat, high-starch diets are having an undeniable effect on this society. The Harvard Nutrition and Fitness Project says child obesity is up 54 percent since the 1960s. Ask yourself this question: Do people who skip breakfast overcompensate later in the day by

eating more, and thus are more prone to weight problems?

▶ **School performance.** As mentioned earlier, schoolteachers can tell within seconds which students return from morning recess having dug a candy bar out of their lunch bags or backpacks. Sugar and reading groups just don't work well together.

▶ **Communication.** Ever notice how much time Jesus spent talking with people over meals? Lazarus, Mary, and Martha . . . Simon the Pharisee . . . Zaccheus . . . the Twelve on Passover night. He knew that people relax more then, that their minds sort of open along with their mouths, and that special closeness can develop.

In tragic contrast, think about the modern child eating alone. Where does he plop down with his bowl of Golden Grahams? In front of the TV. He's silently pleading for communication.

That's why mealtime talk must relate to kids as well as adults; long discussions of job tensions or the family budget are best handled elsewhere. This is a time to ask can-opener questions like "Who had something terrific happen today?" or "How did you feel about that?" or "Let's talk about this coming weekend. What would be fun to do?"

■ **What if the talk turns negative, sarcastic, or complaining?**

Parents must not let the atmosphere be sabotaged. One parent, when his kids were younger, was known to deal with bickering by silently picking up a child's plate, cup, and silverware—and transporting them to the top of the washing machine! The child had tem-

---

WE'RE OUTTA HERE

In this poll, families were asked: Out of twenty-one meals in a week, how many do your family eat together? Here are the answers, and see where your family stacks up.

16-21 meals	8 percent
11-15 meals	18 percent
6-10 meals	45 percent
0-5 meals	29 percent

Source: Parents of Teenagers *magazine poll, February/March 1991*

Q. Do you at least eat your evening meal together?

No	37 percent
Yes	63 percent

Source: USA Today *poll*

porarily lost his or her right to enjoy the family table. And *standing up* for the rest of the meal while looking at nothing but a lonely Maytag was a strong message that pleasant talk would be the wiser route next time.

Also, you should set a firm policy on menu comments: *If you can't say something good, don't say anything.* The parent who *didn't* do the cooking is the better one to enforce this. Erma Bombeck once spoke for every frustrated mom when she cracked, "Why should I take pride in cooking when they don't take pride in eating?" The "eaters" have a responsibility to honor the effort of the "cooker."

■ **Okay, what's the best reason why it's important to eat together?**

Love. Most important of all, regular, reliable meals, whether fancy or simple, send a quiet message to any child that someone is planning for me. Someone cares about my daily needs. Someone is regularly thinking of my good.

Yes, it's a bother sometimes. Yes, it means bending our schedules. But isn't that our calling as dads and moms? "After all," wrote the Apostle Paul, "children should not have to provide for their parents, but parents should provide for their children" (2 Cor. 12:14, TEV).

While all of us in the 1990s

RECIPE FOR BETTER MEALTIMES

1. Plan ahead. Start early enough. Have the right food on hand.

2. Insist on prompt attendance when called. Don't allow a come-when-you-feel-like-it habit.

3. Turn off the TV.

4. Turn off the radio. (The point is to listen to each other, not the meteorologist or disc jockey!)

5. Start with a table prayer, genuinely expressed. Call on a different family member to lead each time. But keep it short.

6. Keep the atmosphere positive. Don't allow "attacks" on the food quality or one another.

7. Don't fight over quantities, especially with preschoolers, who often go on feast-or-famine jags. Hunger will prevail over time. However, if for social reasons you want to require that children "try some of everything on the table," fine.

8. Involve everyone in the conversation.

face particular stresses, we must not forever yield to circumstances. Our children deserve the simple gift of daily bread they
can count on. And as we give it, we find a special joy coming back
our way that frantic, splintered households will never know.

*This material is adapted from "Pizza for Breakfast?" by Dean Merrill, Focus on the Family
magazine, July 1991. Copyright © 1991, Focus on the Family. Used by permission.*

6

How the West Was Done

■ **My wife and I have been talking about taking a Vacation to End All Vacations—a twelve-state, 4,500-mile trip around the Wild West in our '89 Taurus station wagon. I'm all for this "driving vacation," but Emilie isn't sure the two kids can handle sitting in the car for hours on end. Should we go for it?**

By all means, yes. Sure, spending eight, ten hours a day in the car can be a bit much, but you'll be creating some lifetime memories. It will also be a great way to talk together as a family.

When Randy Wilson, a Texas rancher, and his family go on vacation, they drive to Colorado. That way, Randy's certain they'll have plenty of time in the car. (Believe it or not, that's the way he wants it!) One of the kids sits with Dad in the front seat, and as the scenery passes by, long discussions ensue.

■ **That all sounds great, but we're talking about some serious seat time for the two kids. We don't want to endure hearing "Are we there yet?" every hour on the hour.**

Some parents will find this idea sacrilegious, but hear it out. Just a week before Bob Welch took a long driving vacation with his family, he sat down with his pastor for lunch. As he outlined his plans, a look of concern came over his pastor's face.

"Eighteen days," the pastor repeated, nodding slowly. "May I offer a suggestion?"

Bob was thinking he would propose that they pray together. Or that he'd call in the council of elders for the first-ever laying-on-of-hands ceremony in front of a salad bar.

Instead, he locked eyes with Bob and said: "Why don't you borrow our portable TV and video player? It plugs into the cigarette lighter. It kept our kids from going nuts when we took our cross-country vacation."

■ **I'm sure other families have spent three weeks together in a station wagon without a video player—and lived to tell their minister about it in the thirty-six counseling sessions that followed. But traveling the vast expanses of the West with a VCR blaring in the back of the car seems so un-American.**

You're right. Pioneer families on the Oregon Trail, for example, couldn't watch movies as they traveled since their wagons were not equipped with cigarette lighters, thus rendering their video players useless.

■ **Funny, very funny, but you're going to have to come up with more than that.**

All Bob Welch knows is that for him and his family, their Canada-to-Mexico loop was made easier by the technological wonder wedged between their bucket seats. Whenever their fifteen- and twelve-year-old sons started slugging each other, they flipped on a video.

Don't misunderstand Bob. As families hit the Highway to Adventure this summer, he's not suggesting that watching *Babe* a couple of times—okay, six, max—is a ticket to vacation splendor. But while their boys were continually amazed at the beauty along their eleven-state route, twelve hours in the car can get boring from time to time. That's when the movies came in handy.

On the day before the Welches left on their vacation, Bob discovered one of his sons sitting in the back of the car, watching a video.

"Ryan," he said, "you're going to be sitting in the backseat of this car for two weeks. Enjoy your freedom while you can."

His twelve-year-old pulled off his headphones. "It's okay, Dad. I'm just practicing."

The Welches left their hometown in Oregon for eastern Washington to see some old friends. Over dinner at their place, his wife, Sally, and Bob became emotional. It would be the last time for three weeks that they would eat a meal without hearing a chirpy teen say, "Is this for here or to go?"

They headed for Glacier National Park, where they stayed in a cabin so small that they couldn't brush their teeth sideways. The photo caption in the brochure should have said: "Actual size."

But who could be upset with all that fresh air? With that mind-boggling scenery? With fifteen movies yet to be shown? They drove south for about the length of *Groundhog Day* and *Little Big League.*

After five days on the road, their pit stops were Indianapolis 500 caliber. They learned to gas the car, go to the bathroom, and buy chips and Big Gulps in less than five minutes.

After a week they could, with their eyes closed, recite every item on a McDonald's menu—prices included. They knew the WASH YOUR HANDS BEFORE RETURNING TO WORK warnings on the bathroom paper-towel dispensers as well as they knew John 3:16.

After ten days of looking at anti-litter signs, they were convinced that virtually every Rotary Club and wrestling team in America were part of the Adopt-a-Highway cleanup system. The puzzling part was never seeing any of these folks actually cleaning up litter.

In fact, the Welches never saw any folks, period. During one desolate stretch of highway, in the middle of a scene that looked like the backdrop for *Wagons East,* they saw a sign that brought hope to the desperate nomads of the nineties: "Espresso Just Ahead."

In Big Sky land, "Just Ahead" meant roughly 150 miles.

■ **This is starting to sound like the Griswold family in** *National Lampoon's Vacation.*

As the Welches' asphalt marathon continued, the video player came alive with Focus on the Family's *McGee & Me* series. They were on a roll.

By the 2,500-mile mark, Bob discovered that the U.S. has two basic kinds of people: those who can fold road maps and those who cannot.

Bob is a "cannot" sort of guy. His maps were wadded, folded, and refolded so many times that they couldn't tell which state they were in half the time. Sally gave up hope of ever properly refolding any of their maps—or of fitting them into the glove compartment.

Their weary Taurus wheezed over 10,800-foot Wolf Creek Pass as they conquered the Continental Divide and pressed on for the vast painted deserts of Arizona. At the Grand Canyon, they gaped at the amazing mile-deep gorge that's nearly twenty miles wide in spots. Ten hikers a day must be rescued from the canyon, park rangers told them.

By then, Bob and Sally were too tired to become canyon-climbing victims. Their idea of a strenuous outing was sending one of the kids out of the motel room for ice.

THE FIVE BEST REASONS TO TAKE A FAMILY HIGHWAY ADVENTURE

1. It's exciting to open the door to your motel room and see what you got for $24.

2. It's less expensive than flying, unless you count the cost of film developing.

3. It's a great excuse to visit old friends, who will quickly remind you that they're not the only ones getting thinner on top or wider around the waist.

4. It's a wonderful way to compare the merits of the Arch Deluxe and the Double Whopper with cheese.

5. It will improve your sense of direction.

■ **Did the Welches make it home without any more mishaps?**

Ever onward, they endured drenching afternoon thunder-showers and DQ's Blizzards. They blazed across California's Mojave Desert in 108-degree temperatures. They swam in the Pacific Ocean. They did Disneyland for three endless days and nights, the vacation equivalent of sensory overload. With "It's a Small World" ringing in their ears, they headed north toward Oregon.

They were within a mere 700 miles of home sweet home when disaster struck. "That's it," whispered Sally. "We're out of movies."

■ **Out of movies? What a tragedy! What did the Welches do?**

Bob gulped. But, glancing in the rearview mirror at the kids, he realized he must keep his cool. He must be strong. For the others.

They rolled into Santa Rosa to say hello to the wildest–guy-on-Bob's-dorm-floor-twenty-years-ago-turned-Christian. A guy who once saved Bob's life after he'd sliced his leg with a chain saw. A guy who, reaching into his stack of videotapes, saved Bob's life once again.

"Here's *Mighty Ducks 3* and *The University of Oregon Football Highlights—1995*," he said. "That should get you home. Just mail them back when you're done."

ON THE ROAD AGAIN

Whether your family is taking a cross-country flight or a Sunday drive to the lake, traveling with kids is bound to be "eventful." Here are a few tips for families on the go:

▶ **Set reasonable expectations.** If you envision night after night of memorable restaurant dinners with two well-behaved preschoolers, you are probably setting yourself up for disappointment.

▶ **Decide on a trip budget and discuss it with your kids.** Let them know in advance how much they can spend.

▶ **Consider taking a vacation with another family.** This way adults can trade off on child care and enjoy an occasional break from the kids.

▶ **For families with teens, don't insist on around-the-clock togetherness.** Some family members may want to go fishing, while others might prefer to "shop until they drop."

▶ **For families that travel by car,** put a small suitcase or box between children in the backseat to clearly separate "sides."

continued next page

▶ **When traveling by air,** pack an extra change of clothing for each child in a carry-on bag. That way, in case your luggage is delayed, you will be able to get by for a day or two.

▶ **If you don't have a room reservation, start looking for a hotel or motel before 4 P.M.** Tempers fray right around dinnertime when everyone is hungry and many motels are flashing their "No Vacancy" signs.

▶ **Plan—and announce—a treat at the end of the day,** so everyone has something to look forward to: a swim in the motel pool, dinner at a restaurant, or an ice cream stop.

▶ **Avoid fast-food "McBurnout"** by eating picnics in city parks or scenic byways. Not only is this healthier, but it is also a good way to "people-watch" in the cities.

▶ **Before visiting a museum,** look over a brochure or guidebook and tell the children more about what's in store. You can also make a game out of visiting art museums by starting a scavenger hunt for the children. Have them look for a famous painting or painter.

▶ **Once inside a museum or amusement park,** pick out a landmark and set a meeting time in case the family inadvertently loses a member.

▶ **On longer trips, hit the road by 5 A.M.,** when there is little traffic and the kids are likely to sleep. You can drive 150 miles before stopping for a leisurely breakfast.

▶ **Stop every couple of hours** to let the kids burn off some energy. Everyone needs a break. A soccer ball is great to kick around at rest stops.

▶ **Carry a thermos with cold drinks,** so "drink stops" can be minimized. Avoid salty foods, however, which call for lots of drinking—and more stops at restrooms.

▶ **Promote grapes, raisins, and nuts** for drive-time snacking. Sugary items have a way of inducing hyperactivity, especially for smaller kids.

▶ **By all means, have fun,** and don't be afraid to be flexible and depart from a well-planned itinerary. Some of your vacation's best moments may come from those unexpected side trips.

Like thankful pioneers with fresh provisions, they set out for promised land: Oregon Country. When they finally arrived, Bob and Sally were out of energy. They were out of money. They were racked with white-line fever.

But they had done it. The Welches had seen America: Glacier National Park. Old Faithful. Monument Valley. Zuma Beach.

Dennis the Menace. Groundhog Day. McGee & Me. And much more. As they said goodnight to their boys that first evening home, Bob and Sally were both thinking what neither of them said: *All the miles . . . all the money . . . all the sometimes monotonous stretches between "points of interest" had been worth it.*

Now, as time fast-forwards through life and their sons move on to college and careers and families of their own, those memories that the four recorded will stay with each of them forever.

And these memories don't require a portable TV and video player to enjoy.

This material is adapted from writings by Bob Welch and Mike Yorkey, who wrote "On the Road Again" in Focus on the Family *magazine in June 1987. Copyright © 1987, Focus on the Family. Used by permission. By the way, the Welches stayed with the Yorkey family on their Wild West adventure. Since that big trip several years ago, the Welches have taken more modest vacations, including spending a week in the family cabin near the Oregon beach town of Yachats.*

7

Let's Go Camping!

· ·

■ **We send our kids to camp each summer, but someone in my Sunday School class said I should check out Christian camping. I had never heard of such a thing. What can you tell me?**

Let's do a little scene-setting here:

As the summer sun set behind the redwood trees, campers began to emerge from softly lit cabins. They converged on the smooth footpath that wound up behind the main lodge to the outdoor amphitheater where the evening campfire was about to begin.

A counselor set a match to the kerosene-soaked wood pile, and within seconds, the kindling wood crackled as the flames rose into the crisp mountain air. Squeals of excitement erupted from the young campers—and appreciative oohs and ahs from their parents.

■ **Wait a minute! Parents—at a summer camp?**

Indeed, at Mount Hermon—and an ever-increasing number of camps across the country—summer camp is no longer synonymous with kids. Camping in the 1990s has become an attractive vacation option for the entire family.

One of the families enjoying the campfire were the Dedinis of Los Gatos, California, who were at Mount Hermon with their four children.

Dom Dedini thought back to the day a few months earlier when he had gathered the entire family to talk about their summer vacation plans. Rubbing his hands with anticipation, Dom announced that this was the year the family could finally afford a trip to the beaches of Maui.

"If we go to Hawaii, can we still go to Mount Hermon?" asked Jim, his ten-year-old son.

That was a question Dom hadn't anticipated.

"Why?"

"Because if going to Hawaii means we can't go to Mount Hermon this summer, then we don't want to go."

So, by popular demand, the Dedini family returned—for the *eighth* year in a row—to Mount Hermon and the Santa Cruz mountains south of San Francisco.

■ Why had Mount Hermon become a summertime tradition for the Dedini clan?

For starters, both kids and parents had forged friendships with other families around the country, and they looked forward to the time each summer when they could renew old acquaintances and begin new ones.

Also, Mount Hermon was a time for family sharing and spontaneous fun: starlit walks along a quiet trail; late-night talks sitting by the embers of a fading fire; a brisk swim in the cool Pacific Ocean; hikes through a silent redwood forest; and most of all, a chance to have the whole family together at one time, in one place, without the normal household distractions.

Christian family camps—also known in some parts of the country as Christian family conferences—are usually week-long vacations held at a scenic conference center. The goal is to receive spiritual and physical replenishment in a relaxed, enjoyable environment. At most camps, located all across the United States and Canada, meals are provided, activities are planned from morning till night, and families are given the flexibility to do what they want, when they want.

■ What are the accommodations like? Would you characterize them as "early American"?

Accommodations vary according to tastes and budget. So it's your nickel. Some family camps have lush condominium-like suites with all the creature comforts, including daily maid service. Others cater to families willing to "rough it" in rustic cabins and community showers.

Either way, an Aloha vacation just can't compete financially with a family camp. The average cost for a family of four ranges from $650 to $1,500 per week, depending on the accommodations. These rates include meals and activities for the week.

Some of the better known camps are Spring Hills Camps in Michigan, Hume Lake and Forest Home in California, and Sandy Cove in Maryland.

■ What makes camping at a Christian conference center different from other vacation alternatives?

It's the spiritual dimension, reply the camp directors. Bible studies, worship and praise services, as well as prayer meetings, are readily available each day. Each camp works to provide a comprehensive, Bible-based foundation for the week's activities.

Yet, unlike the formal Bible conferences of yesteryear, dress is casual and afternoons are often spent at the ol' fishin' hole with a rod and reel in hand.

A typical day at camp includes a wide range of activities geared toward kids and adults. The day begins with a large "country" breakfast—sometimes served in an open meadow or near a running stream. Then families usually break up for different morning events. The adults may attend a family life seminar, while the teens and preadolescents take off for sports, games, and biblical teaching. The younger children are placed under the caring supervision of trained counselors.

After lunch, families are given the opportunity to do whatever they like. Activities such as softball, tennis, basketball, picnic games, arts and crafts, swimming, fishing, sailing, and hiking are readily available. There are always activities planned, depending upon how much structure you want in your day.

■ But what if I just want to relax?

No problem, Dad. You can "rack out" for a mid-afternoon snooze, if you want to. But you'll probably find too many fun things to do to take a nap. At Mount Hermon, for instance, campers drive through the redwoods on their way to Twin Lakes Beach. After a hearty lunch served by the kitchen crew, families stake out their territory and compete in a sand-sculpturing contest; others hunt for driftwood or wade in the ocean.

At Pine Cove in Texas, the emphasis is on western hospitality. The highlight of the week is "Western Night," complete with western attire, a steak fry, group singing, and hilarious skits.

After dinner, parents usually congregate for the evening meeting, while younger kids head off to their special areas. In this setting, parents can listen to the keynote speaker discuss family topics such as the biblical roles of husbands and wives, or hear a scriptural message related to everyday family experiences.

Each conference strives to minister to every family member. For some, that need may be very real. "We came with real family problems and found direction and redirection," one parent said.

■ I recently remarried, so we're trying to blend two families. How can Christian camping help?

In recent years, Christian conference centers have begun reaching out to blended families. A father of a newly blended family stated it this way: "Mount Hermon is helping us put our families together. The kids had a good time and related well to each other. That gave my wife and me a chance to build on our own relationship."

Many Christian camps have counselors available for couples and families wishing to address specific problems. Speakers and conference staff are always available to spend time with families, talking and praying through special needs.

The key leadership staff at the majority of conference centers are year-round employees who are professionals in the field of camping ministry. But the heart of the summer staff is made up of college students with a great desire to minister and serve the family. They normally go through a comprehensive recruiting and training process before the conference sessions begin.

The impact the young counselors have is impressive. One mother in Texas said, "My daughter loved day camp. The counselors were such a blessing to the children; they are fine examples of living God's Word."

Finally, family conferences are a great place to build memories. They may be family memories, but they may also be personal memories. And the memories are destined to last for years.

And as for Hawaii, well, Dom Dedini figures he'll get there sometime in the twenty-first century. By then, the kids should be married and raising families of their own. But knowing the Dedini family, summer vacation is likely to be a three-generation affair at Mount Hermon.

This material is adapted from writings by Gary Wall of Wheaton, Illinois.

CAMPS FOR YOUR FAMILY

If you are interested in taking your family to camp this summer, a good resource is the *Christian Camp and Conference Guide Pak* published by Christian Camping International/USA.

To obtain a copy, send $14.95 to the Christian Camping International/USA, P.O. Box 62189, Colorado Springs, CO 80962-2189 or call (719) 260-9400.

Christian Camping International/USA also has a web site. The address is http://www.cciusa.org/.

8

Is This the Fun Part?

. . . .

■ **We're planning our summer vacation, and all the kids talk about is going to Disneyland. Should we go ahead and make it a Mickey summer?**

Yes, by all means, but don't forget that it will be hot next summer. Of course, you won't be able to tell that from the Disneyland brochures, because they never show anyone looking hot.

Instead, they show children snuggling up to Goofy and adults lounging beside swimming pools shaped like giant mouse ears, but nobody wearing a sweat-soaked Ralph Lauren shirt.

Fast forward to the month of July. There you are with your family, inching along some thirty-six-lane Los Angeles freeway in your non-A/C-equipped station wagon. You feel like a piece of bread in a giant toaster-on-wheels. A toaster-on-wheels that is, not incidentally, lost somewhere in a large kitchen called California.

You look at the road map. You immediately notice something very strange about the road map, namely that Anaheim no longer exists, having been obliterated, along with most of Southern California, by a melted Snickers bar.

"Daddy," says Megan, your angel-faced five-year-old daughter, "are we almost to the abusement park?"

"That's *amusement* park," you manage through gritted teeth. "And, yes, we're almost there."

Your nine-year-old son Jamie has a question. "Then why," he asks, "does that sign say 'Mexican Border Ahead'?"

You tighten your grip on the steering wheel, wishing you were doing something easier—like pulling lead oar on a slave galley.

"Hey, Dad," Jamie pipes up, "is this the fun part?"

■ **That sounds like our last trip to Disneyland five years ago. Now the kids are talking about going to Six Flags. What's the draw for amusement parks?**

Yes, folks, every summer, families all over the country trade a quiet week of camping for losing their lunches on a 250-foot-high ride called "Free Fall." They forego the solitude of the seashore so they can stand in line for hours with hundreds of sweaty people wearing Six Flags hats. They pass up that inexpensive picnic in the park so they can spend $12.95, plus tax, for the Authentic Davy Crockett Boot Spurs, guaranteed to self-destruct in twenty minutes or 200 feet, whichever comes first.

Amusement parks may be the home of the Quintessential American Family Vacation. From Disneyland to Disney World, from Six Flags in Arlington, Texas, to Kings Island in Cincinnati, America's amusement parks will attract millions of families this summer. Given that, we now offer you a complete guide on how to take such a vacation—and live to show your six trays of slides to obliging friends and relatives:

Planning Your Trip

Package deals are simple and can save you money. But remember, not all of them are created equal. For example, one travel firm might offer, say, the M-I-C-K-E-Y deal. An "M" package might include airfare, lodging at the Disneyland Hotel, and use of a rent-a-car. A "Y" package, on the other hand, might include bus fare, a pup tent in Bakersfield, and a cardboard hitchhiker's sign that says 'Disneyland or Bust.' "

Getting There

The big question here is should you drive or fly. Each has its advantages. Driving is a wonderful way for you to communicate with your children. For example, your child might say, "Are we there yet?" And you might reply, "No, we're not even out of our cul-de-sac yet." This can be repeated numerous times, even before you leave the city limits.

Flying, on the other hand, gives your children the opportunity to see the world from a different perspective and test their inquisitiveness. When you arrive in, say, Orlando, your child might ask you, "What did the man mean when he said our baggage had been routed to Butte, Montana?"

At the Motel

Beware of "extras" advertised on motel marquees. "Continental Breakfast" may sound like exotic cuisine. In reality, it tastes like a donut baked and shipped last week—from another continent.

If you're in a motel and you hear a loud, clanking noise and the room shakes violently, don't panic. You just got stuck next to the ice machine. If you're in L.A., do panic. You're experiencing an earthquake.

What to Wear to the Park

Choose something that will go well with pink cotton candy, soda pop, ketchup, mustard, french fries, snow cones, and various forms of grease, all or some of which will likely wind up on you by the end of the day.

Parking at the Park

In most cases, it is not wise to park your car in the parking lot and attempt to make it to the entrance in the same day. Remember, you're on vacation; don't overextend yourself. Make camp at the midway point the first night, then make the final push the next morning.

Deciding Which Rides to Take

The larger the family, the more difficult it is to agree upon the next ride to take. Families of six or more might consider bringing along a family counselor with a background in labor arbitrations.

Taking Photos and Movies

Photos and movies are essential for an amusement park vacation. After days of hiking miles across 105-degree pavement in search of restrooms, it's easy to become delirious and forget whether you're having fun. Photos and movies, used as evidence, can decide the issue weeks later, when you're more relaxed. Remember: Only take family group shots in amusement parks if you like pictures of a dozen or so blurred ears of strangers.

Finally, don't be a "trigger-happy" videographer. You know the type—the guy who narrates his vacation videos like this: "Okay, here's a shot of Mom as we first meet—oh, you're gonna love this—the travel agent. And look here—slow motion of the agent looking for flight departures on her computer screen!"

Standing in Lines

Amusement park lines are test of fire for parents. You've waited ninety minutes to see a couple of porpoises play volleyball and, right in front of the entrance, your three-year-old quietly announces she needs a bathroom.

What do you do? You have no choice: You take her to that other line, where you wait fifteen minutes and, right in front of that entrance, she quietly announces she doesn't have to go anymore. At this point, we recommend patience, prayer, and Pampers.

What to Eat

On the whole, amusement parks offer the same wholesome food children get at home: pizza, licorice, ice cream, and pop—items from your four basic food groups.

What to Buy

Souvenirs are often the highlight of any amusement park vacation—for at least a minute or two after they've been purchased. That's roughly how long it takes the kid who just said, "I've just gotta have the Dance-n-Sing Snoopy Doll," to realize his life will never be complete if he doesn't have the Daffy Duck Glow-in-the-Dark Suntan Lotion.

The Three Stages of Decline

Watching people at an amusement park is like watching that commercial where, one by one, the battery-powered toys run out of energy. Thus it's important to be aware of the Three Stages of Decline:

- ▶ **Stage 1:** Happy families skipping from ride to ride in the cool, dreamy, early-morning, short-line hours.
- ▶ **Stage 2:** Hot, thirsty, sunburned families arguing over whether to (A) watch a man eat fire while riding upside-down on a motorcycle that's balancing on a tightrope wire strung over a pond of killer alligators, or (B) see something a bit more daring, like Daddy trying to squeeze into a go-kart.
- ▶ **Stage 3:** Tired, drained families with blank expressions on their faces, sitting on curbs half-mumbling, half-singing something about it being a small world after all.

■ **Well, should we go? After all, this all sounds like little Megan was right—maybe such places should be called "abusement" parks.**

Well, of course you should go. Let's face it, anything you do with kids means taking a few risks and enduring a few inconveniences.

Summer vacations with children, you see, were never meant to go smoothly from start to finish. They were meant, instead, to make memories as a family, even if you had to sprint to the bathroom after taking that "Montezuma's Revenge" roller coaster with your son.

When you consider how quickly kids grow up, the risk of a few embarrassing moments seems a small price to pay for the joy of seeing your preschool son gleefully drive a miniature sports car that he's sure he's actually driving. Or watching your daughter's eyes light up when she wins a teddy bear in the beanbag toss.

Besides, time has a way of weeding out the memories of long waits in line and preserving, instead, the memories of the exciting ride that followed. And as for those other vacation pitfalls . . . well, given a few weeks to get over them, most of us wouldn't trade them for all the cotton candy in Opryland.

Remember this: Unlike the Davy Crockett self-destructing boot spurs, family memories come with a lifetime guarantee. So pick up yours now, before it's too late.

This material is adapted from writings by Bob Welch, who's survived Disneyland, Knott's Berry Farm, and Great America amusement parks.

3

. . . .

Dads and Their Teens

The Flourishing Teen Years

■ **Who are those strange creatures inhabiting the rooms that once belonged to my cuddly little boy and my angelic little girl? Why are they always doing odd things? If the teen years are going to be anything like the last six months, what's left of my hair will certainly fall out.**

Whoa, hold on here! Before answering your questions, we must first realize that adolescents are caught in an in-between world as strange as the one Alice found in the looking glass. Trapped between childhood and adulthood, they belong to neither.

But it is even more complicated than that. Though bored with childhood and embarrassed to be associated with it, teenagers are uncertain of the future. Thus they sometimes act like children, even as they try desperately to become adults.

■ **My friends warned me about teenagers. So why do some parents say that the teen years were their most enjoyable years of child raising?**

It's all in your attitude. Don't spend a lot of time looking into the rearview mirror agonizing over things that can't be changed. Instead, concern yourself with learning to be a better parent *now*. Then the teenage years need not be dreaded or feared, but can be enjoyed as a wonderful adventure of growth for both you and your children.

Consider the life of a model teen: Jesus Christ. The description of Jesus' adolescent years is relatively brief. In fact, from the time He confronted the elders in the temple at age twelve until He was baptized by John in the Jordan River at age thirty is covered in one sentence: "And Jesus grew in wisdom and stature, and in favor with God and men" (Luke 2:52).

Scripture is given for our instruction and edification. Therefore, this biblical model can help us with our own children. In Luke 2:52, our heavenly Parent refers to the four major areas of our lives: the physical (stature), the mental (wisdom), and the social and spiritual (favor with God and man). We know that these areas are interrelated and that they must work together if we are to be whole persons. Most adolescents are confused about these major areas of life, and modern society only multiplies their confusion.

■ How is that?

Let's start with their changing bodies. The physical changes in teens' bodies are new, often frightening, and tough to understand.

First of all, teenagers grow at an irregular rate, with girls maturing two to four times faster than boys, both emotionally and physically.

Internally, boys feel certain urges and interests that they express clumsily by teasing girls, hitting them, insulting them, or in some instances of immature bravado, talking dirty. All this seems childish and disgusting to the girls who are only interested in older boys anyway.

The girls aren't secure either, of course. Like kittens who do a figure eight around your legs—leaning all the time—teenage girls need a lot of assurance. They need to lean even when they think they're standing on their own.

Adolescent girls spend hours in their rooms trying to imitate images they find in *Seventeen* magazine—images created by professional photographers and models. The teenager has only her Kmart styling brush and her Cover Girl makeup kit. Consequently, she derives as much frustration as satisfaction from the glossy ads and articles. The magazine girls look coordinated, confident, and comfortable with themselves—everything teenage girls are not.

Today, the teenager who feels lacking in physical beauty or athletic prowess is not only insecure and fearful, but also angry at his or her parents for not supplying the right genetic material or enough money to buy the right clothes. They may even be angry at God for having made them this way.

■ **I've caught snippets of kids talking to each other in their bedrooms, and I've noticed that many of their conversations relate to sexual adjustment. Why is that?**

Some of it has to do with the mystery and magic of these strange urges they feel; some is just bravado born of fear and a sense of inadequacy and ignorance.

Despite all the information about sex available today, you'd be surprised to learn that our young people understand sex little better than we did when we were growing up. They don't know how their bodies work, and they believe the same myths and misinformation that have always been shared between adolescents.

■ **My thirteen-year-old daughter talks a lot of being "independent" of us. I still want her close because it's a nasty world out there. How should I handle this?**

As our children grow older, we should begin loosening the screws—not tightening them. Our natural tendency is the latter, however, especially given the world in which we live. We are bombarded with data about adolescence; almost every magazine and daily newspaper carries some survey about the high rates of teenage pregnancy, venereal disease, AIDS, alcohol, drugs, and teenage suicide.

These statistics are terrifying to parents, but we cannot let them frighten us into tightening the controls just when we should begin letting up. If we do, we create the kind of pressure that brings about explosions within the family.

■ **Yes, but as Christian parents, we have difficulty loosening the screws.**

That's understandable, and it's also quite natural for parents to be fearful about the temptations and problems our children face in today's world. And this, coupled with our desire for them to follow Christ and live by His principles, adds even more pressure. As a result, Christian parents often panic and overreact—then the kids overreact.

One of the great advantages of being in a good church is having Christian friends who have children the same age as your own. As the children grow up together, they spend time in one another's homes, experiencing a type of independence—being away from home without Mom and Dad—in an atmosphere of relative safety.

This kind of support is one of the strongest arguments for choosing a church with a good youth group—one in which responsible, concerned couples and young adults nurture teens in a loving atmosphere. Good youth workers do not drive wedges between parents and children. Instead, they help the young grow into independence while encouraging them to respect their own parents' love and good judgment.

■ **What about peer pressure? Kids are under a lot of pressure these days.**

Concurrent with the need to be independent is the need to be accepted by one's peer group. Much of what young people do— and much of what frightens parents—is simply an attempt to fit into the current youth culture.

The need for acceptance is of major importance in the teen years. Most adults have matured enough to understand that there are certain times in life when one does not need the cheers of a crowd to do what's right. But when you're young, it's tough to comprehend this kind of lone stance.

In the larger scheme of things, the label on one's jacket or jeans is relatively unimportant. Brand X is often as good as the Brand A designer label. In actuality, appearance holds no deep or perma-nent significance for adolescents; they simply wear the uniform of the day to gain acceptance.

■ How can I help my teens "draw the line" as I let them become more independent?

When children are small, we draw the line for them. We tell them what is right and wrong, all the while observing whether we operate by those standards ourselves. They also observe kids whose parents have different values and backgrounds.

During adolescence, our children begin to draw this line for themselves. They experiment to find out what it's like to go beyond the line we have drawn for them. They test our values against the values of others.

Establishing the validity of parental patterns is part of growing up. When our children experiment, they are not necessarily rebelling against our values. Usually they are just trying to get all the facts—by trial and error—before they draw their line.

However, while adolescents are experimenting and examining their options, parents must cut them some slack and honor their personal search for values. Decisions made after this kind of testing are often much more valid than those beliefs assumed without question. And parents who allow their children to express themselves will see less rebellion than parents who are always defensive and condemnatory, trying to force their children into a mold.

One of the great principles of parenting comes from Newton's Law: *For each action there is an equal and opposite reaction.* If parents don't react strongly to everything their teenagers do, then teenagers won't act out contrary behavior with such enthusiasm.

■ The familiar verse—"Train a child in the way he should go, and when he is old he will not turn from it"—is from Proverbs 22:6. Does this mean parents are to make sure their young people are correctly trained in accordance with the will of God?

Chuck Swindoll and others have suggested that in the original Hebrew the intent of Proverbs 22:6 is this: *Train up a child according to his or her bent.* The root word has to do with the bent of the tree. For instance, a willow tree that leans out over a pond toward the southern sun is bent in a certain way. If you try to force it to bend in another direction, you will break it.

There is probably as much wisdom in this interpretation as in the traditional one. Parents should try to raise their children according to biblical patterns, correcting them and disciplining them so that they understand responsible and obedient behavior. On the other hand, children should be nurtured according to their own bent.

We need to be willing to acknowledge that our children are born with different temperaments and different personality types. Parents sometimes try to project their own dreams onto a child with dissimilar bents. Yet trying to mold a child into the patterns of the parent can be one of the most devastating of all rejections. Ultimately, the child feels that nothing he does, especially in the areas in which he excels, can ever please the parent.

■ **Can you give me an example?**

One day a successful doctor admitted with tears and with some anger, "I hate what I'm doing. I've always felt God called me to be a missionary. But my dad was unwilling to let me do it because he had spent so much on my education. He said, 'No, you're going to have to make my expenditure worthwhile. The mission field is out of the question.' "

This doctor, at the height of his successful career, regretted the loss of his great dream—a dream his father had overruled. Wise parents will turn their children over to God, invite His Holy Spirit to speak to them, and then help them achieve the goals He implants in them.

■ **I know I should tell my teens that I love them. Anything else I should be sure to say?**

Tell them: "I'm proud of you." "That was a good job." "I'm so happy that you're my child." Statements like these provide more positive reinforcement than almost anything you could ever do.

■ **What if this is hard for my wife? I'm afraid she always sees the negative.**

Ask her to practice. Ask her to try mouthing the words. Give her the freedom to take a risk. She'll be glad she did. Even when a young person has tried and failed, a parent should take him aside and say, "I know how very much you wanted to do this, and I know how hard you tried. Even though you didn't win, I was very proud of you—of your composure, your sportsmanship, and the way you conducted yourself."

And this advice applies to you as well, Dad. A young man can mow the entire yard, trim all the bushes, weed around all the trees, do the best job possible, but you might see that one little clump of grass that he missed. If you harp on that and never mention all the other work he's done, it will really discourage him and make him feel like giving up. Your son will think, *Why put in all that work if I'm going to get chewed out anyway?*

■ **What if my son doesn't do that great a job on the lawn?**

Why not notice the boy's tenacity and industry? You could simply comment on how much time it must have taken your son to do all that work and thank him for it. Complimenting him in the presence of a neighbor or a friend will probably mean a great deal.

■ **Are there any final thoughts you can give regarding the raising of teens?**

It's halftime, so don't count the score. Don't believe that your children are going to freeze where they are now. They will grow. The grace of God is working in their lives as it has in yours.

Parenting is one of God's great ideas, and parenting teenagers is the best part of it. Just remember: Mind your instincts; parent with confidence; consult His Word; pray a lot; then believe God for the reward.

This material is adapted from writings by Jay Kesler, president of Taylor University in Upland, Indiana.

2

A Promise with a Ring to It

. . . .

■ **I'm terribly worried about how society's preoccupation with sex will affect my three children, who will be teenagers in a few short years. I was not a virgin when I married, and I want to spare my children the emotional pain and sorrow I experienced. What can I do?**

One of the best things you can do is to have a "key talk" with your son or daughter when they hit the teenage years. That's what Dr. Richard Durfield, a Southern California assistant professor at Azusa Pacific University, and his wife, Renée, did with their four children.

It was just a few years ago that Richard took his youngest son, Jonathan, out to dinner for his "key talk." With a flourish, the hostess seated them in El Encanto's main dining room, a nice restaurant in the foothills near their hometown. The expensive furnishings, subdued lighting, and pricy menu told his son that the evening would be a special occasion.

As they scanned the large red menus, Richard mentally walked through what he wanted to say. Jonathan knew they were at El Encanto's for his "key talk," a time when they could discuss any questions the young man had about sexuality. Jonathan already knew the "facts of life"—he had been raised in a home where "no question is too dumb." His parents began telling him about sexual parts in his elementary school days.

But that night would go beyond anatomy to talk about the special meaning of commitment and honor for a young man fast growing up. When the chilled jumbo shrimp appetizers arrived at their table, Richard quietly leaned over.

"Tonight is your night, Jonathan," he began. "This is a special time for you and Dad to talk about any sexual questions that might still be on your mind. Whatever might seem a little awkward at times, well, tonight is the right time to ask. Nothing is off-limits tonight.

"If something's been bothering you about adolescence or whatever, it's okay to talk about it. As we eat through the course of the evening, I want you to just be thinking about any questions you might have."

■ **Did Jonathan have any questions? I think my son would clam up in that situation.**

Jonathan seemed a little uncomfortable because he continued to look around. But as they began talking, he relaxed a bit. Then Jonathan, who was still a few years away from dating, wanted to know *for sure* what "the line" was. How far was *too far?* He had a good idea, but he wanted to hear it from his father.

"A light kiss is about as far as you can go," Richard replied. "Sexual emotions are very strong, and if you're not careful, you'll do things you don't want to. So you need to avoid anything that leads you up to that." For instance, certain types of kissing are going too far, he explained. Kissing a girl on the neck can lead to going much further, counseled his father.

■ **This "key talk" thing is a great idea! Where did the Durfields come up with it?**

About fifteen years ago, when the Durfields' oldest child, Kimberli, was entering adolescence, Richard and Renée had an idea: Have a private, personal, and intimate time with the child to explain conception, the biblical view of marriage, and the sacredness of sexual purity. A time when a mom and daughter or a dad and son can candidly discuss the questions, fears, and anxieties of adolescence. They called it a "key talk."

The Durfields also had another idea. At the time of the key talk, one or both parents would present a specially made "key" ring to the son or daughter. The adolescent would wear the ring, which symbolizes a commitment to God, during the difficult teen and young adult years.

■ Why is it called a key ring?

The purpose of a key is to unlock a door, and the ring symbolizes the key to one's heart and virginity. The ring is a powerful reminder of the value and beauty of virginity, of the importance of reserving sex for marriage.

The ring also represents a covenant between the child and God. A covenant not only obligates us to God, but it also obligates God to us. As long as we honor a covenant, God will also honor it. Throughout history God has blessed those who have remained faithful.

The son or daughter wears the key ring until he or she is married. Then the ring is taken off and presented to the new spouse on their wedding night—that sacred evening when a life of sexual experience begins.

Renée had open and frank key talks with her two daughters, Kimberli and Anna. She described just about everything a child would want to know about sex. Because her daughters were attractive, intelligent, and sought-after, they needed important reasons to remain virgins until their wedding nights.

■ So what happened to Jonathan? Did he get his key ring in that restaurant?

Here's the rest of the story. As the main dishes were taken away, Richard told Jonathan it was time to make a commitment before the Lord. Yes, they lacked privacy, but Richard felt it added to the significance of what they were about to do.

Richard wanted Jonathan to pray—right there at the table—but he had to set things up a little bit. "Now this covenant is going to be something between you and God until you are married," he said. "We're going to include whoever your wife will be in this prayer. We're going to ask God that wherever she is and whoever she is, that He'll be with her also. We'll ask Him to help her be chaste until the time you're married. I want you to ask God for His grace to keep this covenant pure, because even though you may have right intentions, sometimes things go wrong. I want you to pray, and then Dad will pray."

Jonathan turned to his father and took his hands. Richard was pleasantly surprised that his son would act so boldly in a public restaurant, but he realized that was exactly what Jonathan needed in order to stand alone.

Jonathan bowed his head and prayed fervently. Then it was the father's turn. Before Richard prayed, he said, "Jonathan, I have something for you." He took a custom-made 14K ring and slipped it on his finger. Bowing their heads, Richard asked the Lord to honor the covenant Jonathan was making and help him resist temptation in the coming years.

Then Richard read a letter from someone very special, someone who had befriended Jonathan when he was much younger. His father didn't let him know who had written the letter:

Dear Jonathan,

Your dad told me that the two of you are about to have a very important talk. I've been invited to participate in the discussion by way of a letter. I was asked to say a few things about purity—sexual purity—though I don't suppose there's much I can tell you that you haven't heard before.

I'm sure your parents have taught you well. But I want to encourage you to act on what you already know. Believe me, it's worth it to save sex for marriage and keep yourself pure for the woman God wants you to spend you life with. The Lord designed it that way for good reason. Plenty of people who disregarded His plan in that area will tell you how much they regret it.

You're going to need more of this kind of encouragement in the days to come. It's one thing to know what's right. Living by it is something else. Over the next few years, you'll probably face pres-

sure to change or compromise your values—pressure from your friends, from advertising, television and movies, and a hundred other sources. You may even find yourself in situations where it could be easy to yield to sexual temptation.

One of the best ways of fighting back is learning to like yourself. If you feel good about you, you'll have the confidence to take a stand—even if you're the only one! Just remember who you are and what your parents have taught you. There's real strength in knowing that God loves you and has a purpose for your life!

But if you feel inferior to others, it will be that much easier to let them press you into their mold. Don't do it! The rest of your life is ahead of you, and it's worth fighting for. I hope this helps, Jonathan. I'm sure your dad will have more to say on this subject.

You're a lucky guy to have parents who care about you so much! Take advantage of their wisdom and be encouraged by their love. God bless you!

■ **Well? Who wrote the letter? I'm dying to know.**

That letter was signed by Dr. James Dobson, whom Richard had met in the late 1970s when Dr. Dobson was just starting the Focus on the Family ministry. In fact, the Durfields' inspiration for the key talk came from Dr. Dobson's first book, *Dare to Discipline*, in which he described his intention to give his daughter, Danae, a small gold key on her thirteenth birthday that would represent the key to her heart.

When Richard and Jonathan left El Encanto's that night, a couple sitting at a nearby table stopped them. They couldn't help but notice something special *had* happened, they said.

Richard briefly outlined what Jonathan had done, and there were smiles all around. When the father and son stepped out into the cool Southern California evening, they knew something special had happened between Jonathan, his wife-to-be, and the Lord.

■ **My teens are in high school. Is it too late for them to have a "key talk?"**

Key talks should happen when the child becomes interested in the opposite sex. That can be as young as ten or as old as seventeen, although the ideal age is thirteen. Your key talk will be one of the most memorable and moving experiences you'll ever have with your child. It will seem like your hearts bond together.

Obviously, the key ring is a powerful day-in-and-day-out reminder for the child. The more the child values his or her virginity, the more the key ring becomes a precious symbol of the commitment to God and the future spouse.

Young people are romantics. They have a real need to identify their personal self-worth. Wholesome, biblical thoughts instilled during their tender years open an avenue for parents to discuss sex with their children. The importance a parent places on the key talk will greatly influence the child's sexual behavior prior to marriage.

■ **Unfortunately, our seventeen-year-old son is no longer a virgin. Is it too late for him?**

Of course not! The key ring idea is also a great idea for teens who have lost their virginity. Although they've jumped the gun, they can commit themselves to God to remain pure until their wedding day. Teens who have fallen short can become virgins again in the sight of God. Once they're forgiven, it is as though they had never sinned. The Lord tells us in Isaiah 43:25 that "I, even I, am he who blots out your transgressions, for my own sake, and remembers your sins no more."

WANT TO KNOW MORE?

Parents wanting more information about "key talks" should read the Durfields' book, *Raising Them Chaste* (Bethany House), or purchase key rings sold in Bob Siemon Jewelers' display cases. The items are available in most Christian bookstores.

This material is adapted from writings by Richard Durfield, Ph.D., and Renée Durfield, authors of Raising Them Chaste *(Bethany House).*

Kimberli Durfield

When my mother told me she wanted to take me out to our favorite Mexican restaurant for my key talk, I was quite anxious.

Mom talked openly. She even drew pictures on napkins to explain several points. I especially remember her telling me that since sex was not our idea, but God's, it had to be good.

After the talk, Mom pulled out a beautiful silver key ring! She told me this was a sign of the commitment I was about to make. That afternoon, with Mom as my witness, I made a vow to the Lord to remain sexually pure. That ring has been a constant reminder—and gotten me through some tough times!

Anna Durfield

I was so excited about my key talk with Mom—it was like the first night out with just the ladies. I was surprised how I could speak out about my sexual feelings and not feel any guilt. Mom knew where I was coming from and how I was feeling sexually.

At my high school, classmates candidly tell everyone about their sexual experiences. They appear to be happy, but there's a void there. My key talk with Mom—and the promise I made to God—has given me the desire to stay right before the Lord.

I've had strong sexual feelings—I still do. I've had a boyfriend for nearly four years, and we've spent precious moments together. But because I've made a stand from day one of our relationship not to have sex, I've been able to keep my covenant with God.

I'm nineteen and still a virgin. I still have a way to go before I get married, but when I do, I hope God gives me a man strong enough to handle this very healthy lady!

Timothy Durfield

I remember anticipating the day I would make a long-term commitment to God. I felt I was doing something that would make God happy with me. God has always been someone I've wanted to please, and I know if I keep this covenant with Him, God will smile upon me.

I've kept that commitment for three years now. God has blessed me in that I've only gone out with girls who have the same morals as me. I'm still tempted, but that ring on my finger reminds me of my covenant with God and the gift I'll someday give to my wife.

3

Someone Who Is Willing to Wait

. . . .

Here's an interview with someone who has announced to the world that he remains a virgin—A.C. Green, the thirty-three-year-old NBA basketball player with the Dallas Mavericks.

■ **You're tall—six-foot-nine—and like most NBA players, easy to spot in a crowd. Is it true that "groupies" are readily available to you and other NBA players?**

As a professional athlete, I have to deal with groupies in many cities. It seems as though my teammates and I are often confronted by young women wanting to meet us from the time we arrive to the time we depart. They hang out everywhere—airports, hotel lobbies, restaurants, and sports arenas—always trying to catch our eyes.

Not many resist their advances. I don't know how many virgins there are in the NBA, but you can probably count them on one hand. Pro basketball players have a larger-than-life image, and it doesn't help when a former player, such as Wilt Chamberlain, boasts about bedding 20,000 women in his lifetime.

■ **I bet there's a lot of "locker-room talk" about the latest sexual conquests.**

But I don't let that weaken my resolve, because I have chosen to follow God's standard. I've communicated my stand to my teammates. Some—in a humorous vein—have threatened to set me up with women who would make themselves available to me. "Let's see how strong you really are," they joke.

Don't get me wrong. Sex itself isn't bad. It's just a matter of *when* to experience it. God created it for enjoyment, but He also reserved it for marriage. So I'm waiting. The Bible tells me in Philippians 4:13 that "I can do all things through Christ, who strengthens me," and I've taken that verse to heart. I also know that God's Word tells me that He will not give me any temptation too great.

I want young people to hear this message. *It is possible to wait. Not everybody is doing it.* Five years ago, I started the A.C. Green Youth Foundation in Los Angeles. We put together basketball camps, help kids find summer jobs, and try to give inner-city youths some direction. As part of that outreach, several pro athletes—including Daryl Green and David Robinson—along with a Christian rap group called Idle King, joined me to make a video called "It Ain't Worth It."

It's a rap song dealing with teenage love, broken hearts, the dilemma of abortion, and the fallacy of the "safe sex" message. We released it in 1993, and we've been able to get the video into a lot of schools.

■ **What can we do to emphasize self-control and personal responsibility in our schools? Even with so much sex education being taught, teenage birth rates and abortion rates are still very high.**

We need good role models, and while I'm reluctant to put myself on a pedestal, I will take a stand for Christ. I'm proud to say that I am a virgin, and I don't hide the strength God has given me.

Of course, some young kids listening to me have been sexually active for years. That's when I tell them about the concept of secondary virginity. "You may have had sex in the past and think you don't have a reason to wait now," I say. "But there's a better way, and that's following God's way. Perhaps you feel guilty or not worthy, but the Lord can forgive you. After that, you can commit yourselves to remaining pure until your wedding day."

■ **How does your message reconcile with the "safe sex" espoused by your former teammate, Magic Johnson?**

I think the media and society are more willing to accept Magic's message—that kids are going to have sex anyway, and the best approach is to equip them with condoms to lessen the risk of disease.

My message is different. For openers, the facts show that condoms aren't as successful as many would have you believe. And for teens, the failure rate is even worse! It's a lie to say that putting a condom on makes you as secure as Fort Knox. I cringe when I hear that stuff. Condoms have a hard enough time just stopping a woman from getting pregnant, let alone blocking an HIV virus, which is 450 times smaller than sperm itself. It's like water going through a net.

This is what I really like telling kids: You have to learn to respect yourself before you can start respecting other people.

This material is used with permission of A.C. Green.

WANT TO WRITE TO A.C.?

If you would like to contact A.C. Green, write:

A.C. Green Programs for Youth
P.O. Box 1709
Phoenix, AZ 85001
(800) AC-Youth

4

Teens Charting a Different Course

. . . .

■ **At my son's public high school, the pressure to drink after the Friday night football game is pretty intense. What are some ways I can help my son?**

Peer pressure to drink, smoke, and go too far sexually is an age-old problem, but consider what a group of parents and teen students have done to *reverse* peer pressure in Columbus, Georgia.

To illustrate this, let's introduce Erik, a sophomore at Pacelli (pronounced *Puh-CHELL-eee*) High, a private school in Columbus. One afternoon after classes were over, Erik slipped into the classroom of Christi Ham, a religion teacher at Pacelli High.

Visibly distraught, the boy stood near the door. Mrs. Ham asked the student to sit down and compose himself.

"I can't stand it," Erik said in a choked voice, as the teacher patted his shoulder. "I can't fight the pressure anymore."

Gently, Mrs. Ham asked what was bothering him. Was he having trouble with his girlfriend? Was it the pressure to party and drink?

"No," the boy replied. "It's all the pressure *not* to drink."

In a flash, Mrs. Ham understood. Because of a peer counseling group on campus called Teen Advisers, drinking was no longer cool at Pacelli. The sophomore, who liked to down beer at weekend parties, was tired of hearing his classmates tell him to abstain from alcohol.

■ **Really? Do you mean that the Pacelli Teen Advisers turned peer pressure into a positive force?**

That's right. The message not to drink or do drugs was coming from the students themselves—not parents and school officials, a concept that makes the Teen Advisers so interesting.

■ **How did Teen Advisers start?**

The Columbus program began in 1987 when Richard and Dee Dee Stephens' eldest daughter, Mary Lawson (that's her first and middle name), was attending Pacelli, a Catholic high school with more than half of its students coming from Protestant denominations.

Back then, bitter arguments between daughter and parents marked every weekend. Why? Mary Lawson wasn't allowed to go out to parties. A popular cheerleader, she yearned to be accepted by the "in crowd," but that crowd usually huddled around a beer keg every Friday and Saturday night.

As Christian parents, Richard and Dee Dee wanted to do something *proactive* about the peer pressure. They were convinced that if several high school students would take a stand against drinking, drugs, and premarital sex, more would follow. In addition, they were sure impressionable freshmen and junior high students would readily listen to upperclassmen.

That spring, Dee Dee and another mother, Kit Newlin, asked the principal of a Columbus-area junior high if they and several students could talk to an eighth-grade class about dating. The moms were joined by four Pacelli High students, including Mary Lawson (who came around to her parents' point of view) and Kit's daughter, Missy. They answered questions the eighth-graders had written anonymously on three-by-five cards.

The first panel was so well received that Dee Dee telephoned eight more students and asked if they would be interested in talking to junior-highers about drinking.

Dee Dee mentioned one little catch, however: The teens had to agree not to drink for the rest of the school year. "I asked another junior whom I *knew* was drinking to take the pledge," remembers Dee Dee. "I knew if she would do it, ten kids would follow her. She said yes, and since then, I've found that more kids will take this step if they know their friends are going to stand with them."

■ What changes did the Stephens see in their daughter?

When Mary Lawson inked her pact, she received a dose of self-confidence to stand up against negative peer pressure. "I made a commitment that I knew I had to live up to," she says. "And I did."

■ Then what happened?

The Stephens started having the teens over to their house at least one Sunday afternoon a month to talk about how to avoid drinking, sexual pressure, getting along with parents, and the importance of self-esteem.

They did skits and games (which are described in the Teen Advisers' manual; see the sidebar to order one), and they worked on their "presentations" to freshmen and junior high students, which happens several times a month in schools around Columbus.

"Our seniors and juniors," says Dee Dee, "are saying to the younger students, 'Hey, we've been there, and we're going to tell you what it's like not to drink and *not* to get physical with your boyfriend or girlfriend.' When you're a freshman, you will listen to someone two years older, even more so than your parents."

In a way, this arrangement sets up an unexpected system of accountability. How? A Teen Adviser *knows* the freshmen are watching him closely to see if he backs up his word.

■ But what happens if a Teen Adviser stumbles and parties heartily?

"If you know someone who breaks the contract, you're bound to go to that person and ask him to turn himself in," says Rusty

Walker, a Pacelli senior. "If that doesn't work, you're supposed to turn him in yourself. If you don't, then you've broken *your* contract."

Teens who have slipped up appear before the Teen Adviser Honor Council, a panel of six elected by other TAs. Notice again that accountability is coming from teen to teen. (Although Teen Advisers espouse abstinence, sexual purity is often not part of the contract because the teens don't feel comfortable discussing the sex lives of their friends.)

"We want those who have broken their contract to be honest," explains Rusty, who's also an Honor Council member. "If they are sorry and want to remain with the group, they have to apologize to all the Teen Advisers. They also have to tell their parents—perhaps the toughest part of all. Then they are given a punishment, which is usually a Saturday afternoon of community service."

Another student, Becky Davidson, says signing the contract is a big commitment. "It's not fun and games. Even if there had ever been times when I wanted to break my contract, I wouldn't have because not only had I signed it before other teens, but also I had signed it before God."

■ Can you describe one of these "peer-counseling" sessions?

Let's say it's Monday morning in Mrs. Rivard's eighth-grade class at St. Anne's, a parochial junior high school. This is the first class of the day for the thirteen- and fourteen-year-old students, who are dressed in their blue-and-yellow school uniforms. Ten Teen Advisers walk in and sit before the students. Mrs. Rivard introduces the group, then adds, "The Teen Advisers are here to talk to you about drinking and to answer the questions you wrote out last week."

The eighth-graders appear excited, but they also take pains to be cool. They didn't notice Dee Dee slipping into the back of the classroom, where she monitors all the Teen Advisers' panels.

The TAs are given permission by Pacelli to miss class several times a month to speak before various junior high classes in the Columbus area. Because of the success of the Pacelli program, school authorities recognize that the Teen Advisers reach younger students in ways adults never will.

"Drinking—and the pressure to drink—is one of the top problems facing teenagers today," begins Randi Dean, a senior. "And alcohol is the most widely used drug," chips in cheerleader Kristie Wheeler. "It kills more people than any other drug."

Several other TAs pick up the beat. "The younger you are when you start drinking, the greater the chances you'll become an alcoholic," says Adam Conard. "After an adult starts drinking, it can take five to fifteen years to become an alcoholic. Once a teenager starts drinking, it can take only six to eighteen *months* to become an alcoholic."

Rusty Walker says everyone on the panel has taken a firm stand against drinking, noting that all the Teen Advisers had signed one-year contracts not to drink alcohol.

"When you get to Pacelli," Rusty tells the rapt eighth-graders, "don't plan on drinking beer if you want to be cool. That won't be the way to go. You know those beer commercials with the hard-body guys and Swedish bikini teams? Well, those aren't the usual drinkers. A beer drinker is usually a couch potato with a big beer belly."

The eighth-graders giggle, and then one raises his hand. "Have you ever had anything to drink?" he asks.

Nearly everyone on the panel nods yes. Most say they tried beer or hard liquor at a friend's party while they were in junior high. One girl says her mom offered her sips of bacardi rum while the family was vacationing in Florida. "Imagine having the pressure to drink from your parents!"

Dee Dee leans over to a visitor. "Four years ago, when Teen Advisers heard this question, they usually answered, 'I was getting drunk last year, but now I'm not.' Now, it's 'I had a beer back in junior high.' That's how I have seen the pendulum swing in just five years."

■ How do the Teen Advisers talk about sex, since sexual purity is not necessarily part of the contract?

Sometimes it depends on the audience. One time the Teen Advisers did a "sex panel" at a Columbus public school eighth-grade class, and the reception was rather cool. The eighth-graders may have listened to the Teen Advisers' pro-abstinence message, but they weren't buying it. When the TAs talked about the consequences of an unplanned pregnancy, one eighth-grader raised her hand and described her seventeen-year-old sister's pregnancy and safe delivery of a little boy. The father married the sister, she said, and they were doing just fine.

■ That sounds like one of those "take-that" statements hurled at the panel.

It was. Jennifer Young remembers being taken aback for a moment, but after a quick, silent prayer, she plunged ahead. "I am really happy that it worked out for your sister," she said, "but she's an exception. She's maybe the one out of one hundred that works out, but for the other ninety-nine, their lives are ruined." She also told the eighth-grader it's okay not to do it, that she's a virgin, and she is going to save herself until marriage.

The Teen Advisers continued that "wait-until-marriage" theme at another sex panel before a seventh-grade class at St. Anne's. "We want to tell you that safe sex is sex with the person you marry," began Shawn Scott, a senior.

The Teen Advisers then shared statistics about the low effectiveness rate of condoms and the danger of AIDS and sexually transmitted diseases. "And there's no condom that protects your heart, your mind, and your self-esteem," said Lauren Jones. "When you start having sex, pretty soon that's all you'll have in common. You can't go back to kissing because sex is progressive."

The panel then entertained questions from the seventh-graders:

► **"How far should you go on the first date?"** Their answer: Although it's expected to kiss on the first date, you certainly don't have to, the panel agreed. Anne Stephens, a junior and one of Dee Dee's three daughters, said she went with a guy for four months before they kissed. "That made it a lot more special."

► **"When should I start dating?"** You should talk it over with your parents, the panelists replied. Group dates are the best because that won't put you in a compromising position.

► **"Should I go out with a guy even if I don't like him?"** Shawn took this one. "Guys don't want 'pity dates,' " he said. "You'll both end up having a lousy time."

The strapping, six-foot, 180-pound Shawn then turned the discussion to premarital sex. "I'm eighteen, and I'm a virgin. So don't let people out there tell you no one's a virgin anymore," he said. The seventh-graders didn't make a sound as they hung onto his words. "I think being a virgin makes me more of a man. It takes more character and more will power not to have sex these days."

■ **How have parents reacted to Teen Advisers?**

They've seen big changes. One father, Joe Wheeler, is the father of a sophomore girl, Kristie. "When my boys went to Pacelli before Kristi," said Joe, "it was: 'Who can spin the most doughnuts in the parking lot and drink the most beer?' My oldest son was the class president, and it took him fifteen years to get off Skoal chewing tobacco. He started chewing when he was on the football team because it was the macho thing to do in those days. He didn't quit until the birth of his first child.

"You should see this school now," continued Joe. "It's as calm as can be, like back in the fifties. Fifteen years ago, if a boy stood up

---

HOW CAN I LEARN MORE ABOUT TEEN ADVISERS?

These days the Teen Advisers program has spread all across the country as parents have learned about Pacelli High's success story. And just before he left office, President Bush presented the Stephens with the 987th "Point of Light" award in a White House ceremony.

To learn more about Teen Advisers, including information on a manual for starting a Teen Advisers group at your high school, please write:

Teen Advisers
P.O. Box 6468
Columbus, GA
(706) 322-6186

and said he was a virgin, they would have laughed him out of the school.

"What I like is that Kristie is getting a good education. She doesn't have to worry about all this drinking and drugs stuff. Yup, this school has really turned around."

This material is adapted from "Charting a Different Course" by Mike Yorkey, Focus on the Family *magazine, November 1992. Copyright © 1992, Focus on the Family. Used by permission.*

5

Choosing a College— Already?

. . . .

■ **The high school years pass quickly, and I'm already worried about my children's college education. When I ask my ten-year-old son, "What do you want to be when you grow up?" the answer depends on the season and his outfit for the day—a fireman, professional football player, or famous basketball player. But won't that innocent question take on a greater meaning in a few short years when teachers, counselors, and even their friends begin asking for real?**

Yes, it will. Carol Kuykendall, a mother of three and author of *Give Them Wings*, remembers when her son Derek, a high school junior, sat in his counselor's office, discussing his future.

"Have you given any thought to what you want to do when you grow up?" Derek's counselor asked him as they casually discussed a schedule change.

Derek's eyes widened as he realized it was not a grandmotherly question about childish dreams. He suddenly had no answer at all.

"I just want to be a high school student for now," he moaned.

Kids, like adults, get caught off guard with the realization that the years have passed so quickly, and suddenly it's time to make important decisions.

"Everything starts counting now," parents warn their teenagers as they enter high school, but we parents walk a tenuous line when we pass along that kind of advice.

■ **So how do we encourage without pressuring?**

Our role as parents is to encourage teens through a series of stressful and confusing choices so they can find a path that seems right for them. In high school, that means determining areas of interest and ability, and thinking about options beyond high school.

If college seems to be that option, as it is for nearly 60 percent of all high school graduates, choices become even more important. However, we should assure them that few choices are irreversible. We change our minds; we change classes; we change majors; some people even change schools; and the average American adult changes jobs six times. Many kids are frightened that a choice made in tenth grade may affect them for the rest of their lives.

Even if it's the wrong choice, remind your teen that changes are possible.

■ **I'm about to enter this maze with my high school-age daughter. What's my first step?**

Take advantage of the resources schools have to offer. High school counselors have been in the business of helping students through this stage longer than you have as a parent. They offer good materials, including brochures that ask the student some questions to determine interests and strengths: "What are your patterns of choices as they have developed over the years in school, jobs, hobbies, or other activities?" "What's important to you?" "What bugs you?" "How much time do you spend studying?" "Do you enjoy learning?" "What are your most favorite and least favorite subjects in school?"

■ **As we talk about what college to attend, what are some things to keep in mind?**

Give your children a choice. Instead of predetermining your

teen's university, the best things you can do are to gather and give information, identify and state your boundaries or limitations to those choices, and then offer encouragement and support while a choice is made.

You might pray that at least two colleges that are acceptable to you will accept your high school senior, and then leave the final choice to him or her. At that stage of growing independence, teens need to have ownership of the decision. Otherwise, they won't buy into it with the same sense of personal commitment.

Some parents who decide that a certain prestigious college is the only right choice act as if acceptance will become an A on their report card of parenting. They don the sweatshirt of that school or proudly place the decal on the back of the family car.

As parents, our goal should be to help our sons and daughters find a school (or other post-high school choice) that's right for *them*. We don't want to set up a situation for failure by pressuring them into choices that aren't right; we want to help them succeed in a college that matches their abilities and prepares them for the vocation they have chosen.

■ **Right now, we are in the "gathering information" phase, and brochures, applications, and financial aid forms are burying us. How can we keep track of this paper blizzard?**

The amount of information that begins to accumulate regarding college choices and applications quickly overwhelms a high school student. If you're drowning in a sea of paper at your house, purchase a sturdy, portable file box with folders and start keeping all the information together, but in separate files.

As you network with other parents and talk with your child's counselor, you'll be able to pass on helpful advice in the areas where your teen is willing to accept it. For instance, tell your teen that most colleges don't insist on well-rounded students; they prefer well-rounded classes made up of lopsided students who excel in one or two areas. Most colleges believe that consistently good grades in quality courses are still the best indicators of potential in college; and they especially dislike the choice of "Mickey Mouse" courses during the senior year.

■ **Our family definitely has financial limits on what we'll be able to do for our two boys. How do we declare those limits?**

You need to define your limitations early in the process. For each family, those boundaries will be different. You may recognize that finding a good college that meets the needs of your children for their first year away from home is a high priority and wise investment. Or, your budget may say that all you can do is send them to a community college close to home for the first two years.

You may want to actually write out your boundaries. For example: No more than $10,000 a year from your pockets; the rest will have to come from scholarship money, student loans, and so on. No coed dorms. No more than a day's drive from home. No big-city colleges.

At any rate, your children should know the total budget allotted for their four years of school. Beyond that, they should know that they will have to share the responsibility of finding financial aid. The fact is, many of the more expensive private institutions offer more financial aid than public institutions.

■ **We're in a quandary because the nearest state university has a student population of 30,000. We don't feel at all comfortable sending our daughter to that campus next year.**

That's why you should consider small schools. Our children need the nurturing, individual attention, and personal challenge found in classes and dormitories at smaller schools, ideally 3,000 students or less. Though some students thrive amidst the stimulation of a large university, you may want a place where your children are less likely to slip through the cracks, at least for their first year away from home.

At large universities, your children may find themselves in some classes with 500 other people. Nobody will know if they miss the class; worse, nobody will care. Smaller classes provide an opportunity to know professors personally and to write essay answers to tests (rather than true/false or multiple choice), which teaches students to express themselves and develop their critical-thinking skills.

■ What about the so-called "liberal arts" colleges? Should we keep an arm's distance from them?

If your children don't go through high school with a passionate, clear leaning toward a specific career, a good liberal arts college would best prepare them to become competent, knowledgeable, disciplined people who can write and speak effectively, work well with others, and think critically within any chosen field. A liberal arts curriculum can educate for life, not just a specific job.

■ The $64,000 question in many parents' hearts is: Christian college or non-Christian? What are the pros and cons?

This is an all-important consideration. For a young student leaving home for the first time, a Christian school offers the most nurturing environment and a proper balance between academic excellence and Christian commitment.

■ What about geographical location?

If money is not an issue and your teens desire to go away from home or out of state, feel free to encourage that choice. Geographical distance increases their potential to gain independence, if they are ready. Remember that if they don't make that adjustment to leaving home now, they'll have to

---

SHOULD I SEND MY CHILD TO A CHRISTIAN COLLEGE?

This is what a president of a Christian college had to say on the question:

"If you give me your children for only one year of their lives, give me their freshman year—their first year away from home—when they are most vulnerable and impressionable, bombarded with choices and trying to develop views about life and values and truth and who they are. Let me surround them with some Christian mentors and role models during this tough time of transition."

And here is what Dr. James Dobson has to say:

"I strongly believe in Christian education, especially at the collegiate level. The single greatest influence during the college years does not come from the faculty. It is derived from other students! Thus, being classmates with men and women who profess a faith in Jesus Christ is vital to the bonding that should occur during those four years."

make it at some later date.

Though the decision of where to send your children to college is important and profoundly shapes their future, keep in mind that when we surrender ourselves to God, He weaves all our circumstances together for good.

This material is adapted from Give Them Wings *by Carol Kuykendall and published by Focus on the Family. Copyright © 1994, Carol Kuykendall. Used with permission.*

A STUDENT'S COLLEGE-PLANNING TIME LINE

Junior Year of High School

February and March: Develop a preliminary list of ten to twelve colleges that sound interesting. Start collecting information from those schools, noting deadlines, tests, and information required for admission. Review your senior year plan to make sure you are completing all academic courses required by the colleges in which you are interested.

Spring break: Visit college campuses, if possible, noticing the differences between large and small, rural and urban schools. Seek to identify the personalities of each school. Visit classes, eat in the cafeteria, talk with students, and stay in a dormitory.

May: Take advanced placement tests if you qualify. High scorers receive college credits.

Summer: Plan additional campus visits, if possible.

Senior Year

September: Narrow your list of schools to a manageable number—four to six. Line up teachers to write the recommendations that will accompany your applications. Start thinking about your essays.

November: Take the SAT.

December: Complete and send in applications.

January: Last chance to take the SAT and achievement tests for the fall freshman class. Final deadlines for most applications are between January 15 and March 1. Have your high school counseling office send transcripts of your first semester grades to colleges to which you've applied.

March and April: Acceptance and rejection letters are sent. Continue to do your best work in school; colleges check for signs of senioritis.

This Father-Son Thing Is Not an Act

. . . .

Editor's note: Jeoffrey Benward and his son, Aaron, form the Christian singing duo called Aaron Jeoffrey. In this story, Jeoffrey Benward talks about how his son decided to follow in his footsteps.

Five years ago, my son, Aaron, was graduating from high school. Like any father, I was curious about his plans. Aaron was a National Merit scholar, all-state in basketball, and a terrific soccer player. It seemed like a good time for a father-and-son chat.

When we sat down at our kitchen table, I prefaced our conversation by saying, "Aaron, I know you're experiencing a lot of emotions and feelings, but I'd like to talk about what you want to do with your life, and what God wants you to do, as well."

Aaron took the longest time to respond, and then he said, "Dad, I feel called to become a singer—just like you."

I had been involved in the music ministry for fourteen years, and like any father, I was flattered that he wanted to follow in my footsteps. Yet I felt apprehensive because I knew the pressures of the music business. I had experienced the highest highs and lowest lows. I knew how elusive "success" can be.

"There are a lot of people doing what you want to do," I said. "To be noticed by a record company, you either have to be first, great, or different."

Then a thought suddenly came to mind: *Why doesn't Aaron sing with me?*

"Aaron, don't answer me right away when I ask you this question. There is no pressure to say yes or no, but I would like you to think about us becoming a duo."

We agreed to take two weeks to pray about it, and when we got back together, Aaron said, "Dad, I've really thought and prayed about what you asked me. I *would* like to sing with you because I think God can use our relationship to touch people's lives."

His response thrilled me because God had been placing the same desire in my heart. Still, he was eighteen years old, and putting together a singing career would be a long-term project. Aaron began attending Belmont University in Nashville, but on weekends he started traveling with me. At first he'd sing only one song with me, "A Man of God," which always drew the biggest cheers of the evening.

For the next three years, we tried to get our duo—called Aaron Jeoffrey—off the ground. We worked on developing our own sound, which I would characterize as "blue-eyed soul," but every major Christian label in Nashville turned us down until Star Song caught the vision of where this thing could go.

Since then, we've recorded three albums. Lyrically, we're positive and fun to listen to. We've created records that we love, and it's music that every generation can enjoy.

As we've toured, we've been amazed to watch our father-and-son relationship affect our audiences. After one concert, a thirty-five-year-old man came up to Aaron, and with tears running down his face he said, "I just lost my dad a few weeks ago. I wish I could have had what you and your dad have. I'm going to go home and try to be a good father to my son." That's why we make appeals to fathers to be shepherds of the

DISCOGRAPHY

Name of group: Aaron Jeoffrey
Members: Jeoffrey Benward, 45
Aaron Benward, 23
Albums: "Aaron Jeoffrey," and "After the Rain"
No. 1 hits: "Promise Me," "Heavy on My Heart," and "After the Rain"
Hometown: Franklin, Tennessee

family, but we're not heavy-handed, since we've experienced our own ups and downs.

About a year ago, our relationship went into the tank. We were getting caught up in petty disagreements about when to make a record, who was going to write the songs, how much we should tour—things like that.

Since I can be intense and Aaron is laid-back, I was wearing on him, but he was also wearing on me. Instead of dealing with it, we continued to ignore each other. This was the first time as father and son that we weren't addressing our differences openly and honestly.

I remember sitting in the office of our manager, and she looked at both of us and said, "I just have to ask you two something. Are you okay?"

"No, we're not," replied Aaron. I agreed with him, then things became really emotional. We had stopped being vulnerable. We were not fun to be around. I looked at Aaron and saw a twenty-one-year-old grown man, who was married and about to become a father. All those emotions swept over me, and I reached out to hold my son. Then we wept and got down on our knees in that office, and through our tears, we prayed for reconciliation.

Afterward, I said to Aaron, "My relationship with you means more than making records. If it ever gets to the point where making records overshadows our relationship, I want to quit."

I meant that a year ago, and I still mean it today.

This material was originally written by Mike Yorkey for Jeoffrey Benward.

JEOFFREY BENWARD ON PERFORMING

You may be wondering why a guy in his mid-forties would want to share a stage with his energetic son. Well, I do know my limitations. We were working with a Hollywood choreographer, and she gave us each a little dance move. Aaron picked it up the first time, but I still don't have it. Since then, I've made a promise to myself that if I think I can still make a move like I could twenty years ago, I better realize that it's just a memory.

But one thing I've noticed is that our audiences give me a lot of liberty. I'm having fun up there, and I think they sense that.

7

Seizing the Moment

. . . .

by Bob Welch

On a cool August morning, two golfers blow on their cupped hands to ward off the chill. They stand on the tee and look ahead toward their target, lost somewhere in the yellowish light of sunrise. It's 6 A.M.

The hole is arrow-straight with a slight dogleg right at the end. Water left. Trees and beach grass right.

And lots of sand.

Lots and lots and lots of sand.

You see, this golf hole stretches seven miles long. My sixteen-year-old son and I created it last summer by sticking a soup can in the sand about 12,320 yards north of my grandfather's beach cabin on the Oregon coast.

Par 72, we figure.

This sea monster makes the 948-yard sixth at Australia's Kooland Island Golf Course—the longest in the world, according to Guinness—look like a miniature golf hole by comparison.

But this challenge is more than man vs. monster. It's also father vs. son, as it's been since the knee football games began nearly sixteen years ago.

Ryan steps to the first—and only—tee. Like a young gymnast, he fears nothing. Thwack. He hits one straight down the middle. *When did he get so strong?*

I step to the tee like a forty-one-year-old man who fears nearly everything, particularly a water trap on my left—the Pacific Ocean—that spans 70 million square miles and covers one-third of the earth's surface. When God made the sea and saw that it was good, He obviously wasn't taking into consideration my hook.

But I, too, hit straight and long. I may be aging, but I refuse to go gently into the good night.

The Thrill of Competition

We're off into the morning mist. The gallery is decidedly uninterested, as most of the feathery fans are too busy ripping the innards from washed-ashore crabs to pay much attention to us.

That's fine; we're not here for glory, we're here for the same reason one man in an office will shoot a crumpled memo into a waste basket and another man will slap it away as if he were David Robinson. We're competition freaks who do crazy things involving sports.

But we're also here because the father part of this twosome is increasingly aware that time and tide wait for no man.

He sees a son who, Lord and admissions directors willing, will be off to college in a couple of years to do more mature things, like painting his entire upper body in school colors for home football games.

This father-son stuff won't go on forever, this dad has realized lately. He's heard all those sermons about parents being the bows and children being the arrows, and he knows the archer must soon let go. Plus, he's read the late golf guru Harvey Penick's book that encourages golfers to "Take dead aim." The axiom, the father has come to understand, goes beyond the golf course to life itself.

What's more, the same father determined months ago that a minus-tide on this particular morning of the family vacation would stretch the fairway to its optimum width. A couple hundred yards is a gloriously wide margin of error for someone who once broke a car windshield with a wild hook.

Fairway Jaunt

Down the windless beach we head—two waves at different points in our journey to shore. I see Ryan as a silhouette against the western sky and think, *When did he get to be so tall?*

We each carry but one club—a driver, for maximum distance. I hit the ball farther in the air, but Ryan takes better advantage of the hard sand with line drives that hit and roll forever. At Big Creek, three miles after teeing off, he has a full stroke on me, 26 to 27.

We each wear a fanny pack filled with extra golf balls that unmask my spoken bravado. Ryan has packed three extra balls. Me? Twelve.

As the early morning sky turns light blue, the match remains tight. The sun bursts through the trees at the four-mile mark, turning the surf to a frothy white. The smoke from a state campground flavors the cool air.

We play Rules of Golf with Beach Alterations: Every shot may be placed on a wooden tee, of which we've brought many. But anything in the water—be it ocean, tide pool, creek, or lagoon—cannot be removed without a one-stroke penalty. Seaweed, logs, and dead gulls are not considered loose impediments and thus, cannot be moved.

Hit, walk, hit, walk. The journey continues. Past motels. Past cabins. Past deep-thinking walkers who stroll the fairway as if they were on a beach.

We make small talk. In the months to come, as Ryan grows more independent, there will be time for deeper things; for now, it is enough that we comment on blocks of sandpipers, rib each other relentlessly about who will win, and compare hunger pains, which our Big Hunks soon fix.

Then it happens. Near Yaquina John Point, with a mile to go, disaster strikes Ryan. It is the long-distance golfer's equivalent of a sailor's mast breaking: His last tee snaps in half. He must now hit off the hardpan sand with a driver, a difficult task.

Half of me wants to console him and loan him a tee; half of me wants to exploit this advantage for all its worth. Being the sensitive midlife father I am, I smile like the Grinch Who Stole Christmas and push the thrusters to Full Exploit. This is, after all, a kid who loves to beat me at everything from arm wrestling to Yahtzee. Who only occasionally loans me my pickup. Who chides me for thinking PFR is a medical acronym, not a Christian band.

I must cling to my dignity any way I can get it.

Ryan doesn't grouse; he simply buckles down and does his best. *When did he get so mature?*

Clubhouse Finish

A hundred yards out, with the seaweed-flag now in sight, we are dead even. Father and son. Sixty-two shots apiece. After we each hit four more shots, Ryan is twelve feet and I am three feet from the hole. The pressure mounts.

Ryan lines up his putt, steps over the ball, strokes and—misses. He looks to the sky in agony before tapping in for a 4-under-par 68.

So it comes to this: After seven miles and sixteen years, I can make this simple putt to remain The Family Beach Golf King.

I stand over the ball that I teed off with four hours earlier. (Amazingly, Ryan and I have each used only one, though the sand has all but worn off the dimples.)

All is quiet. A few crabbers watch curiously from their boats nearby Alsea Bay. The air is still.

I stroke the putt. As if pulled by a soup-can magnet, the ball rolls straight for the cup, for the jaws of victory, for the gentle reminder to my worthy young foe that, in the sea of life, I'm more than just some fortysomething flounder. Then suddenly, inexplicably, the ball veers left like a sickly crab and dies two feet away.

Huh?

We tie.

But after a handshake and a maple bar, I realize that we have come a long way, father and son—much farther than seven miles. We have shared a sunrise, something we've rarely done. We have made a memory that may be told around beach fires for years to come.

"You know I purposely missed that last putt."

"No way, Dad."

"Sure. You didn't think I actually wanted to beat you, did you?"

Above all, we have taken dead aim and hit life's real target which, in God's eyes, has nothing to do with swinging a golf club and everything to do with seizing a moment.

No, I realize as the incoming tide erases our footsteps on the beach, we don't tie.

We win.

In a rematch the following year, Bob Welch lost to Ryan by more than ten strokes.

4

Dads and Their
Wives

1

It's Always Courting Time

. . . .

■ **I've been married three years, and I'm finally learning that a good relationship doesn't just happen. In other words, I have to work at it, right?**

In marriage, little things make big differences. For example, fellows, there's a dramatic difference in referring to your one and only as a "vision" instead of a "sight." There's also just a day's difference in time, but light years of difference between telling your beloved she looks like the first day of spring compared to the last day of a long winter.

On the serious side, let's say you go on a diet and exercise program to lose forty pounds. Over a period of ten months, you'd have to lose around two ounces a day to meet your goal. People who are successful at whatever they do reach their objectives by a series of little things they do every day.

Some of these "little" things will make a dramatic difference almost immediately, while others will take time. A lot depends on the condition of your marriage at the moment and whether you take the steps grudgingly because you've got "nothing to lose" or whether you take them with a loving, expectant attitude. But please hear this: Regardless of your attitude when you start the procedures, the process of doing them will ultimately produce results.

■ **What are some of those little things I can be doing?**

The "Golden Rule" clearly says you should do unto your wife as you want your wife to do unto you. Please notice the instructions say we are to initiate the action. There really are many instances when husbands need to "spoil" their wives.

Fellows, a little thing like calling your wife during a coffee break is no big deal either, but over a period of time, little things do make a big difference. A simple little thing, even like regularly opening the car door, can tell her that you think she is special.

Now, obviously, she's physically capable of opening it, but you should personally feel good when you're privileged to do such a simple little thing like opening that door for her. It serves as a constant reminder that she is important, and you want to be constantly aware of taking the action steps that say, "I love you."

Look for those things that can ease your wife's path and make your own life and marriage happier. If your wife is working outside the home, then dealing with the children, preparing the evening meal, and doing the laundry do *not* fit under the category of "women's work." These tasks are family responsibilities and *opportunities.*

If the family includes you, your wife, and a couple of children, that means four people created the work. If four people created disorder in the home, but only one is doing the work, an impossible burden is placed on that person. You function as a team. It's that simple.

When your wife does *anything* that makes your trip through life a little easier, a sincere "thank you" is important and appreciated. If you expect her to do something because it's her "job," the odds are long that it will be done reluctantly, poorly, or not at all. If you express appreciation, results are far better. Those little thank-you's are indications of *class.*

■ **My mother told me many times that we might not all be rich and smart, but we can all be kind and courteous. Is that what you mean?**

The sixteenth-century French writer De Sales was right: "Nothing is so strong as gentleness; nothing so gentle as real strength."

The next thing you have to know is when to apologize. Many times husbands act considerably less than mature (would you believe childishly and selfishly?) when they hit a snag in their relationship, and stubborn pride (hardheaded arrogance might be more accurate) erects a serious roadblock in the marriage.

■ **Give me an example.**

Perhaps you say, "If she showed more affection, I'd come home earlier." Meanwhile she says, "If he came home earlier, I'd show more affection."

Remember, when disagreements take place, who makes the move to make up isn't important. The one who makes the move demonstrates the greater maturity and love, as well as the greater concern that the marriage not only will survive, but also thrive in an atmosphere of love and understanding. And when you are wrong, the most important words in your vocabulary are "I'm sorry, Honey. Will you forgive me?"

■ **I received an unusual present from my wife for our anniversary. When I arrived home from the office one Friday, very tired from a hard day, she said, "Honey, we need to run one errand before dinner this evening." Then she gave me directions by a circuitous route, and we finally ended up at one of the nicest hotels in Dallas, where my wife had arranged a special weekend of relaxation together. That's one anniversary I'll never forget!**

You're a fortunate husband. But let's say you can't afford something so extravagant. Similar options may include taking her to that incredible restaurant she's always wanted to visit, or giving her complete freedom for the day. Get up early with the kids, prepare their breakfast, and take care of their every need. Your wife could visit friends, shop a little, have lunch out, catch a movie, walk in the park, or "live it up" in general.

In the meantime, you're back home looking after the kids and gaining a new appreciation for your wife. The kids win too because they get to know you much better.

With careful budgeting and planning, most couples can squirrel away money for a heavy date or a short weekend trip where you can devote 100 percent of your time and attention to each other.

■ **I always forget our anniversary, unless my wife does some serious "reminding" for a week leading up to our special day. How can I do a better job of remembering?**

We all like to feel important and be remembered on our birthdays, anniversaries, Valentine's Day, Christmas, and other special holidays. But we should also remember those occasions when there are no occasions. Drop your wife a note in the mail, "just because." Pick up a single rose and take it home, "just because." When you have occasions to choose gifts, choose them with care, thinking of what your wife would really want.

If you're the recipient of a gift you are less than enthusiastic about, don't forget that she chose the gift to please you. So, Dad, if she gave you cologne for your birthday, slap it on after you shave. Don't leave the bottle on the shelf until next year so you can pitch it out during spring-cleaning.

If she gave you a sweater, and you don't particularly enjoy wearing sweaters, go ahead and wear it occasionally anyway. That's just a gracious way of saying, "Thank you for loving me and thinking of me when you bought this gift."

Please understand that whether the gift is a ten-carat diamond, a cruise around the world, or a two-dollar bauble, it isn't the gift itself but the thought behind the gift that really counts. As the medieval character Sir Lancelot said, "The gift without the giver is bare."

In short, don't get carried away with "things" to give your wife, but do give yourself. From time to time, a simple gift, or card, or—even better—a handwritten love letter shows marvelous devotion to your wife. Its cost is zero; its value enormous.

■ **I can't help but think that this courtship-after-marriage stuff takes a lot of time.**

You're right, but the return on this time investment is enormous. Not only are the ongoing rewards exciting, but also it takes considerably less time to maintain a loving relationship than it does to repair a broken one.

This material is adapted from Courtship After Marriage *(Thomas Nelson) by Zig Ziglar. Phyllis Guth lives in Allentown, Pennsylvania.*

THE MANY FACES OF LOVE

Love is:

► Rising at 7 A.M. on Sunday morning to prepare breakfast for the entire family.

► Getting up in the middle of the night to feed a baby.

► Performing tasks for your wife's elderly parents that they are no longer able to do for themselves.

► Taking time out from a busy schedule to listen to a friend.

► Going along with your wife's choice of a vacation spot.

► Making your children's friends welcome in your home, even when it's inconvenient.

► Overlooking your wife's foibles.

► Being accepting of your in-laws, even when their ideas clash with yours.

► Picking up after yourself without any prompting.

—Phyllis Guth

2

Asking the Right Questions

· ·

■ **I've heard that one aspect of building intimacy in a marriage is learning to ask the right questions. Well, here's a question. Where do I start?**

Have you ever had a conversation like this with your wife?
"What do you want to do tonight, Honey?"
"I don't know. What do you want to do?"
"I don't know either. Don't you have any plans or ideas?"
"It doesn't really matter to me. Whatever you want to do will be fine with me!"

■ **Yes, all the time. What should I do about it?**

Read this interchange and see if it sounds better to you:
"What's the most fun we've ever had on a date?"
"Oh, the time we rode our bikes and you took me to that little bagel shop for lunch."
"Well then, how would you like to do that again?"

The smile on her face will say it all!

■ **So, what's the difference between *good* questions and *great* ones?**

Ultimately, it boils down to *how* they are asked and *when* they are asked. Here are some key components of great questions:

1. Use questions that cannot be answered with a yes or no. Nothing will slow down a conversation more than asking questions that can be answered with one word. Such questions will fail to engage the personality, mind, or opinions of your wife.

2. Ask razor-sharp questions. Vague questions will shut down openness and cut off communication. The best questions do more than seek information; they seek *specific* information. For example, which of the following questions makes you eager to respond?

"So, how was your day?" or "Which part of your day did you enjoy the most?"

3. Know why you are asking a question. Before asking your wife a question, it helps to ask yourself, *What is motivating me to ask this question right now?* Often, the tone of a question will get more of a response than what's being asked. For that reason, it may be better to ask a question later—or never.

WHEN SHE SAYS . . .	SHE REALLY MEANS . . .
"We need"	I want
"Do what you want."	You'll pay for this later!
"Sure . . . go ahead."	I don't want you to do that!
"I'm not upset."	Of course I'm upset, you jerk!
"The kitchen is so inconvenient."	I want a new house.
"The trash is full."	Take the trash out!
"How much do you love me?"	I did something today you're really not going to like.
"Nothing is wrong."	Everything is wrong.
"I don't want to talk about it."	Go away. I'm still building up steam.
"Am I fat?"	Tell me I'm beautiful.
"I'll be ready in a minute."	Take off your shoes and find a good football game on TV.
"You have to learn to communicate."	Just agree with me.
"Are you listening?"	Too late. You're dead.

4. Avoid leading questions. Great questions are two-way streets, not dead ends. It's easy to ask questions that compel a person to come to *our* conclusions, instead of getting a sense of what she is genuinely thinking and feeling.

The best way to avoid using leading questions is to wholeheartedly listen to your wife's responses. She can tell when she is being heard or merely being humored.

5. Don't ask a good question at a bad time. The husband who has learned to ask great questions knows that the best time to ask them is not when *you* want to ask, but when your wife is willing to respond. Discerning the times of openness in your relationship with your wife is an art you can spend a lifetime perfecting. Yet it is essential to effective communication.

6. Use *would* instead of *could*. When asking for your wife's help, *would* is always more effective than *could!* For instance, what would you think if your wife asked you, "Could you put a new light bulb in the hallway?" She simply may want an old light bulb replaced, but you might respond, "Can I? Of course I can fix a stupid little hallway light!" In your mind, she is questioning your ability; in her mind, she is simply asking for help.

The most vibrant marriages are those that have developed the skill of asking questions. Such husbands and wives are passionate about learning all they can about each other. They are grateful for what they know, but they are also eager to learn and discover more!

WHEN HE SAYS . . .	HE REALLY MEANS . . .
"You look nice tonight."	I want to have sex.
"Boy, am I hungry!"	Make me something to eat and serve it to me on the couch.
"It's too expensive."	You could get a neat computer for that!
"It's a beautiful day."	It's too hot to do yard work!
"I have a surprise."	I bought something really stupid.
"Are you still awake?"	I want to have sex again.
"You can't mow the lawn when the grass is wet."	There's a game on the tube.
"Why don't you stop working?"	You're always too tired to have sex.

Remember . . .

Good questions create interest; great ones inspire a response. Good questions open conversations; great ones open souls. Good questions raise issues; great ones evoke dreams and visions. Good questions elicit ideas; great questions uncover needs.

All you have to do is ask.

This article is adapted from Now We're Talking *by Robert C. Crosby and Pamela Crosby and published by Focus on the Family. Copyright © 1996 by Robert C. Crosby and Pamela Crosby. Used by permission.*

REMEMBER WHAT'S IMPORTANT TO A WOMAN . . .

► Make sure you have time to listen. She can tell when you are really interested and when you are merely humoring her.

► A woman needs to know that a man is genuinely listening . . . listening with his heart and not trying to figure out how to "fix" her problem.

► She needs to feel free to share her opinion and to help her husband understand without him getting frustrated or angry.

► A woman needs to feel valued by her husband beyond all of his human relationships.

► A woman values relational moments far more than occupational achievements.

► A woman is deeply affirmed when a man makes a noticeable effort to hear her heart.

REMEMBER WHAT'S IMPORTANT TO YOU . . .

► When men become uncaring or distant, it is usually because they're afraid of something.

► Men are more motivated to achieve goals than to absorb moments.

► Men fear nothing more than failure.

► Men are motivated by feeling significant.

► Men want to manage their own problems and be "Mr. Fix-It!"

► Men want to "get to the bottom line."

► Men tend to "report" more than converse. Just listen to a man on the phone. Usually, his comments are brief, utilitarian, and to the point. "Okay . . . got it . . . be there at 8 . . . see ya soon."

WHAT WE MOST ENJOY TALKING ABOUT

Men	Women
Facts	Feelings
How things work	Resolving and building relationships
Objects and things	Friendships
Sports	Self-improvement ideas
Computers and cars	Husbands and kids
Accomplishments	Areas of need

3

Date Your Mate!

· ·

■ My wife, Kam, and I recently enjoyed a rare weekend away from the kids at a resort hotel. While lounging beside a huge swimming pool, we watched a hundred-plus people tanning, swimming, playing, reading, and otherwise enjoying themselves. As far as I could see, the pairs having the best time weren't the married ones. As a matter of fact, most of the married couples appeared rather bored. If they were having fun with each other, you'd never have known it by looking at them.

We watched one couple in their sixties playing around in the water, giggling, splashing, and enjoying one another immensely. I assumed, because of their age, that they were married. But we soon learned it wasn't so—they, too, were just "dating." Then I saw Kam reading her book in her lounge chair, and I knew she wouldn't be in the mood to frolic in the pool that afternoon. Whatever happened to all the fun in marriage?

The sad fact is that many couples become bored and uninterested once they are married. For them, dating and romance are all but nonexistent.

In fact, they believe there's a clause on the marriage license stating, "Once married, you shall no longer date. Furthermore, if you decide to do anything resembling a date, it shall be called 'going out' and shall never be too exciting!"

That's why, with the right spirit and motivation, dating can help strengthen a good marriage as well as encourage a troubled one. Many Christian marriage counselors are convinced that the lack of dating and romance in marriage is one of the major causes of a broken relationship. Marriages usually don't collapse overnight. They become bankrupt gradually because they lack daily deposits of love, communication, and affirmation.

■ **Okay, we want to add life to our marriage by bringing romance and dating back into the picture. What are some of the benefits of dating my wife?**

Dating will strengthen your relationship. Relationships are strengthened through time spent together, honest communication, and positive memories. Dating provides all of these. Dating builds up marriages and helps solidify their foundations. Enduring relationships aren't constructed out of fleeting emotions and occasional passion. They are built on quality time spent together, each partner investing in the other.

■ **We would like to date once a week, but it's a real stretch for us financially. As we're making new priorities, what should we keep in mind about the importance of dating?**

Almost without exception, those couples who manage to date regularly find this time of shared experience has brought them closer together. It's not always easy nor inexpensive to find a baby-sitter, but they place high priority on their weekly dates. And the value they add to their marriage can't be measured in financial terms.

Dating also enriches life. Life was given to us by our Creator to be lived to its fullest. And He gave us a great playground we affectionately call "Earth" to use and enjoy while we have the opportunity. Setting time aside to enjoy one another is not only pleasing to God but also enriches the quality of our lives. You are bound to be a much better husband or wife when you invest time in your marriage, giving it higher priority than the television set, the PTA, the office or church activities, or the golf course.

Dating creates positive memories. Quality relationships are rich in positive memories. Since our world does a good job of dispensing negative experiences, it's up to us to do an even better job of providing positive ones.

Finally, dating gives you something to look forward to. You will come to a point where you view your date nights as sacred. Those nights will give you something exciting to anticipate. Actually, when you get depressed about work or tired of the bills, what best lifts your spirits is the awareness that you'll soon be spending special time with your wife. What can be better than getting out of the house and being alone with the one person you love more than anyone else?

■ **What are some other benefits to dating?**

One of the best ways you can demonstrate love to your children is by expressing affection to your wife in front of them. When children have observed their parents placing priority on dating and romance, they will carry that expectation into their own significant relationships.

■ **Sometimes I just don't see the value of taking Kam out on a date. What's a good "word picture?"**

Consider this story. Two construction workers were busy working on a huge brick-laying project. A passerby was curious about the future of the building. She stopped the workers and asked, "Just what is it you're building?"

The first worker told her he was simply laying bricks to finish a construction project. When she asked the second worker the same question, he stood and proudly explained to her that he was helping to build a great cathedral. He was able to see the big picture and was excited about the outcome. He viewed his job as a worthy task.

As you think about your own marriage, you might want to answer that same question, "What are you building?" What you want to be able to say is "I'm building a great marriage, day-by-day, year-by-year, brick-by-brick!"

50 CREATIVE DATING IDEAS

Feel free to add, subtract, or delete from this list. You may find some of the more outrageous ideas helpful in stretching your imagination.

1. Sketch your dream house floor plan and talk about possibilities for each room.

2. Write the story of how you met. Get it printed and put it in a family picture album.

3. List your wife's best qualities in alphabetical order.

4. Tour a museum or art gallery.

5. Notice the little changes your wife makes in her appearance.

6. Float on a raft together.

7. Take a stroll around the block—and hold hands as you walk.

8. Stock the cupboards with food your wife loves to eat. (But only if she isn't on a diet.)

9. Give your wife a back rub.

10. Rent a classic love-story video and watch it while cuddling.

11. Build a fire in the fireplace, turn out the lights, and talk.

12. Take a horse-drawn carriage ride.

13. Go swimming in the middle of the night.

14. Write a poem for your wife.

15. Remember to look into your wife's eyes as she tells you about the day.

16. Tell your wife, "I'm glad I married you!"

17. Hug your wife from behind and give her a kiss on the back of the neck.

18. Stop in the middle of your busy day and telephone your wife for fifteen minutes.

19. Create your own special holiday.

20. Do something your wife loves to do, even though it doesn't interest you personally.

21. Mail your wife a love letter.

22. Build a snowman together.

23. Watch the sunset together.

24. Sit on the same side of a restaurant booth.

25. Picnic by a pond.

26. Give your wife a foot massage.

27. Put together a puzzle on a rainy evening.

28. Take a moonlight canoe ride.

29. Tell your wife, "I'd rather be here with you than any place in the world."

continued next page

30. Whisper something romantic to your wife in a crowded room.
31. Have a candlelight picnic in the backyard.
32. Perfume the bed sheets.
33. Serve breakfast in bed.
34. Reminisce through old photo albums.
35. Go away for a weekend.
36. Share a milk shake with two straws.
37. Kiss in the rain.
38. Brush her hair.
39. Ride the merry-go-round together.
40. Dedicate a song to her over the radio.
41. Wink and smile at your wife from across the room.
42. Have a hot bubble bath ready for her at the end of a long day.
43. Buy new satin sheets.
44. Tenderly touch your wife as you pass one another around the house.
45. Reminisce about your first date.
46. Plant a tree together in honor of your marriage.
47. Go kite-flying.
48. Attend a sporting event you've never been to together.
49. Take time to think about her during the day, then share those thoughts.
50. Drop everything and do something for the one you love—right now!

A SIMPLE WAY TO MAKE YOUR WIFE HAPPY

by Yanira Alfonso

I was busy running around the kitchen trying to finish dinner one Friday evening after a long week of work. I anxiously waited for the sound of the garage door. Throughout the years, this familiar sound had become a sweet, pleasant indication that my husband was home.

On this occasion, his arrival was no different. I heard the garage door open. My heart did its usual happy, silent dance, as my ears tuned to the sound of the downstairs door opening and the thump, thump of his walk up the stairs. "Honey, have you seen the package outside?" he yelled.

"What package?" I responded.

When my husband walked into the kitchen, he was carrying an opened box containing a dozen beautiful red roses! My eyes lit up, and I held my face in astonishment.

I did a quick mental check. No, it wasn't our wedding anniversary or my birthday.

"Ohh, hhoww swweet!" I exclaimed. "It's not even our anniversary!"

Then I threw both hands around my husband's neck and gave him a big hug and a kiss. I had received roses before, but getting them when it wasn't our anniversary, a holiday, or my birthday made them so much more special—not to mention how much more special it made the man who had delivered them.

So don't wait to bring your wife flowers. Bring them today! It's one simple way to say "I love you" and make her very happy.

This material is adapted from writings by Doug Fields, author of Creative Romance *(Harvest House) and from writings by Yanira Alfonso of Loganville, Georgia.*

4

The Language of Love

· ·

■ Not long ago, I sat down at the kitchen table with my wife, who was in obvious pain. With tears streaming down her face, she sobbed, "I've tried to express what's wrong in our marriage, but I just can't seem to explain it. What's the use in bringing it all up again?" Our communication was at rock-bottom. Where had I blown it?

Before that question can be answered, you need to make a decision to understand what's happening in your marriage—or not happening. Start by asking several questions. Why is your wife feeling so frustrated in her attempts to communicate with you? Why is she having such a difficult time sharing her feelings with you?

■ I don't know. I have to say that it's a real struggle for us to understand each other—particularly when we discuss important issues.

First off, you need to know that males and females think and speak differently, much differently. In order for you to begin spanning the communication gap between you, you need to start using emotional "word pictures."

■ **"Word pictures?" What's that?**

Word pictures can supercharge communication and change lives, whether in marriage, families, friendships, or businesses. Indeed, word pictures have the capacity to capture a person's attention by engaging both their thoughts and their feelings.

Have you ever tried to express an important thought or feeling with your wife, only to have her act as if you're speaking a foreign language? Have you ever asked, "Why can't she *feel* what I'm saying?"

■ **Yes, I have. Give me an example of how we use the same words but speak a different language.**

Let's say you have an idea that will get you nominated Husband of the Year. That idea is to do something adventurous with your wife—like go shopping!

One can't be sure what emotional and physiological changes ignite a wife upon hearing the words, "Let's go to the mall," but it would be like if someone offered you two tickets to go see Michael Jordan and the Bulls play basketball.

Here's what happened to Gary Smalley when he offered to go shopping with his wife, Norma.

That next Saturday morning, as we drove up to the mall, Norma told me she needed to look for a new blouse. So after we parked the car and walked into the nearest clothing store, she held up a blouse and asked, "What do you think?"

"Great," I said. "Let's get it." But really, I was thinking, *Great! If she hurries up and gets this blouse, we'll be back home in plenty of time to watch the USC-Notre Dame football game on TV.*

Then she picked up another blouse and said, "What do you think about this one?"

"It's great, too," I said. "Get either one. No, get both!"

But after looking at a number of blouses on the rack, we walked out of the store empty-handed. Then we went into another store, and she did the same thing. And then into another store. And another. And another!

As we went in and out of all the shops, I became increasingly anxious. The thought even struck me, *Not only will I miss the halftime highlights, but at the rate we're going, I will miss the entire season!* And that's when it happened.

Instead of picking up a blouse at the next store we entered, she held up a dress that was about our daughter's size. "What do you think about this for Kari?" she asked.

Taxed beyond any mortal's limits, my willpower cracked, and I blurted out, "What do you mean, 'What do you think about a dress for Kari?' We're here shopping for blouses for *you*, not dresses for Kari!"

That night, I began to understand a common difference between men and women. I wasn't shopping for blouses . . . I was hunting for blouses! I wanted to conquer the blouse, bag it, and then get back home where important things waited, like Saturday afternoon football!

My wife, however, looked at shopping from the opposite extreme. For her, it meant more than simply buying a blouse. It was a way to spend time talking together as we enjoyed several hours away from the children—and Saturday afternoon football.

Like most men, I thought a trip to the mall meant going shopping. But to Norma, it meant *shoooooopppping!*

■ **Boy, that sure explains why I don't like to go shopping with my wife. What are some of the other innate differences between men and women I should know about?**

Do you know that women talk more than men? Of course, you do. But researchers have found that from the earliest ages, little girls talk more than little boys. One study showed that even in the hospital nursery, girls have more lip movement than boys! And in the playground, Harvard researchers found that 100 percent of the sounds coming from the girls' mouths were audible, recognizable words, but for little boys, only 68 percent of their sounds were understandable words. The remaining 32 percent either were one-syllable sounds like "uh" and "mmmm" to sound effects like "varoom!" "yaaahhh!" and "zoooom!"

■ **I guess that's why I grunt and rattle the newspaper when my wife tries to talk to me. Are we really that brain damaged?**

No, but our brains are different. Specifically, medical studies have shown that between the eighteenth and twenty-sixth week of pregnancy, something happens that forever separates the sexes. Using heat-sensitive color monitors, researchers have actually observed a chemical bath of testosterone and other sex-related hormones wash over a baby boy's brain. This causes changes that never happen to the brain of a baby girl.

The human body is divided into two halves, or hemispheres, connected by fibrous tissue called the *corpus callosum*. The sex-related hormones and chemicals that flood a baby boy's brain cause the right side to recede slightly, destroying some of the connecting fibers. One result is that, in most cases, a boy starts life more *left*-brain oriented.

■ **So where does that leave little girls?**

Little girls leave the starting blocks much more two-sided in their thinking. And while electrical impulses and messages do travel back and forth between both sides of a baby boy's brain, those same messages can proceed faster and be less hindered by the brain of a little girl.

■ **So you're saying that men are basically brain damaged.**

Well, not exactly. What occurs in the womb merely sets the stage for men and women to "specialize" in two different ways of thinking. And this is one major reason men and women need each other so much.

The left brain houses more of the logical, analytical, factual, and aggressive centers of thought. It's the side of the brain most men reserve for the majority of their waking hours. It enjoys conquering 500 miles a day on family vacation trips; favors mathematical formulas over romance novels; stores the dictionary definition of love; and generally prefers clinical, black-and-white thinking.

On the other hand, most women spend the majority of their

days and nights camped out on the right side of the brain. It's the side that harbors the center for feelings, as well as the primary relational, language, and communication skills. It enables them to do fine-detail work, spark imaginations, and make an afternoon devoted to art. Perhaps you now can begin to understand why communication is difficult in marriage.

■ Yes, I can. So how do I boost my communication skills?

By using the power of emotional word pictures, as mentioned before. Word pictures can help a man move beyond "facts" and begin to achieve total communication with a woman. This same skill not only will help a woman get a man to *feel* her words as well as *hear* them, but it also maximizes her innate relational abilities.

If a woman truly expects to have meaningful communication with her husband, she *must* activate the right side of his brain. And if a man truly wants to communicate with his wife, he *must* enter her world of emotions. In fact, a world of colorful communication waits for those who learn the skill of bridging both sides of the brain. Word pictures won't eliminate all the difference between men and women, but

SOME SAMPLE WORD PICTURES

Need some help coming up with word pictures? Maybe these will spark some ideas:

► "With the job I'm in, I often feel like I'm walking on a desert trail on a hot summer day. After struggling through the heat and cactus all day, I come to the end of a path, and there's a beautiful pool of cool water. At last I'm at a place where I can drink and be refreshed. That's what it's like being with you. After ten years of marriage, I still like being with you, which is like coming upon an oasis."

► "There have been times over the years when I've faced hailstorms that I thought would turn into tornadoes. But like the shelter of a storm cellar, I can always run to you to protect me from hardship. You're as solid as a rock, and I know you'll always be there when the storm clouds blow into my life."

► "Sweetheart, when you live with a brand-new, gleaming white Cadillac convertible, there's no desire to rush and drive a Yugo."

they can enable us to unlock the gateway to intimacy.

This material is adapted from The Language of Love *by Gary Smalley and John Trent, Ph.D., and published by Focus on the Family. Copyright © 1988, 1991, Gary Smalley and John Trent, Ph.D. Used by permission.*

5

Become a Marriage Mentor

■ At church the other day, the pastor came up to my wife and me and asked if we would consider becoming marriage mentors. He said that since we were married veterans, we could help smooth the way for young couples. Annette and I were flattered that Pastor Steve thought enough of us and our marriage to approach us. What kind of couples will we be mentoring?

You'll probably wind up meeting a couple like Tom and Wendy, who are in their mid-twenties and married for just a few months. They dated for nearly two years before getting engaged. They had the blessing of their parents, attended premarital counseling, and were on their way to living happily ever after—or so everyone thought.

But marriage for Tom and Wendy, like the majority of newlyweds you'll be mentoring, wasn't all they hoped for. Each of them, for different reasons, felt let down. Unlike the majority of couples, however, Tom and Wendy talked openly about their feelings in their Sunday School class. Their expectations of marriage were not being met, and they were determined to do something about it.

So on a cold January day four months after their wedding, Tom and Wendy approached the pastor and asked for help. Bundled up against the cold, they came into his office and began to shed their coats. As Wendy sipped hot coffee to thaw out, she said, "We have talked to friends and family about what is going on, but we both decided we need more objectivity."

Tom joined in: "Yeah, everybody who knows us just says 'give it time' or something like that." Tom went on to say that their marriage was not on the rocks and no major overhaul was needed. "I just think we need a little realignment," he said.

The pastor gave them several exercises to help them explore their misconceptions of marriage and then recommended a few resources. Then he introduced the idea of linking up with a marriage mentor couple.

"What's that?" Wendy asked.

He told them how meeting from time to time with a seasoned married couple could give them a sounding board and a safe place to explore some of their questions about marriage. Like most newly married couples, Tom and Wendy were very eager to find such a couple. After a bit of discussion, Pastor Steve suggested you and Annette. They don't know you very well, but they respect your marriage from afar and thought you would fit the bill.

■ What's the general philosophy behind marriage mentors?

Throughout human history, mentoring has been the primary means of passing on knowledge and skills. The Bible is also filled with examples of mentoring (Eli and Samuel, Elijah and Elisha, Moses and Joshua, Naomi and Ruth, Elizabeth and Mary, Barnabas and Paul, Paul and Timothy).

Today, there's a great need for a network of mentors who will rise up to become guardians of the next generation of marriages.

But mentoring is in short supply these days. In our modern age, the learning process has shifted. It now relies primarily on computers, classrooms, books, and videos. In most cases today, the relational connection between the knowledgeable and experienced giver and the receiver of that wisdom has weakened or is nonexistent—especially in the early years of marriage.

■ **If people need help in their marriage, why don't they contact their pastor or their parents?**

Pastors can—and certainly do—help young married couples, but the demands of church sometimes mean that young couples get lost in the shuffle. And parents—well, let's just say that the vast majority of young marrieds do not want to admit to their parents that something has gone awry so early in a marriage.

"What I need is someone to talk to who has walked down the path I'm just beginning," said Lisa a few weeks into her new marriage. "Whenever I go to my mom or dad with a situation, they end up being a parent or teaching me something I don't really need to learn."

While a mother and father can certainly serve a helpful function in the life of a new bride or groom, they usually cannot offer the distance and objectivity that a mentor gives. For this reason, it is important first to realize exactly what a mentor is *not*.

- ► A mentor is not a mother or father.
- ► A mentor is not a friend.
- ► A mentor is not "on call" for every little crisis.
- ► A mentor is not a know-it-all.
- ► A mentor is not committed long term.

■ **If a mentor couple is not these things, what is a mentor couple?**

The relationship between a mentor couple and newlyweds has a natural cycle of its own, which is not always predictable. Each mentoring relationship takes on its own style and personality. The amount of time couples spend together and the content they discuss can rarely be prescribed.

However, it's recommended that the two couples meet a minimum of three meetings throughout the newlyweds' first year together: at three months, seven months, and one year after the wedding. These times provide the basic structure upon which additional meetings, meals, and phone calls can rest.

■ **Some friends of ours mentored a young couple and said they learned a lot about their own marriage. Is this what is known as the "boomerang effect"?**

Indeed, an interesting aspect about marriage mentoring is that it can actually help the mentor couple.

"I don't know how much we helped Doug and Sarah," said Joan, "but we sure got a lot out of it." Joan laughed as she described being a marriage mentor couple along with Larry, her husband of eighteen years.

"Helping a young couple seemed to spark a lot of things in our own marriage that we had neglected," Larry added.

THE PROOF IS IN THE PUDDING

Drs. Les and Leslie Parrott recently received this letter that sums up the life-changing effect a mentoring couple can have on a young marriage:

Dear Les and Leslie,

How can we ever thank you for helping us find a marriage mentor couple! Our mentoring relationship with Nate and Sharon ended up being the most important thing we have ever done to build up our marriage. It was nice to have another couple know what we were going through and remain objective at the same time.

Someday we hope to give back the gift that Nate and Sharon gave to us by mentoring some newly married couples. We think every couple just starting out should have a mentor.

Something wonderful happens when a more mature couple reaches out to a new couple. Some call it the boomerang effect. By helping another couple live out their dreams, one's own dreams for marriage are reawakened and fulfilled.

Once you take the time to listen to a questioning couple, your own "answers" become clearer. You will also be refreshed by this relationship. Almost by osmosis, the vim and vigor for marriage that a new couple enjoys will begin to rub off on you. Simply being around their energetic spirits will revive and rejuvenate your marriage. There is also an overwhelming sense of having done good, of helping a new couple build a love that will last a lifetime.

■ How can we become a mentor couple?

Easy. Just follow these simple directions:

1. Pray that God will direct you in ministering to engaged and newly married couples.

2. Contact your pastor about how you can serve as a mentoring couple in your local congregation.

3. Volunteer to begin a marriage mentoring program that would augment the existing ministry to young couples in your church.

4. Write to Les and Leslie Parrott about receiving information on beginning a mentoring program:

Drs. Les and Leslie Parrott
Center for Relationship Development
Seattle Pacific University
Seattle, WA 98119

Information is available on recruiting, selecting, and training marriage mentors.

This material is adapted from writings by Drs. Les and Leslie Parrott, who have been married thirteen years and have coordinated 300 mentor couples in the Seattle area. They are codirectors of the Center for Relationship at Seattle Pacific University.

6

Divorce War

. . . .

■ We've been going through horrible marital difficulties, and my golfing buddy—who's been twice divorced—told me that the last thing I want is to end up in divorce court. I've always felt that a court of law is where everything gets hashed out, where you get your say before an impartial judge. He chuckled and said, "You're so naive."
Why was he laughing at me?

Because you never *have* experienced the stark coldness of a divorce courtroom. When the gavel falls, the judge sits down, and the trial begins, you and your wife—who had once said before Almighty God and hundreds of witnesses the words "I do" to each other—begin the painful process of saying "I don't."

You will sit within fifteen feet of each other, avoiding eye contact at all costs. Though legally still married, you will become petitioner and respondent, not husband and wife; enemies, not allies. The connection between you will be as lifeless as the brick on the courtroom walls. And to think that you once called each other sweetheart.

■ **That's why my friend said, "I wish you could sit in divorce court; it will get you thinking about what you have." But you don't understand how it's a war every time I come home from work.**

Then you need to address those issues—most likely with a third party present, such as a pastor or a counselor. You don't want to end up in court, however, becoming just another statistic. Each day in hundreds of courtrooms across America, divorce wars are fought between warring couples. It isn't pretty. But then to understand the importance of wearing a seat belt, sometimes you need to look at a mangled car.

■ **Okay, describe a typical court proceeding.**

More often than not, the man and woman are your typical middle-class family. They're nice-looking and dress well. They're not part of a dysfunctional family, a counselor has ruled. They're simply a couple who have decided to split up because of "irreconcilable differences."

A judge will decide who will get everything from their house to their Grolier Multimedia Encyclopedia on CD-ROM. But the big question is who will get custody of their children.

■ **Oh, yes, I forgot about the children. They are the contested prizes in divorce court, right?**

Very much so. As a trial unfolds, a chasm of contrasts will separate then and now, wedding and dissolution. The two will be flanked not by a best man and maid of honor bearing rings that will unite, but by attorneys armed with evidence that will divide.

There will be no photographer capturing each priceless memory, only a court reporter recording each verbal volley.

There will be no triumphant music, only the tinny sound of testimony spoken into microphones.

There will be no festive throng of family and friends, only empty benches and a handful of supporters waiting in the lobby.

Between sessions, the two will gather with their friends and families in the lobby, like boxers going to their respective corners.

The woman's attorney will argue that the father is an irresponsible parent, as shown by the raising of their twelve-year-old and fourteen-year-old sons. He doesn't believe in structure and discipline. He doesn't care if the kids do their homework or not. The mother, the attorney says, has cared enough to set boundaries, build structure, and require accountability.

■ **I bet that father didn't take that accusation lying down. I know I wouldn't.**

You're right. The man's attorney will counterattack. He will argue that the woman has been abusive to the children. She has hit them, screamed at them, locked them out of the house in their underwear. The husband, he will say, has cared enough to help the boys with their homework, calmly handle friction, and cook an abundance of meals, particularly pancake breakfasts.

On topics ranging from pearl necklaces to dented trucks, from flunked classes to stapled cats, the attorneys will continue their assaults, dropping smart bombs to do damage in strategic positions. Pierced ears, paddles, and broken pickle jars—these are among the subjects that will come into play in deciding which parent will be best for the children, who have no say in the matter.

At one point, the mother will be put on the witness stand. "Was there a time when your husband put you into a bedroom?" asks her husband's attorney.

"Yes, he threw me into the bedroom."

"Do you remember why you were placed in the bedroom by him?"

"He was angry at me."

"Do you know why?"

"No."

"Wasn't it because he just separated you from having a fight with one of the older children?"

"No."

Minute by minute, hour by hour, day by day, the evidence will grow like a gnarly tree. The judge will hear about the time the three-year-old was slapped for pushing the VCR buttons during

The Hunchback of Notre Dame. The time he cried when being shifted from one parent to another. And the time he was allowed to ride in the back of a pickup truck.

What's true? What's not? Amid this family's chaos, it will be difficult to tell. While the battle continues, the propaganda war will heat up, each side describing incidents in vastly different ways.

Between sessions, one of the young witnesses will look at the stockpiled ammunition on the attorneys' tables, piles of notes and documents.

"This," says the little boy, "is a mess."

When a seven-day trial finally ends, the court reporter will have typed the equivalent of 1,400 double-spaced pages. The judge will have listened to about thirty witnesses. The attorneys will have entered 110 pieces of evidence, everything from belts allegedly used for hitting to father-son photographs. And the man and woman will have spent about $35,000 in attorney's fees; one attorney charges $95 an hour, the other $145.

■ What happened at the end of this trial?

Two weeks after the trial ended, the judge, "with considerable trepidation," granted custody of the child to the mother and gave the father liberal visitation rights. In his decision, he mentioned a recent case in which the state had to remove a child from the care of a mildly retarded man and woman. The couple had tried courageously to overcome their handicaps and be good parents, but it was not within their capacity. How sad, the judge pointed out, that two mentally sound people could hardly do better.

"For a variety of reasons, I hope never to see another case like this one," he said.

■ Hearing all this makes me wonder how the same couple who promised themselves to love each other nearly twenty years ago could become such bitter enemies.

Divorce was hailed in the 1970s as a great mender of wounds. But divorce hasn't become the panacea that it was thought it would be. In fact, divorce devastates families.

The sad irony is this: The time and place to prove one's proficiency as a parent isn't during a divorce proceeding in front of a judge, but in a family setting in front of the children themselves. For all the time, money, and energy that goes into divorce trials, all it really proves is the high cost of divorce—in terms of money and human casualties.

In the end, divorce is worse than war. In war, at least you have a winner.

This article is adapted from writings by Bob Welch of Eugene, Oregon, who watched several days of a divorce case proceedings.

7

Commitment to Love

. . . .

Editor's note: Clebe and Deanna McClary were young newlyweds with life ahead of them. And then tragedy struck.

Deanna McClary: I remember my wedding day just like it was yesterday. More than thirty years ago, on March 26, 1967, we were married on Easter Sunday before our families and friends in Florence, South Carolina.

My heart pounded as I walked down the aisle with Daddy. I looked for Clebe because, in keeping with tradition, I hadn't seen him all day. In his Marine dress blue uniform, standing at parade rest with his hands behind him, he looked more debonair than ever.

At nineteen years of age, I felt a deep sense of satisfaction as we met in front of the altar. Why? Because I had saved myself for Clebe. The white dress I was wearing represented the purity I was offering to Clebe as my wedding gift.

Clebe McClary: After we exchanged vows and the minister pronounced us husband and wife, he said I could kiss the bride. When the audience chuckled, I got cold feet.

There were 600 people there. The church was packed, and the lights were on. When the minister told me to kiss the bride, I said, "I'm not kissing in front of all these folks. Momma and

Daddy are sitting out there."

I threw the veil back, smiled at Deanna, and said, "Let's go." With that, we turned and walked down the aisle to the surprise of our friends. Outside the church, I could see my convertible with the top down.

My lovely wife turned to me and said, "Clebe, I'll lose my veil if you don't put the top up."

It was a beautiful sunny day, and I couldn't see any reason not to enjoy it. "I'm not putting the top up, Deanna. Let's go!"

But the brand-new Mrs. McClary said, "I am not riding to the reception in that convertible with the top down, Clebe. I'll just ride with Daddy."

I thought about that for a minute. "You ride with your daddy," I said, "and you can just go home with your daddy."

Deanna: We hadn't been married more than two minutes when we had our first argument. I decided to ride with Clebe and just hang on to my veil—*and* my husband.

On my honeymoon night, I disappeared into the bathroom to slip on my negligee. I discovered that Aunt Gee-Gee, whom I had entrusted with my suitcase to protect it from pranksters, had sewn up my negligee! I had to sit in the bathroom and painstakingly remove hundreds of stitches.

Clebe: Our honeymoon lasted only a few days because I was on a short leave from Marine Corps training. I had just passed Officer Candidate School at Quantico, Virginia, becoming a second lieutenant at twenty-six years of age. I knew that Marine second lieutenants were being shipped directly into action in Vietnam as quickly as we could be trained and processed. I also knew that second lieutenants led platoons into battle and were usually the first to die in combat.

I wanted to be where the action was. I was a patriot, born and bred. Antiwar protesters burning the American flag and refusing to support our country during the war sickened me. I couldn't do much to stop the protesters, but I could step forward and serve my country. So shortly before we got married, I enlisted.

Deanna: Clebe said he was thinking about volunteering for reconnaissance duty. That sounded like some kind of suicide mission to me. A friend had told me that recon teams led the way, scouting areas behind enemy lines in advance of the troops. I made Clebe promise me he wouldn't ask for recon duty, although we both knew he would be good at it.

Clebe: When I got orders for Vietnam, I was anxious to go. Once there, I was given my supplies, and almost all of them had come from dead or wounded Marines. There was blood on my guns and holes in my uniform. At first, the shock sort of dampened my patriotic enthusiasm, but then I realized that this blood and these holes represented fellow Americans, some who had already given their lives in this war, maybe while wearing these same clothes.

How could I let them down? They had given their best, and as a second lieutenant in the U.S. Marine Corps, that was my responsibility, too. I knew then that I was in the right place, and I was eager to meet my troops and get down to business.

Deanna: The first letter I got from Clebe had this return address: Lt. Clebe McClary, First Recon Battalion, Alpha Company. *I could not believe it.* I wrote and told him how upset I was, but in his next letter, he said, "I feel more secure in this position. This is the place for me."

Clebe: If you slept at night while on patrol, you got your throat cut. So I napped only during the day. Besides, 98 percent of the fighting in Vietnam took place at night.

A fight was usually quick. It didn't take a man long to fire 400 rounds and throw 4 grenades. My men were disciplined, well-trained, and prepared to fight hand-to-hand, if necessary. Our recon motto was *Swift, Silent, Deadly.* Yet we refused to leave an injured or dying man behind.

Deanna: Almost every day, Clebe would write a fascinating letter, telling me all about his exciting—sometimes terrifying—adventures. Although I wrote just as often, my life and letters were rather dull compared to his.

Eventually, he started sending audiocassettes. Hearing his voice was great, but it was also sad. I would cry hearing his voice, knowing I couldn't touch him.

One tape was a horrifying experience and gave me an all-too-real insight into what our men were going through over there. Clebe was talking into the recorder, but at one point he suddenly shouted, "Gotta go! Incoming." He left the tape recorder running, and all I could hear was the boom of enemy bombs in the background. I fast-forwarded that tape to see if he came back!

Clebe: On my last patrol in Vietnam, we went into an area where few men had been. Our recon crew of thirteen men landed at Hill 146 near a small tea plantation in Quan Duc Valley. Once on the ground, I cleared the stakes out of a punji pit and climbed in. I had my radioman and corpsman in the foxhole to my left and three men in a foxhole on my right.

We had been sent out ahead to report enemy activity, but then the operation was canceled. The weather turned bad and choppers couldn't get in to lift us out. For two days we were on the hill, knowing full well that the enemy was out there, watching and waiting.

The third night, March 3, 1968, was Deanna's birthday, but it was not a time of celebration for me. The night was total quiet. I could hear my heart beat. At midnight, I thought I heard enemy movement. I grabbed my shotgun, but before I could organize my men, a grenade soared into the pit, with shrapnel hitting me in the face, neck, and shoulder.

"Call for air support!" I yelled to the radioman.

To my horror, I saw about a dozen of the enemy running up the hill. They were "sappers"—North Vietnamese strapped with explosives. They were on a suicide mission, having been told to die for Ho Chi Minh that night. Their goal was to jump into our foxholes with their exploding satchel charges, killing us all.

Suddenly, a sapper jumped into the air in front of me. I swung my shotgun around and fired, but I must have shot him low because he still kept coming. He fell into my punji pit and exploded. Blinded by blood and choking on bits of my own teeth, I realized my left arm was gone.

I got up and started running to another foxhole, but a hand grenade took my legs out from under me. I lay in the dirt, pretending to be dead, when I heard an NVA soldier walk up to me. He pointed his AK-47 and tried to shoot me in the head. The bullet passed through my neck, however. Then he stuck an enemy flag right next to me.

Someone once said, "Courage is a strong desire to live, taking the form of a readiness to die." I was willing to die for my country and my freedom, but two powerful desires drove me that night: To see my men get off that hill and to see my beautiful Deanna one more time.

A few minutes passed. I felt a buddy start dragging me. A chopper had come in, and he got me in halfway when it lifted off. Five more minutes and probably no one would've gotten off that hill alive.

Deanna: When I saw a Marine officer and a physician at my front porch, I was sure that Clebe was dead.

The officer, Maj. Burleson, caught me by the shoulders. "He's alive, Mrs. McClary! He's alive!"

I felt numb as Maj. Burleson read the official telegram: "Mrs. McClary, your husband, Lt. Clebe McClary, has suffered a traumatic amputation of his left arm and shrapnel wounds to all extremities. His prognosis is poor. His outlook is very dim."

Clebe: The nurses wouldn't let anything shiny in front of my eyes. They didn't want me to see what I looked like. They thought I'd give up hope if I looked into a mirror.

As I lay there, I actually thought it would be better if I died. Deanna and I didn't have any children, and I figured she would be better off without a mangled husband to care for.

Deanna: It took almost two months before Clebe was in good enough shape to be flown to Bethesda Medical Hospital in Maryland. The staff tried to prepare me for what he was going to look like.

I walked down a corridor and thought I heard Clebe's voice. I peeked around a door and saw two men. Since one had two arms dangling, I knew he couldn't be Clebe. The other had his head bandaged, one eye, and no arms! I stared at the huge red-and-pink scars, the jagged stitches, the broken teeth, and lips so swollen that they were turned inside out.

I'm in the wrong room, I thought. Just as I turned, I heard a voice. "Dea, Honey, it's me. I know I'm not too pretty to look at, but I thank God I'm alive to be with you."

Clebe: Deanna hadn't recognized me because my right arm was in a cast and bound against my body. After hearing my voice, she rushed to my side and told me how much she loved me. Lying in that hospital bed, I was all too aware of the many wives who turned around and kept on walking, never looking back. But Deanna sat down next to me and promised we would always be together.

Deanna: And we've stayed together for three decades. It's true; I invested a lot in Clebe's life and recovery. But he was doing even more for me. For almost three years, as I worked with him every day in rehabilitation, I saw his strength and determination, and I fell more and more in love with him. Although he was just scabs and scars and stitches, with metal sticking out of his body, he was still the most handsome man in the world to me.

Clebe: I see now that love really is a commitment. It's a conscious decision to make the best of whatever comes along in your relationship. I've often asked myself what would have happened if I had come home in good shape to a wife who had been disfigured in a terrible car wreck. Would I still be with her? Would I have sat there for nearly three years, exercising her arms and legs, helping her learn to walk again?

Deanna: Love is a decision, not based on feeling but on commitment. Yes, we've gone through some incredibly difficult years, but we have made the decision that surrender is not an option when you plan to win. We would not—and did not—quit.

Clebe: I have a saying that has helped our marriage: FIDO, which stands for "Forget it, drive on." If something goes wrong in our marriage or we have an argument, we deal with it and then drive on. We don't keep digging up the past. We learn from it, but we don't dwell on it.

Deanna: I had a lot to learn in this area because in our first decade of marriage, I wanted to keep talking about all the "what-ifs" and "if-onlys." Clebe would listen to me and then he would say, "That's over with, and we can't change a thing. Let's learn from it and move forward."

Our youngest daughter, Christa, was married in 1996, and I told her that love wouldn't be an emotional high every day. In fact, I said there would be times when she wouldn't even *feel* in love, but you make the decision to stay in love, and as you do, your marriage grows richer and more beautiful every year.

I am more in love with Clebe today than I have ever been. Our relationship has matured and strengthened over the years, and I am very secure in his love after thirty years of marriage. It's a great feeling—a priceless treasure.

I watched as Clebe escorted Christa down the chapel aisle, and I'll be there when he does the same for our daughter Tara. Such a sight allows me the privilege of reliving that momentous day in my life when I too stood before God and made my vows to the man I loved. Seeing Clebe walk down the aisle, a black patch over one eye, his left sleeve hanging limply at his side, I know that he is still that same debonair fellow I married thirty years ago.

We've talked about getting married all over again—really doing it up big with hundreds of friends. Clebe says that this time he won't be so foolish when he gets the chance to kiss the bride.

Clebe: That's right. I told Deanna that she better believe that I'd kiss her this time around!

Clebe and Deanna McClary travel around the country speaking before thousands of people each year in churches, schools, businesses, and military installations. Their books, Living Proof *and* Commitment to Love, *have reached people all over the world. You may contact the McClarys by writing Clebe McClary, P.O. Box 535, Pawleys Island, SC 29585, or by calling (803) 237-2582.*

AGAINST ALL ODDS

Sixty years ago, on a warm day in Butler, Missouri, James and Lou handed a justice of the peace two bucks and vowed to love each other for better or for worse.

They got the worse.

Today, we married types complain about the hardship of juggling careers, kids, and Mastercard payments. It was never that simple for Jim and Lou, not when you spend your honeymoon working at a sawmill and your first home is a dirt-floor tent.

They met in 1936 at a church conference in Iowa, where Jim was raised. He was nineteen; Lou was seventeen. Since Jim couldn't forget about the Missouri farm girl, he hitchhiked to see her. After that visit, he scrounged up $50, bought a 1926 Chevrolet coupe, and went to propose to her.

Five people showed up for the wedding. Louie's father, not excited about losing a daughter he cherished, refused to come. But he did give the couple $5, which was all they had to start their married life.

continued next page

At the time, the country was still in the throes of the Depression. An uncle gave Jim a job in his sawmill. Jim worked six days a week, made $14 a month, and was nearly killed when a steam engine exploded.

In 1940, Jim and Lou were living in the basement of her folks' house in Nevada, Missouri, where Jim would walk five miles to his dollar-a-day service station job. One Saturday night, he came home from work, slumped in the chair, and told Lou, "There's got to be something better in the world."

The next morning, they packed their bags and began a four-month trip to Seattle, hitchhiking and hopping freight trains. Once, they were riding in the back of a watermelon truck that crashed. They survived. Another time, they were nearly beaten by club-wielding "railroad bulls," brawny men hired by the railroads to keep uninvited passengers off the freight trains. From North Dakota to Spokane, Washington, they rode the rails. They worked their way to Seattle by picking apples. They survived.

In Seattle, Jim got a job in a lumber mill. But he was laid off when World War II started. He found a job as a pipe fitter in a shipyard and, after four years, was able to afford the couple's lifelong dream—a home. Jim built it himself, painstakingly nailing every board in place. But before the house was finished, the state announced that a new freeway was going to be built right through their living room.

The house was moved. A few months later, as the two were finally enjoying the fruits of their labor, disaster struck: The house burned down. The local newspaper interviewed Jim at the time. "Well, we started our married life in a tent," he told the reporter. "I guess we can do it again."

And, of course, they did. Soon, they were blessed with a son. He was born mentally retarded. But Jim and Lou didn't wring their hands and become recluses. Instead, they founded a school for teaching children with disabilities, the first in the state.

Their son is now married and living with his family in another city. "The Lord," said Jim, "has been good to us."

They attribute their long marriage to some simple things. "Learn to give and take," said Lou.

"Think of the other person," said Jim.

No, this couple didn't become wealthy, start a chain of successful franchises, or coauthor a best-selling book. But perhaps their greatest accomplishment was staying married for sixty years despite odds that would have sunk most marriages. They made a promise and kept it.

—*Bob Welch*

8

PMS: How Husbands Can Manage the Mood Swings

- -

■ Certain times of the month, my wife yells at me and the kids. I've seen my wife close the drapes and hide out, battling despondency, fear, and paranoia. I've seen her on the edge of panic. I've seen her cry, become angry, clean obsessively. Other times, she can't lift a finger.

When I ask her what's wrong, she mumbles something about PMS. I know it's something to do with her menstrual cycle, but beyond that, I'm clueless. What am I dealing with here?

Your wife is correct in noting that PMS—Premenstrual Syndrome—is affecting her behavior, and PMS affects women in varying degrees. Some women experience mild headaches, while others battle their emotions. Medical experts estimate that up to 80 percent of all women have had PMS symptoms at some point, but only 8 percent experience symptoms severe enough to require medical treatment.

In spite of these statistics, much uncertainty surrounds PMS, and medical professionals still do not agree on its cause or treatment. Because of this, many women who suffer from PMS don't receive appropriate care because a number of physicians, especially those who don't specialize in the treatment of PMS, aren't sure how to prescribe treatment.

■ **Is PMS serious? I know it can take Kerri down for the count.**

Though its symptoms vary in range and intensity, PMS can be a debilitating affliction, not only for women as individuals, but for husbands and families as well. That's why it's crucial that you understand what PMS is and how to deal with it practically. Your wife needs to know that she's not crazy, that it's not all in her head, and that she can do something about PMS. Even more important, though, she needs to be encouraged not to give up hope, because help is possible for the PMS sufferer and her family.

■ **What exactly is PMS? I'm a total beginner on this stuff.**

PMS is assumed to be a physical and psychological disorder that occurs regularly, in the same phase of a woman's menstrual cycle (between ovulation and the onset of menstruation), followed by a symptom-free phase. Common PMS symptoms include fatigue, depression, tension, headaches, and mood swings, to name just a few (see the list on page 241 for a more extensive list of symptoms). Symptoms can range from a couple of days to a couple of weeks.

Women emotionally stable at any other time of the month often find themselves barely able to cope during PMS. For some, PMS is analogous to being thrown into the middle of a great sea and being left alone to survive. It's all they can do to tread water and simply breathe.

To truly qualify as PMS, symptoms must be severe enough to interfere with some aspect of daily living. It's easy to use the term "PMS" as an excuse for unacceptable behavior or a catchall for problems, but PMS does not necessarily cause all physical or emotional problems. In fact, genuine PMS sufferers experience their symptoms *cyclically* and *repeatedly* in direct relationship to their menstrual cycles and do not experience those same symptoms after the onset of menstruation. The pattern is unmistakable.

■ **Those descriptions sound like Kerri. What can I do about it?**

If you think your spouse suffers from PMS, the first step is diagnosis. PMS may affect the emotions, but in order to treat it, both of you need to approach it objectively. In other words, "Just the facts, Ma'am."

The best way to get the facts is by having your wife chart her menstrual cycle, along with any physical or psychological symptoms she experiences during this time. This may sound laborious and painstaking, but it's the only way to get an objective representation of her symptoms. By charting her cycle consistently over a period of several months, she may detect an obvious pattern; this pattern will help determine whether PMS is the culprit.

If her ob-gyn diagnoses PMS (hopefully, she is seeing a PMS-sensitive physician), she can take practical steps toward gaining control. PMS doesn't have to be endured; it can be controlled—if she is willing to follow some simple guidelines.

■ **What would those guidelines be?**

Your wife will have to fundamentally change her diet and exercise habits. Let's take a closer look at these ideas:

► **Eat healthy.** During PMS times, some women tend to crave quick-energy foods. Sugar is one. However, some believe refined sugar can trigger or intensify PMS symptoms because it actually produces a "high high" along with a corresponding "low low."

The result can be an emotional roller coaster ride that drains both energy and emotions. A diet rich in complex carbohydrates, such as fruits, vegetables, grains, and legumes, on the other hand, results in a slower release of sugar into the bloodstream. This provides a more stable blood sugar level, with a corresponding stability in mood and emotion.

Though it's important to eat the healthiest foods possible throughout her cycle, it's even more important during PMS. Quite simply, her diet at this time should be low as possible in caffeine, salt, sugar, and alcohol, and high in complex carbohydrates. Vitamin supplements are a good idea as well, but have your wife consult a physician or nutritionist about proper doses.

► **Exercise regularly.** It's no secret that regular exercise—thirty to forty-five minutes, three times a week—both energizes and relaxes. Physical exertion gives her body an opportunity to release pent-up tension and anxiety while allowing the brain to produce endorphins that relieve pain and elevate mood. In fact, many medical experts agree that exercise is one of the best treatments. And exercise is free!

By taking charge of her diet and exercise habits, and by keeping a record of these changes over a period of a few months, she may begin to recognize noticeable changes in her PMS symptoms. If symptoms haven't eased, consult a PMS-sensitive doctor. Keep in mind, however, that there's no quick fix with PMS. Adjusting your habits and routines requires planning and discipline, but if she's willing to make the adjustments, she'll find herself gradually gaining control of her symptoms.

■ **I have to tell you: PMS has nearly destroyed our marriage. After going through monthly ups and downs, experiencing the emotional wounds, I'm beginning to give up hope that our marriage will ever be what God intended.**

More and more men are aware that PMS is not just "a woman's problem." It's also your problem too. PMS may be a physiological problem originating in a woman's body, but its impact is profoundly felt by those closest to her—husbands, children, friends, family.

Though statistics aren't available, some health professionals suspect that PMS is one of the primary contributors to marital breakdown. Common problems and struggles encountered by all couples are often magnified many times when PMS enters the picture.

These struggles may be bad enough in a marriage in which the husband understands PMS, is sympathetic, and can provide support. Unfortunately, that's not always the case. More often than not, men don't have a clue about what's going on because PMS has never been explained to them and they have no comparable cyclical alteration of their lifestyle.

Even if men suspect PMS is affecting their marriages, they view it, not as something to solve together with their wives, but as something to blame. Sometimes they blame their wives. A vicious cycle of guilt and blame ensues, and the marriage spirals downward.

■ How does PMS affect children?

A moody and unpredictable mother creates insecure, tense, or anxious children. Children crave consistency, and when their mom isn't consistent in her moods or reactions, the children become confused. Sometimes too children feel responsible for their mom's misery, especially if she's prone to outbursts such as, "You're driving me crazy!" And, in extreme cases, the mother may go too far and lash out physically at her children.

PMS affects another important relationship—a woman's relationship to the Lord. Christian women suffering from PMS often experience a profound sense of spiritual shame. They convince themselves that the discord caused by PMS is their fault and begin to dwell on self-condemning thoughts: *If only my spiritual walk were stronger. If only I could trust God more. If only . . .*

On and on it goes, and an already low self-esteem plunges deeper into an abyss of feeling unworthy and disgraced.

■ Give me some hope here. What should I be doing to help my wife get through this?

PMS may affect the family, but it doesn't have to tear it apart. This is where communication becomes extremely important. Your wife needs to learn how to communicate her physical and emotional needs to you, preferably during a time when she's not experiencing PMS. On the other hand, you should be open about your feelings and let your wife know how PMS is affecting you.

Communication may involve devising strategies that can take the load off your wife. If finances permit, you might arrange for a house-cleaning service or baby-sitter during your wife's PMS. If not, everyone in the family can pitch in and help with household chores. And it's always a good idea to establish a strong network of support—close friends or family members—who are willing to step in and give a hand. These strategies should be worked out before your wife's PMS sets in, so the added stress of decision-making isn't foisted upon her during that time.

When communicating to children about PMS, it's important to be positive. Reassure them that they're loved and accepted, even when her balance is off-kilter. Let them know that she's going to be okay and, most of all, that they're not the source of your problems.

Finally, your wife doesn't need to be weighted down by guilt or shame. God knows her exactly as she is. He understands her anxieties and her fluctuating emotions, and He does not condemn her

---

HUSBANDS AND PMS

"I have bad days, but I just pull myself out of them," men often complain. "Why can't she do the same?"

Sounds a bit like Professor Henry Higgins in *My Fair Lady*—"Why can't a woman be more like a man?" The fact is, with PMS, it's not a matter of willpower. Many women who experience PMS are strong-willed, capable individuals who just happen to experience severe symptoms. No matter how hard they try, they simply can't make up their minds not to have PMS.

That's not to say they can't *manage* their PMS. They can. But in the meantime, there are some things men can do to assist their wives as they recover. Here are some suggestions:

▶ **Get informed.** Find out as much as you can about PMS. Accompany your wife to her medical appointments; ask questions; read the literature. The more you know, the better equipped you'll be to participate in helping her gain control.

▶ **Be supportive.** Learn what kind of support your wife needs; it's different for every woman. Accompany your wife on a walk or jog; give her a break from household duties; whip up a snack (healthy!) and invite her to join you.

▶ **Be objective.** Don't take mood swings personally—this only complicates the situation. Recognize that PMS is a normal part of a woman's life and treat it as such. When you discuss emotions or feelings, don't blame or accuse. Simply express your thoughts and feelings. No doubt she'll appreciate your openness and respond positively.

for them. Keep that in mind if you find her struggling spiritually.

In Romans 8:35 the question is asked, "What shall separate us from the love of Christ?" The answer, of course, is *nothing* because "in all these things we are more than conquerors through him who loves us."

Probably the best thing your wife can do for herself during her PMS is simply believe. Believe that in spite of how bad she feels, in spite of her imagined sense of unworthiness, God still loves her. If nothing else, PMS can become a vibrant example of what Christianity is all about—"the just shall live by faith." And even during her worst moments, she can choose to believe that nothing shall be able to separate her from the love of God. Not even PMS.

This material is adapted from writings by Stephanie Bender, M.A. (in Clinical Psychology), who lives in Boulder, Colorado, where she is director of Full Circle Women's Health, a clinic offering counseling for women suffering from problems associated with PMS, postpartum depression, and menopause. If you would like a packet of free information, call toll-free (800) 418-4040. While the clinic has successfully treated thousands of women, Stephanie Bender is not a medical doctor, and any medical questions should be directed to your physician.

OTHER SYMPTOMS RELATED TO PMS

Psychological Symptoms	Physical Symptoms
anger	bloating
loss of control	weight gain
sudden mood swings	acne
emotional overresponsiveness	dizziness
unexplained crying	migraine headaches
irritability	breast tenderness
anxiety	joint and muscle pain
forgetfulness	backaches
decreased concentration	changes in sex drive
confusion	food cravings
withdrawal	constipation
rejection-sensitive	diarrhea
depression	sweating
nightmares	shakiness
suicidal thoughts	seizures

9

Working Moms

■ **After our first child was born, my wife, Pam, returned to her job with the insurance company, but we never felt right putting Max into day care. Pam is pregnant again, and we have really been struggling with whether she should return to her job. She wants to stay home and raise the kids, which is great, but I don't know how we'll be able to survive without her salary. What should we do?**

You're smart to be asking yourselves if Pam should be working outside the home because many couples don't. In too many marriages today, it's a given that Mom *will* work outside the home. It doesn't have to be that way, you know.

A working mom (*all* moms are working moms, but we're referring to moms employed outside the home) has it really tough. After putting in an eight- or nine-hour day, she returns home for the "second shift." It's a recipe for marital stress, but more importantly, kids *need* their moms to be there all the time. We're not trying to heap any more guilt on you, but if Mom isn't raising the kids, who is?

■ **So you're saying that Pam should stay home with the kids, right?**

Afraid so, and that's the tough part for young families these days. The kids need her, plain and simple. If the children are old enough, you should explain to them that a stay-at-home mom means no trips to Disney World, but you'll be able to visit local museums and city pools.

■ **But aren't both parents working these days? Won't Pam be the only stay-at-home mom on the block?**

That's what the popular culture would have you believe, but that's not necessarily true. According to the U.S. Department of Labor and Statistics, 41.3 percent of all married mothers with preschool children are full-time homemakers. Another 20 percent work part-time, some only a few hours a week. You add those two figures up, and that means 61 percent of all mothers with preschool children are spending most of their time raising their kids.

Of course, exceptions exist, and there are some families in which the mother *must* work. Some areas of the country—especially the major cities on each coast—have stratospheric housing costs, and it's all a family can do to make the monthly house payment.

■ **Why are housing costs so high? Growing up, we could afford a home on just my dad's salary.**

It goes like this. As housing costs went through the roof in the 1970s and the 1980s, fathers responded by working longer hours and taking second jobs. When inflation and housing prices continued to soar, families responded by sending Mom back into the workforce. When that wasn't enough, banks relaxed their lending policies with 90 percent mortgages and low adjustable "start" rates in order to qualify more families.

Then we had the S&L crisis and bank failures across the country in the late 1980s and early 1990s, and throughout this decade, we've seen real estate values flatten in much of the country or actually depreciate. That's because there's very little families can do to increase income these days.

■ **I feel like we can never get ahead because my pay raises have been 2 or 3 percent. Am I spinning my wheels?**

In terms of getting ahead of the inflation curve, the answer is yes, you are spinning your financial wheels. George Will, in a *Newsweek* column, said Americans' real after-tax income has risen a barely perceptible 0.5 percent since 1973. The nearly twenty-five years of income stagnation is unprecedented since the start of the Industrial Revolution.

"As many workers' real incomes have declined, families have maintained living standards by sending more mothers back into the workforce, with consequent family stresses and a pervasive erosion of the sense of well-being," wrote Will.

■ **That sure sounds like my situation. But we're caught in that trap and need her income.**

Then you need to sit down and ask yourselves, *What is Mom really earning?* As you consider the cost of your wife taking the job, you need to do a little calculating.

Start by deducting payroll taxes, child-care expenses, new clothes, wear-and-tear on a second car, cleaning help, and meals away from home (that includes restaurant lunches and dinners, plus take-out food, since Mom is often too wiped out to cook dinner). Once you subtract these expenses, your wife will probably net $200 to $400 a month, if that. Divided by 160 work hours a month, your wife will be only netting $2 an hour. Could she save the family $16 a day by cooking at home and shopping for bargains? You bet she can.

■ **I see your point. As we go through our budget, what other arguments can I marshal for my wife's staying home with the kids?**

Consider the intangibles. Sure, stay-at-home moms are pooped out by the end of the day, but moms employed outside the home are even more frazzled. Working moms have less time to serve at church, less energy to pursue a relationship with God, less personal time, and less motivation for romance. Disciplining and loving the children will get pushed aside because of tiredness. As the late Green Bay Packer coach Vince Lombardi once said, "Fatigue makes cowards of us all."

■ What if we *have* to have some extra income?

Could your wife operate a side business at home? Look for novel ways to bring in that extra money. Could she start an at-home business or work part-time a couple of hours a week? It's estimated that 26 million of the U.S. population—10 percent of the population—now work at least part-time in their home. Many of them are women who jumped off the career track to become mothers and raise a family.

For instance, our family (the Yorkeys) have a little side business. We string tennis rackets out of the home, which allows Nicole to be there for Andrea and Patrick. The couple of hundred bucks we earn each month has been a real boost to the family finances.

■ We've decided to bite the bullet and keep Olivia home with the kids. But it's been a rather interesting turn of events. One day at work, I had one of those days. At 10 A.M., a computer blip swallowed half my morning's work and refused to give it back. At 11:30, my supervisor stopped by to examine my "to do" pile. Within five minutes, my work area was declared a national state of emergency.

As the clock struggled toward 5 P.M., all I could think about was enjoying a quiet evening with the family. I drove home, grabbed the mail, and sat in the La-Z-Boy. Then I called out to Olivia, who was fixing dinner in the kitchen. "So, Honey, what did *you* do today?"

"What did *I* do today?" she screamed. At that moment, I knew I was in trouble. In fact, that innocent question put me in the doghouse the rest of the evening. Why did Olivia get so ticked off at me?

Because it was a dumb question, even though we guys think it's like asking, "How was the weather today?" You see, when you came home, you had this romantic image of what home life would be like. You pictured your wife waiting at the front door when you arrive, her hair permed, her lips pursed. The children would be sitting at the table, newly washed smiles on their faces. They would be talking politely to each other.

"No, Jeffrey," Stephen would say, "we're not allowed to eat the rolls until we say grace and start dinner."

"I'm sorry," his little brother would respond. "I was wrong. It won't happen again." The two would exchange hugs.

When you greet the children, they would say in chorus, "Hi, Daddy!" Then they would run into your arms and ask to rough-house.

When you sit down for dinner, your wife would place a beautiful plate stacked high with baked chicken, mashed potatoes, and stewed vegetables in front of you. You would smother the delicious food with brown gravy. The dinner conversation would be stimulating and scintillating, focusing on the upcoming NFL playoff games or the church Christmas play.

After eating delicious banana creme pie for dessert, the children would beg to be put to bed early. "We want you and Mom to have some quality time alone," they would say. "You've probably had a tough day."

But that isn't reality for husbands and wives, and you should understand the stresses that Olivia experienced as she was with the kids all day.

■ How should I handle my home arrival?

Think about it. Usually when you park the car, half the neighborhood kids are running around in your yard. When you enter the house, you see the other half, raiding your refrigerator. The hallway is strewn with toys, and kids you don't know are in your children's bedrooms. Your wife is in the laundry room, piling clean clothes high atop a table.

If you walk down to the basement and find her in the laundry room, don't ask, "So what's for supper? Chicken?"

That question is liable to light her fuse, but if you really want a close-up view of a nuclear explosion, then go ahead and ask the time-honored question that every husband has asked: "So, what did *you* do today?"

You're liable to have a huge screwdriver brandished in your face.

"What did I do today?" she will respond, waving the screwdriver. "What did I do today?"

"Um, yes," you will respond defensively. "I just thought. . . ."

"Somehow, I knew you were going to ask that question. So I kept a little list. Here, read this!"

You can read her list on page 249. Look it over closely: You'll have a greater appreciation of what your wife does when she stays home with the children while you're at work.

■ **Gee, I know Olivia doesn't have time to watch soap operas and eat bonbons. What's the best way to tell her that I was insensitive?**

A simple apology always works. Say something like, "I'm sorry, Honey. I really am. Sometimes I get so caught up in my world that I forget how important yours is."

And look for ways to build your wife up. When you are at public gatherings, your wife will sometimes be asked, "So, do you work?" When she hears that loaded question, tell her she can respond this way:

"It may interest you to know that I am socializing two *Homo sapiens* in the dominant values of the Judeo-Christian tradition in order that they might be instruments for the transformation of the social order into the teleologically prescribed utopia inherent in the eschaton."

Seriously, your wife can hold her head high and say that as a homemaker, she is reminded of the fact that no one can shape the mind of a child like a mother can. It's true: She has the most powerful, most influential role on earth. The pay may be poor, but don't we all parent out of love?

A MOM DESCRIBES WHAT SHE DID TODAY

3:21 A.M. Woke up. Took Jeffrey to the bathroom.

3:33 A.M. Got you to quit snoring.

3:49 A.M. Went to sleep.

5:11 A.M. Woke up. Took Jeffrey to the bathroom.

6:50 A.M. Alarm went off. Mentally reviewed all I had to do today.

7:00 A.M. Alarm went off again. Ignored it.

7:10 A.M. Alarm went off third time. Contemplated doing something violent to the alarm clock.

7:19 A.M. Got up. Got dressed. Warned Stephen to get up.

7:24 A.M. Made our bed. Warned Stephen again.

7:29 A.M. Rousted Stephen. Told him he had two minutes to get his clothes on and start eating his cereal.

7:37 A.M. Fed boys a breakfast consisting of Cheerios, orange juice, and something that resembled toast. Scolded Jeffrey for mixing them.

7:46 A.M. Woke Rachel.

7:48 A.M. Had devotions.

7:49 A.M. Made Stephen's lunch. Tried to answer Jeffrey's question, "Why does God need people?" Warned Stephen to get ready for school.

8:01 A.M. Woke Rachel.

8:02 A.M. Started laundry.

8:03 A.M. Took rocks out of washing machine.

8:04 A.M. Restarted washing machine.

8:13 A.M. Planned grocery list. Tried to answer Jeffrey's question, "Why do some people go to church and others don't?"

8:29 A.M. Woke Rachel again.

8:30 A.M Helped Stephen with homework. Told him to remember his lunch.

8:31 A.M. Sent Stephen to school.

Rest of morning: Teacher phoned, wondering why Stephen had no socks. Ran over to school with a pair. Returned library books. Explained why a cover was missing. Mailed letters. Bought groceries. Turned radio on. Heard report warning of "gale-force storms in the area." Phoned Sherri and Julie about storms. Planned birthday party. Ruth phoned, wondering if I'd heard about the big sale on chicken whole fryers. Phoned Sherri and Julie. Told them about the big chicken sale. Cleaned house. Wiped noses. Wiped windows. Wiped Rachel's bottom.

Teacher called, wondering why Stephen had no lunch. Made a peanut-butter

continued next page

sandwich and took it to him. Watched Rachel fling lunch spaghetti on kitchen floor. Cleaned spaghetti off linoleum floor.

12:35 P.M. Put wet clothes in the dryer.

12:36 P.M. Sat down to rest.

12:39 P.M. Scolded Jeffrey. Helped him put clothes back in dryer.

12:45 P.M. Agreed to baby-sit for a friend. Cut tree sap out of Rachel's hair. Regretted baby-sitting decision. Killed assorted insects. Read to the kids. Clipped ten fingernails. Sent kids outside. Watered plants. Swept floor. Picked watermelon seeds off linoleum. Explained to Jeffrey why he shouldn't singe ants with magnifying glass. Read to the kids.

3:43 P.M. Organized task force to clean kitchen. Cleaned parts of the house. Accepted appointment to local committee because the secretary said, "We thought you'd have extra time since you don't work." Tried to answer Rachel's question, "Why are boys and girls different?" Listened to 224 more questions. Answered a few. Cleaned out dishwasher. Briefly considered supper.

5:21 P.M. Husband came home looking for food, quietness, and romance.

This material is adapted from writings by Phil Callaway, editor of Servant *magazine and the author of* Honey, I Dunked the Kids. *He lives in Three Hills, Alberta, with his high school sweetheart, Ramona, and their three children. Material has also been taken from* Daddy's Home *by Greg Johnson and Mike Yorkey. Copyright © 1992. Used by permission of Tyndale House Publishers, Inc. All rights reserved.*

10

Nag, Nag, Nag

· ·

■ **I gotta tell you, my wife is on my case all the time. If she's not telling me to ease up on the accelerator, then she's reminding me to skip fatty foods. How can I get her to lay off?**

Actually, you may have a serious problem if your wife *isn't* nagging you. She's doing you a big favor by reminding you to wear a coat in cold weather or slap on sunscreen on a bright day.

Or so University of Chicago researcher Linda Waite seems to think. Waite, like a growing number of scholars, has been intrigued by mounting scientific evidence that women and (particularly) men live longer and enjoy better health when they are married. Waite believes there are a number of reasons for this, but one of her explanations is sure to get under the skin of every red-blooded American male.

"Marriage provides individuals—especially men—with someone who monitors their health and health-related behaviors and who encourages self-regulation," Waite says, adding that married men benefit from having "someone who nags them."

■ **Yikes! Waite's suggestion that a wife's nagging does a man good has to be every husband's worst nightmare.**

While most men can see the benefits of having a wife who "reminds" them to get a regular checkup or eat a high-fiber diet, the last thing most men want is for some expert to legitimize the kind of merciless hounding normally associated with the term "nagging."

Indeed, most men identify with the sage words of King Solomon, who compared a woman's nagging to "constant dripping on a rainy day" and concluded that it would be better to live on the corner of a roof "than share a house with a quarrelsome wife" (Prov. 21:9).

In her defense, Waite's chief aim isn't to encourage women to pester their husbands mercilessly—or to see men take up residence on their roofs. Instead, she wants to raise public awareness of research showing that a man's life expectancy is more adversely affected by being unmarried than by being poor, overweight, or having heart disease. Waite thinks such findings need the same sort of attention given to cigarette smoking and lack of exercise.

■ **What is some of the research showing regarding the benefits of being married?**

Scholars at the National Institute for Healthcare Research (NIHR) recently compiled a weighty report showing that divorced men are especially likely to experience health problems. When compared to married men, divorced males are twice as likely to die prematurely from hypertension, four times as likely to die prematurely from throat cancer, and seven times as likely to die prematurely from pneumonia.

According to the NIHR, divorced men also have significantly higher rates of depression, substance abuse, auto accidents, and suicide. "Being divorced and a nonsmoker is only slightly less dangerous than smoking a pack or more a day and staying married," observes NIHR president Dr. David Larson.

■ **All nagging aside, why does marriage offer men such health benefits?**

Waite says marriage gives men a sense of obligation to others, which discourages them from high-risk behaviors, such as driving too fast and drinking too much, and encourages them to make and save more money, which can be used to buy better health care and safer surroundings, among other things.

In addition, marriage offers a network of help and support that can be helpful in dealing with stress and in recovering from illnesses and accidents. In other words, "Two are better than one," as Solomon observed, "because if one falls, the other will lift him up."

But the research goes on to show that all twosomes are not alike—that married couples fare better than men and women living together outside of marriage.

For example, Waite says married men and women each report higher physical and emotional satisfaction with their sex lives than either single or cohabiting men and women. Washington State University researcher Jan Stets reports that women in cohabiting unions are more than twice as likely to be victims of domestic violence than married women. And data from the National Institute of Mental Health show that cohabiting women have rates of depression more than three times higher than married women and more than twice those of other never-married women.

■ **So why does living together not offer the same benefits that marriage provides?**

In large part because the absence of a permanent commitment hinders the development of qualities such as self-sacrifice, empathy, and trust that are critical to the success of an intimate union.

This is but one reason why a recent research review by Robert Coombs of UCLA found that the link between marriage and long life is due more to the fact that marriage fosters good health than to the possibility that healthy people are more likely to get and stay married. Indeed, Waite says there is actually some evidence that men who would otherwise be at higher risk for premature death are more likely than other men to marry and remain married.

As with all research of this kind, it is important to recognize that these findings reflect averages. They in no way suggest that every unmarried person is doomed to bad health or that getting married gives one immunity from the negative consequences of eating pork rinds, for instance.

But all things considered, stable marriage is good for one's health. That's not just an opinion—it's the nagging truth.

WHAT THE DICTIONARY SAYS

nag v. 1. To annoy by constant scolding, complaining or urging. 2. To torment persistently, as with anxiety. Usage: *She is always nagging me.* **nagged, nagging, nags.**

This material is adapted from writings by William R. Mattox, Jr., a contributing editor at USA Today *and a consulting editor at the Family Research Council in Washington, D.C. Bill says he enjoys the benefits of married life with his wife, Jill, and has never considered moving onto the corner of his roof.*

What If Beer Ads Lasted Longer Than Thirty Seconds?

. . . .

by Bob Moeller

Every fall and into the New Year, football is at the height of its season, and with all the college bowl and NFL games cluttering up the screen, it can mean only one thing: tons of beer commercials.

Why are these thirty-second beer spots aired so often? Because they feed the fantasy of what a "real man" looks like and what he does for entertainment.

Notice that the advertisements always feature young, virile, noticeably single men in their twenties, thirties, and sometimes forties. These macho figures live out exquisite fantasies with alluring young nymphs, who appear the moment they pop the lid of a Coors Light. The chicks are there to meet their every need.

What you won't see are wives, children, or—heaven forbid—babies. That would spoil the fun, pop the fantasy. The message is clear: The good life is free of commitments, kids, and conscience. Order another brewski, bring on the babes, and forget the tired wives, irritable teenagers, and monthly bills.

But what would happen if the commercials stayed on the screen longer than the customary thirty seconds? Let's say the macho man and the barroom babe fall in love. Their overpowering physical attraction to one another can't be denied. They decide to get married. As months turn into years, he sees what to him is a tragic and unforgivable thing: She starts to age. At twenty-nine, she no longer looks twenty. Worse yet, she's had a baby. He's bothered that her waistline has lost its snap and her bloated legs are criss-crossed with varicose veins.

Hey, wait a minute, this wasn't in the script, the macho man says to himself. *Life is young chicks, good buddies, and a party in the offing. It isn't measles, crabgrass, and clogged sinks. I deserve better. I'm a gift to women. They need me. I'm outta here.*

But the truth is the macho man has developed his own problems. He suffers from a Budweiser tumor (translation: a beer belly). His bloodshot eyes resemble a Los Angeles freeway map. What happened? This once virile young stud is growing older himself.

To deny reality, he heads back to the bar to find another twenty-two-year-old beauty who will keep the illusion alive that he's still young. Perhaps he repeats this cycle two or three times more before he realizes what a fool he's been. He abandoned the wife of his youth to chase a beer commercial that lasted only thirty seconds.

The kids are grown up now. The "ex" is remarried and living in New York. All he's left with is a six-pack.

As he puts another Miller Lite to his lips, he realizes just how cold a cold one can be.

This material was written by author Bob Moeller of Libertyville, Illinois.

5

Dads and Their
God

1

Finding New Friends on the Block

. . . .

■ **The big buzz word in the last few years is "men's account-ability groups." What's it all about? Why are some men getting together just to talk?**

Anyone watching Morrie Driesenga lead a Wednesday morning men's group in Holland, Michigan, would never guess that this retired salesman once tried to fill the spiritual void in his life with alcohol. Today, Morrie credits the special friendships he built with other men for helping him break that destructive pattern.

"I had grown up in the church, but I made wrong choices," he says. "My new life began when I literally dropped to my knees and said, 'Help me, Lord.' After I quit drinking, it was my friends' quiet encouragement and warm handshakes that helped me stay sober."

When Morrie was elected to the board of elders, he invited the pastor out for a cup of coffee. "What can you teach me about prayer?" he asked, and within weeks, Morrie began meeting with the pastor and two other men every Wednesday for breakfast.

"We always begin with Scripture," Morrie says, "and then the leader asks individuals how we can best pray for them. That makes it easy for us to open up about what's going on in our lives."

Morrie is just one of many men who are gathering in churches, homes, workplaces—even restaurants—on a regular basis. Men's groups have been around since Jesus' disciples met in the Upper Room and broke bread with the Master, but in recent years the trend has accelerated. Men are again understanding the need to talk about their feelings and develop deeper relationships with their own gender.

■ Why is that?

"Men have very few friends whom they feel they can reveal everything to," says Steve Largent, the NFL Hall of Fame pass receiver who is now a U.S. Congressman from Oklahoma. "A lot of men don't have anybody—not even their wives—whom they feel comfortable to talk with. By developing relationships with other men, they can open up and express themselves freely."

The momentum behind the Christian men's movement—driven by the Spirit of God—has picked up in recent years. Several ministries have been effective: Promise Keepers, Career Impact, Priority Living, Christian Business Men's Committee, and AbbaFather, to name a few. The latter ministry is the outreach of the Reverend Gordon Dalbey, author of *Healing the Masculine Soul.*

Men's souls have been torn, he says, between a women's movement that requires they abdicate masculinity to gain sensitivity and a deluge of Rambo-like media portrayals. Only by holding up Jesus Christ as the model for authentic manhood can men attain genuine masculine virtues, says Dalbey.

■ I've heard about the so-called men's movement started by author Robert Bly back in the early nineties. What's different about the Christian men's movement?

The Christian movement takes several guises. Some are "men-only" Bible studies, with time set aside at the end for prayer. Others are less structured; guys eating out together, chatting over food, and discussing their relationships with their families or the progress of their spiritual growth. Some men attend once-a-year retreats; others prefer a large-group setting at weekly breakfast meetings.

At Cherry Hills Community Church in Denver, more than 300 men squeeze into an auditorium every Tuesday morning at 6 A.M. to hear executive pastor Bob Beltz talk about biblical masculinity. "We started with six men in 1980, and our group has slowly grown," says Beltz. "Now we just can't fit anyone else in the room."

But another trend is three or four men meeting in an "accountability group."

■ Why would a self-reliant man submit to one?

Because it means giving permission to raise tough questions, such as:

► "How is it really going with your wife?"
► "How are you spending your free time?"
► "Are you reading your Bible regularly?"
► "What are you doing to make sure your kids grow up knowing the Lord?"

Said one husband, "When your wife asks those questions, it often feels as though she's nagging. But when someone else sits down across from you and asks the same questions, it shows he cares for you."

Craig Wierda, who meets with three other men in Michigan, is surprised at how quickly he adapted to the closeness. "Once men experience the caring atmosphere, they go with it," he says. "Men for years have been islands, not wanting other people to get close. We haven't had anybody share what's inside because we live in a culture that says we have to go it alone."

■ But isn't it second nature for men to keep their feelings bottled up? I know it is for me.

You, like many men, were probably raised by fathers who told us never to let our guards down, lest we reveal a weakness. Some of us make an unconscious choice to keep friendships at an arm's-length level, while too many of us never heard our fathers say, "I love you."

One time, at an Adventures in Fatherhood retreat in California's Sierra Nevada mountains, several dozen fathers and their sons gathered around the evening campfire. A father stood up and described how he had never heard his father tell him that he loved him. He added that his father had never heard those three simple words from *his* father.

Then the father called his seventeen-year-old son to stand beside him. "Son, I'm going to break a generations-long tradition in our family. I'm here to tell you that I love you." With that, he gave his son a bear hug.

■ **That's touching, but I would still find it hard to be that expressive.**

Then consider this: Dick Savidge, director of pastoral care at Cherry Hills Community Church, says, "We are starting to redefine masculinity. I think any time you are willing to be open and honest in front of other people, it's an important step toward God's power setting you free. I don't think a man can make it without reading the Bible consistently. I also believe holding one another accountable is a biblical concept."

Bart Hansen, a Southern California real estate developer, agrees that accountability is scriptural.

"I know the friendship of David and Jonathan in the First Book of Samuel is an example of two becoming accountable to each other. Especially in chapter 20, where they confided in each other when faced with Saul's treachery."

Hansen also quotes Ecclesiastes 4:9-10, which says, "Two are better than one, because they have a good return for their work: If one falls down, his friend can help him up. But pity the man who falls and has no one to help him up!"

■ **What other Scriptures support accountability between men?**

A couple can be found in Proverbs:
- "A man of many companions may come to ruin, but there is a friend who sticks closer than a brother" (18:24).
- "Do not forsake your friend and the friend of your father, and do not go to your brother's house when disaster strikes

you—better a neighbor nearby than a brother far away" (27:10).

■ How do women feel about this movement? Do they feel threatened?

Not at all. A Los Angeles woman in a Bible study group with a half-dozen other women said all of them shared the same concern: Although they knew their husbands attended church and made the right noises, *they had no idea where their men were with God.* Each expressed regret that their husbands weren't in accountability groups. They so loved what they were experiencing that they hoped their husbands would share with other men and thus be encouraged to grow spiritually.

Perhaps that's why Dr. Howard Hendricks, professor emeritus at Dallas Theological Seminary, once said, "A man who is not in a group with other men is an accident waiting to happen."

Bruce Hosford, a Seattle real estate developer, has taken that advice to heart: He belongs to three small groups. For a while, one of his groups was real small: just he and Denny Rydberg, a good friend. "Denny and I have lots in common, and we would meet for lunch each week. We called it the 'Ultimate Small Group,' and we checked in with each other to see what's going on in life."

In recent years, Hosford and Rydberg have expanded the group to five. "We've gone through a half-dozen psalms, and sometimes we'll raise tough questions such as homo-

---

MAKING SENSE OF THE MEN'S MOVEMENT

Any men's movement without a spiritual foundation is bound to fail. Dr. James Dobson, writing in his book *Straight Talk,* says he's concerned about the men's movement phenomenon and its emphasis on intimacy without a spiritual anchor. His advice:

► A man's number-one responsibility is to evangelize his own children.

► A Christian man is obligated to be the ultimate decision-maker in the home.

► Most men in the throes of a midlife crisis are long-term workaholics.

► It is a mistake to tamper with the time-honored relationship of husband as loving protector and wife as recipient of that protection.

sexuality. Believe me, that makes for some interesting discussions. We always have a timekeeper, though, and we always spend the last ten minutes praying for one another."

Hosford also meets once a week with several University of Washington students in their early twenties. "It's amazing how open these college guys are: the struggles of living in a frat house, the dating scene, and the difficulties of being a follower of Christ at a large public university. These guys are willing to be vulnerable, and that is not typically male."

Accountability groups often help in unexpected ways. Anthony Munoz, the former NFL All-Pro offensive tackle for the Cincinnati Bengals, used to meet weekly with six close church friends. A few years ago, Anthony was in the middle of contract negotiations with the Bengals.

"Things were going slow between me and the club, and I had this group to bounce things off," remembers Munoz. "One of the guys owned a small company, and he shared with me the management side of business. Not only was that beneficial, but I also really grew a lot during that time."

THE PROMISE KEEPERS

No discussion of men's groups would be complete without mentioning Promise Keepers, a nonprofit organization that motivates and equips men to keep their word with Jesus Christ, their wives, children, church, and community.

The organization was founded by former University of Colorado football coach Bill McCartney, who's greatest triumph was not beating Nebraska at Folsom Stadium but filling it with more than 50,000 men at a weekend Promise Keepers event.

These days, Promise Keepers has grown to nearly two-dozen cities. The organization has recruited some blue-chip talent for the two-day conferences: Gary Smalley, Dr. John Trent, evangelist Luis Palau, pastors E.V. Hill, Jack Hayford, and Dr. Dobson have all addressed at one time or another the critical issues facing men in the nineties.

If you haven't been to a Promise Keepers event, put it on the daily planner now. Call (303) 964-7600 for more information, or write Promise Keepers, P.O. Box 103001, Denver, CO 80250-3001.

For Morrie Driesenga, meeting with other men has been a real blessing too.

"It's an old cliché, but we truly have cried together and laughed together as we've talked—and prayed—about our families, our frustrations, and our praises. When any of us are out of town, we know we're missing a special time."

This article is adapted from "Finding New Friends on the Block," by Mike Yorkey and Peb Jackson, Focus on the Family magazine, June 1992. Copyright © 1992, Focus on the Family. Used by permission. Peb Jackson is a senior vice president with Young Life in Colorado Springs, Colorado.

WHAT DO I DO NOW?

For many men, the word *accountability* conjures up fears of having to tell secrets about yourself, secrets you don't want anyone else to know.

Some may think, *What if it ever gets out that I've been in one of those adult bookstores or massage parlors? The whole church would know. My life and marriage would be ruined.*

Accountability can be a scary word, and no one should make you share something you don't want to share. But if you're thinking about starting or joining an accountability group, keep these things in mind:

▶ **Discuss your options.** Talk to your pastor or the person heading up the men's ministry about the possibility.

▶ **For the first couple of months, expect things to be a little "surfacy."** It takes time to build relationships—and trust.

▶ **Don't betray confidences.** Remember that "what's said here stays here."

▶ **Don't let the group get too big.** Three or four is a good number. Any bigger, and the dynamics of a large group discourages intimacy. You'll also find it difficult to have enough time to hear from everyone.

▶ **Meet with people you enjoy.**

▶ **Keep the group diverse, but pay attention to the dynamics.** Perhaps an unemployed carpenter, a workaholic surgeon, and a struggling salesman might not be the best combination for a successful give-and-take relationship.

2

The High Calling—
and Cost—of Serving

■ "George, I want a divorce."

As those words shot across the restaurant table, I stared at my wife in disbelief.

You've got to be joking, I thought. But the look on Donna's face told me, *This is for real, buddy.*

"I've found another man—a man who can meet my needs," she said calmly.

Few would have predicted our marriage was headed for a cliff. We were an active couple who gladly served our local church in a variety of ways. We were your basic pillars of the community.

Years earlier, I approached the church elders with an offer of help. I was duly appointed chairman of the Christian education committee, and I felt sure God was rewarding me for my faithfulness. Other people in the church noticed the new George as well, and they slapped my shoulders with encouragement. The more strokes I got, the more I took on.

I took on too much. Why couldn't I have seen that all my church activity caused me to neglect Donna and our marriage?

Unfortunately, too much church work *can* interfere with the home front. When a husband ignores his wife and kids at the same time another man pays attention to her, the devil is exploiting a weakness in the marriage.

If you are gone several evenings a week serving at church, your wife may be home alone playing the comparison game. If the right man comes along at the right time, it might not be too long before "What if . . . " swims through her mind.

If he calls her the most wonderful person in the world, he'll melt her heart—and manipulate her emotions. What's especially frightening as this sin develops is that even if your wife brought up some reason that their budding affair wasn't right, he could convince her that God wanted His followers to be happy. It is absolutely amazing what mental gymnastics our minds will go through to justify actions that we know are against God's commandments.

■ **That's what happened in my case. The romance progressed. They held hands, they embraced, they kissed, they did everything but. There was no intercourse; that was a line Donna said she never could have crossed.**

But the lovers' triangle caught the eye of my church pastor. One evening he called me over and broadly hinted that Donna was involved with another man. I rejected that notion out of hand. *My wife is a Christian. There's no way she'd ever do something like that.*

But there was a way, and the deceiver had lulled Donna into believing the answer was to divorce me and start over. Our three children? She told me she and her new beau could deal with that.

George, you're in a battle royale for your marriage. Marriage troubles can happen to "involved" Christians. This is no time for acting wishy-washy. You need to get with a pastor or Christian counselor and discuss these issues head-on. For instance, you may turn to her and state, "Tell me you don't love me! I have to hear it from you first!"

Perhaps this will be the time when Donna reflects deep inside and *knows* she loves you and that the other relationship was an out-of-hand infatuation. Or perhaps the counselor will guide you through another approach to repairing your marriage. Either way, you need to pray for her *and* your relationship. You are fighting for your family's life.

■ **I'm like George in that I'm heavily involved in church as an elder. I'm careful to always assure my wife that I love her. Is there anything else I should do?**

Look for caution signals, folks. Days, weeks, and months can pass by in a blur. If your wife complains that you never take her out, she's not lamenting the lack of restaurant meals in her life. Actually, she's making a plea for attention. You would do well to take her out for a nice dinner—pronto.

Amidst all of the distractions, it's easy for spouses to neglect giving time to the marital relationship. When that occurs, Satan tries to create some opportunities to fill the void. George got his strokes from heavy church involvement. Donna got hers when another man pursued her.

Feelings of neglect and fleeting thoughts of "there's something better waiting out there for me" have separated thousands of couples. Don't let the greener-grass syndrome happen to you.

The lesson here isn't to eschew serving in church. Rather, it's this: *The deceiver can use Christian service to cause one or both of the spouses to neglect each other. In fact, he can use anything. Be on guard.*

■ **I remember the time an avalanche of church service buried me so deep I didn't even know I was smothered. How could I turn my back on Awana, the church board, or the growing youth department? I couldn't.**

Frankly, my wife, Elena, was a church widow. My old friends never saw me. One night after dinner, they dropped by and did an "intervention" on me. Just like family members or a professional counselor who confronts an alcoholic with his problem, my wife and friends jolted me into realizing what I was doing.

They said I was working and serving too much and not attending to the needs of my family. I felt shocked and betrayed—especially since my wife was the one who arranged it. How could she do that to me?

She was doing you a favor. Although the process is painful, you need to poke your head above the clouds and see that they were right. You need to rotate off several committees, make yourself unavailable for more meetings, and put your life back in balance.

Perhaps you've seen overcommitted church friends go through burnout—or terrible trials. You've heard them tell you in your men's group that they're struggling with the occasions when they volunteered once too many times. Since they're purportedly doing "the Lord's work," what can you say? That's why overinvolvement in church work can be so insidious.

One survival key is giving your spouse permission to wave the flag when things are out of whack—and not dismiss her pleas for more time together. That's an arrangement the Gaites have made.

"Every six or eight weeks, we try to get away for an evening—a day, if we can manage it," Trent says. "When Mary's feeling the stress of a busy schedule, my life reflects it too. That's one reason why I try not to get too busy myself. If I'm running as fast as she is, then I'm less able to notice when we're out of balance."

Like a battle commander who keeps some fresh troops in reserve, Trent doesn't deploy all of his forces in the day-to-day stresses of normal family life. He holds something back; perhaps that's a smart idea you can use.

■ Yes, but using the gifts God has given me—and seeing lives change for Christ—can be a heady experience. I've found it rewarding and addicting. How can I stay in balance?

Let's assume for a moment you're aware of some of the dangers, such as the great time demands on your marriage and your children. But you're also telling yourself that God has placed you in the body of Christ to be a blessing to others.

How can this be illustrated? Perhaps this drawing will help. Picture your marriage like two overlapping pyramids.

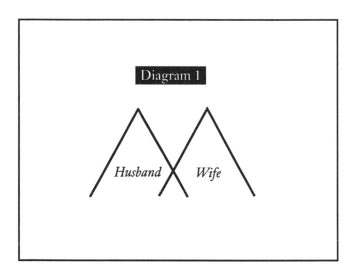

The ideal is to serve in the church while staying in touch with your spouse.

As you can see, there's a slight overlap. This is the point where you and your wife are doing things in tandem. It doesn't have to be a lot, just enough to keep you from living two separate lives under the same roof.

Greg Johnson and his wife, Elaine, have tried to keep this type of balance throughout their marriage. On a dozen occasions over the years, they have led a small group Bible study in their home. Greg enjoys using his Youth for Christ background to introduce "seekers" to Christ. He is also able to use his Bible college education to point out insights about Scripture.

He and Elaine are a good team. God gave her the gift of hospitality, and she has put it to good use. She has always created a warm, comfortable atmosphere to make everyone feel at home.

For the last couple of years, however, they haven't led a Bible study. Why? Life has gotten too busy with two teenagers, and they realize that they need to save their free evenings to reconnect as a family—and as a couple.

Not that they've dropped their efforts to evangelize. What

they've noticed is that their children's sports programs have put them into contact with many nonchurchgoing families, and they've been able to reach out to their new friends. There's something about standing on the sidelines and cheering on your sons and daughters that makes for a great mixer.

These two pyramids also clearly illustrate how most of their time is spent apart. Life is hectic but not stressful. They manage to keep 80 percent of their evenings and weekends free for family activities. It's a balance they are comfortable with.

Don't think that the way to serve God is by attending church meetings. Don't place more value in that than in being a faithful servant at home.

Now, let's take a look at a second set of pyramids that illustrates two lives serving separately.

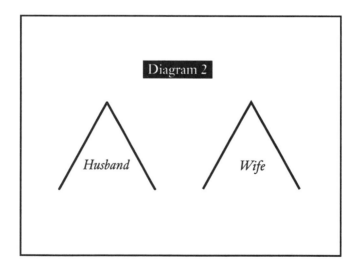

Though this arrangement is occasionally unavoidable, a prolonged period of serving outside the home will strain most marriages. If you find yourself falling into this pattern, ask some questions: Why am I serving so much? Is it because this is the only avenue where I am appreciated? Has my spouse dropped hints that

I may be doing too much? How have I responded to a plea for more time at home?

To prevent church involvement and service to others from overwhelming your marriage, you must develop a clear strategy. Here is a simple, yet effective start:

- ► What are your spiritual gifts? (Examples: leading, teaching, administrating, or giving.) What do you like to do? Write down areas where you are currently serving or would enjoy volunteering. Have your spouse do the same.
- ► Is there some overlap? Can you combine some areas and serve together? After you find areas of common interest, start serving together as soon as your schedule allows.
- ► If not, what can be altered to change the present situation? Being in the Lord's service should be a win/win situation. Adults should want their marriage to be a model of servanthood. The reason? First, it's biblical. You're a member of the body of Christ, and therefore, you have responsibilities to serve. Second, your children—and others—need to see someone as an example of what true servanthood is.

In addition, you'll enjoy the fulfillment that comes from expressing the gifts God has given you. It's fun to be used to meet practical or spiritual needs. And finally, it can allow you and your spouse to spend more time together instead of apart.

See? It's a win/win situation.

This material is adapted from The Second Decade of Love *by Greg Johnson and Mike Yorkey. Copyright © 1994. Used by permission of Tyndale House Publishers, Inc. All rights reserved.*

3

Let Prayer Change Your Life

. . . .

■ **I'm a relatively new Christian, and my pastor has been encouraging us to make prayer a regular part of our day. Why should I make that commitment? What kind of power is behind prayer?**

When Becky Tirabassi became a Christian over twenty years ago, she asked herself the same questions. She was a footloose twenty-one-year-old Californian living paycheck to paycheck. Yet, as a new Christian, she remembers praying for impossible opportunities, blindly trusting God's power to intervene.

For instance, she believed He wanted her to return to her parents' home in Ohio to show them her new life in Christ and get a fresh start on life. There was just one little problem: Becky had no money.

■ **What did she do about it?**

Becky told all her coworkers at the auto dealership about her desire to return to Ohio. After hearing her dramatic conversion story, they looked at her as if she were on drugs, which Becky had been for much of her party-going years.

One of the used-car salesmen chuckled when Becky said she felt God wanted her to return to Ohio. Her faith in prayer was so childlike that his skepticism didn't embarrass her. But a few days later, the salesman dropped by her desk and said, "You won't believe this, but I have a friend in Ohio who has a twenty-nine-foot motor home in storage not far from here. Since he doesn't have the time to fly out and drive it back to Ohio, he was wondering if you would be interested in doing that for him."

Would she? Of course, she would!

Within a couple of days, Becky loaded her bike, kitchen utensils, clothes, and the rest of her worldly belongings into the luxurious motor home. Then she headed east, extremely glad that the owner was paying all the fuel costs for that gas-guzzler. Though it may have seemed coincidental to some, Becky felt that Jesus had literally provided a way home for her—knowing that she didn't have the money to do it on her own.

■ **Stories like those seem too incredible for me. My prayer life is haphazard and inconsistent. Sure, if something big is happening in my life, I am on my knees. But I have a thousand excuses for not praying:**

"I'm too busy."

"I'm too tired."

"It doesn't do anything."

"It takes too much time."

"It's boring."

"Prayer is for old people."

So what can prayer do for me? I already know that I am saved.

Becky Tirabassi used all the same excuses until February 1984, when she attended a conference workshop on prayer. Sitting in the back of the auditorium, she heard one speaker say, "Prayerlessness in the life of a believer is sin." The statement stunned her, but she knew as a Christian that *either I believe this as truth, or I don't believe it.*

At the end of that workshop, Becky remained seated, not wanting to leave as the same person she was when she entered. She had been given her most powerful resource—a direct communication link with God. With prayer, she could request His help and hear Him express His love toward her.

At that moment, Becky told God that she would pray for one hour a day for the rest of her life. *After all He had done for me*, she thought, *it was the least I could do!*

■ **How did Becky get started?**

That first morning home, she walked into her kitchen after sending her son and husband off for the day. A little baffled, she thought, *What do I do now?*

She collected paper and pen and made a fresh pot of coffee. She turned off the radio, took the phone off the hook, and set the alarm on the stove to ring in one hour. She had made her first "appointment" with God.

■ **If I go for this "appointment with God," what should I do during that time?**

Why not write out your prayers? Writing will keep you from daydreaming or becoming distracted. Now only does journaling your prayers keep you accountable and organized, but as you fine-tune your system, you'll also discover that written prayer is a practical, tangible way to stay focused—a one-stop place where you can journal your conversations with God each morning.

Becky Tirabassi recommends using a three-ring binder and calling it your *Prayer Notebook*. You can divide it into four sections: Praise, Admit, Request, and Thanks.

In the **Praise section,** use the Psalms—the written prayers of the psalmists—as a pattern for your praise prayers. By reading four to five psalms a day and rewriting some of the verses as your personal praise prayers, your heart will be opened to the Word at the start of each appointment with God.

The **Admit** section is where you can confess your sins in writing. Begin by reading Psalm 139:23-24: "Search me, O God, and know my heart; test me and know my anxious thoughts. See if there is any offensive way in me, and lead me in the way everlasting."

Be honest with God and agree with Him about your shortcomings (or sins). Openly discuss your temper, your impatience, and other missed marks with the One who already knows them. He is waiting for your confession so He can forgive, change, and transform you with His powerful Holy Spirit.

By meeting God every day, you will gain assurance that integrity, blamelessness, and holiness are assets in the life of a believer. You can finish your Admit section encouraged by the promise of Romans 12:2 that His Holy Spirit is renewing your mind each and every day.

■ **What about my prayer requests? Where does that all fit in?**

Use the **Request** section of your notebook as your detailed, specific prayer request list. Psalm 5:3 reads:

Morning by morning, O Lord, you hear my voice; morning by morning I lay my requests before you and wait in expectation.

So each morning, lay your requests before God and wait expectantly for His reply. Sometimes God says yes and sometimes He says no, but no matter the outcome, He still loves you. Know that for certain requests, you may receive an answer within minutes. For others, it will be years! For some, you will have to continue to wait.

The **Thanks** section is where you can daily acknowledge God's touch of love. It is the place where you tell Him that you love Him, where you notice His hand upon your life, and where you record His answers to your prayers.

■ **Why in this time of great need for revival, especially in the United States, does a power source for transformation and change—namely prayer—receive so little attention?**

The reasons for not praying are based upon many misconceptions: prayer is boring; prayer is only for the pious and spiritual; God doesn't always answer prayer.

If you harbor those misconceptions, chances are that you will be a powerless Christian who finds Bible reading and praying too time-consuming for your daily life.

Can you examine your own prayer life in the privacy of your heart? Perhaps it is time to:

▶ Let God convince you that prayerlessness in a believer's life is sin. First Samuel 12:23 says, "As for me, far be it from me that I should sin against the Lord by failing to pray for you."

▶ Admit your helplessness.

▶ Confess your sin and accept God's forgiveness.

▶ Be encouraged that you are not alone in the world, but that you may be a trailblazer for prayer in your home, youth group, church, city, or state.

■ **How am I going to find time to pray? I have so little free time already.**

Maybe you've tried, but after setting the alarm clock to get up a half-hour earlier, you hit the snooze button over and over.

Former Nazi death camp prisoner Corrie ten Boom once said, "Don't pray when you feel like it, but make an appointment and *keep it.*"

Look at your weekly schedule and then set aside non-negotiable time. Granted, one hour is unrealistic for busy dads, but how about ten minutes a day for starters? No matter how long you spend with God, you will discover the incredible importance of prayer in your life.

Your perspective on Him will change as well. He will not be too small, or too strict, or too far away. Instead, you will find Him near. He will always be with you. You have His word on that.

VOLUNTEER FOR THE NATIONAL DAY OF PRAYER!

If you're making a commitment to pray more in your life, then also consider volunteering in the annual National Day of Prayer (NDP) campaign. Mrs. Shirley Dobson has been chairman of the NDP Task Force since 1991.

Held the first Thursday in May, the National Day of Prayer features hundreds of prayer breakfasts, noontime rallies, and prayer gatherings. Each year, volunteers are needed to organize NDP events in their hometowns or cities.

More than 15,000 different prayer rallies are held on the National Day of Prayer. If you or your church would like to request a National Day of Prayer resource kit, please call toll-free (800) 444-8828.

■ **Final question: Becky Tirabassi mentioned that she started praying for one hour a day in February 1984. Has she missed a day yet?**

As of this book's writing, Becky says she hasn't missed a day since making that vow more than thirteen years ago.

This material is adapted from writings by Becky Tirabassi, author of Let Prayer Change Your Life Workbook *(Thomas Nelson). She and her husband, Roger, and son, Jacob, live in Newport Beach, California.*

4

Singer Steve Green:
The Comeback Kid

. . . .

Editor's note: If you ask Steve Green what's the downside of being a successful Christian artist, he'll tell you that a lot of people know very little about him.

Sure, some are aware that Steve can sing in English or Spanish with equal dexterity, since he was born and raised in Argentina as a missionary kid. You figure he's a great family man because you've seen the warm, fuzzy pictures of him and his wife, Marijean, with their two handsome children, Summer and Josiah.

Let's face it: Steve Green is one guy who appears to Have It All Together. His voice can belt out "Mighty Fortress" or cause the hankies to come out during "The Letter." His concerts—he schedules more than 100 dates a year—appeal to everyone from three to ninety-three. He's a regular at Promise Keepers weekends, and he and Larnell Harris collaborated on a song about racial reconciliation ("Teach Me to Love"). Steve was also featured on the cover of Focus on the Family *magazine (September 1996).*

But behind his amazing voice and engaging stage presence, there's something Steve Green wants you to know about him. When you hear this story, you'll understand him and his music ministry much better.

Steve Green's Story

In the summer of 1983, Steve, then twenty-seven, was an up-and-coming singer in a hurry. He and Marijean were part of the backup group for Bill and Gloria Gaither, but Steve's classically trained voice was attracting notice. Sparrow Records offered him a recording contract, and the buzz in Nashville circles was that Steve Green, solo act, was ready for orbit.

But Steve's spiritual life was stuck on the launch pad, where it had been ever since his college days. Steve, who had never spent much time in the U.S. until he attended Grand Canyon University in Phoenix, had discovered the *Norte Americano* lifestyle to be very appealing. While his four brothers and sisters attended Bible colleges and pursued careers in ministry, Steve daydreamed about becoming a doctor or lawyer—money-making careers that could fuel his newfound aspirations.

"Although I grew up in a spiritual home," he says, "I turned my back on the level of commitment to Christ that I had seen in my parents. I just wanted to be a 'regular Christian,' someone who wanted to know the Lord but also wanted freedom from the restraints that I felt inhibited me: rules, regulations, all the things that good Christians don't do. My desire to be free was really a license to sin. I disobeyed the Lord in a lot of areas. I rebelled and grieved the heart of God."

Growing up, Steve wasn't allowed to go to the cinema. When he was on his own, Steve was attracted to randy movies on cable TV, something new in the early eighties. Consequently, with his thought life running rampant, Steve's prayer life evaporated to nearly nothing. Yes, he still uttered a quick grace before meals, but his prayers didn't reflect any deep love for the Lord or a desire to be close to Him.

In early August 1983, Steve flew to Phoenix to attend his younger sister's wedding. For the first time in several years, the entire Green family (Steve had two brothers and two sisters) was together, but it didn't take long for everyone to notice that his older brother Randy had been through some sort of "revival" experience. For several days leading up to the wedding, Randy cornered each family member and asked where they stood with the Lord. Were they tracking with Him? Had they *really* given their hearts and lives over to Jesus Christ?

When Steve heard from other family members that he was next, he kept a wary distance from Randy. But one afternoon, the family jumped into a car to visit a hospitalized relative, and suddenly Randy had a captive audience.

"I couldn't get away," remembers Steve, "and he didn't care *who* heard him. He kept talking about the importance of holiness and the shortness of time, but I kept changing the subject. He kept changing it back. Finally, I became angry with him and yelled, 'Just stop talking!' "

Randy, who was sitting in the front seat, began crying. He turned around and told Steve that he was not resisting him, but the Holy Spirit. He said God wanted to use Steve, but He couldn't because there was something bottled up inside of him.

"You're a liar!" Steve steamed. "God can look at me right now and see there's nothing wrong with my life!" But no sooner were the words out of his mouth than Steve thought he sounded hypocritical and empty.

That night, sleep did not come easily. Steve tossed in bed, reliving his conversation with Randy. His older brother had peeled away a layer of his heart and exposed the hypocrisy that his life had become. *Wait a minute*, thought Steve. *I sing with famous people, and the audience cheers for me every night. They tell me that God is using me. No, I can't be that bad.*

But as Steve stared at the ceiling, he knew that he *was* bad. His brother's words haunted him, and worse yet, he had seen right through him. No one else had ever talked to him like that before. *Doesn't he know who he's talking to?*

Something powerful was tugging Steve's conscience, and after another hour of internal debate, he fell out of bed and dropped to his knees.

"Lord, I give up. I'm a hypocrite and I've sinned against You. I've lived a dual life. I've made a mockery of You. I don't love You, and I hardly know You. And my brother is right. I've said no to You for so many years that I don't even know how to say yes, but if You will help me, I'll say yes. And if You can do in me what You've done in my brother, please do it, because from now on, I'm Yours."

The next day, he called Marijean and asked her if she had spent any time with the Lord that day.

"No, I haven't," she replied. "Why do you ask? *Something's different here.*

"Has something happened to you?" she asked.

"God is doing something in me, but I'm not sure what it is. We'll talk about it more when I get home."

When he boarded a plane later that day, he started writing down his thoughts and prayers in a journal. "Is the cost of surrender too high?" he wrote. "Not if I'm sick of a bland relationship with no burning love and no power." Then Steve asked God to revive his first love for Him at any cost.

When he and Marijean were reunited, he started the story from the very beginning, confessing things to Marijean that she did not know about her husband of five years. Driven by a newfound passion for God and a clean conscience, Steve spent the next two weeks making restitution with those he had wronged. He was saying good-bye to an old life.

That *adios* prompted Steve to start a solo career. Several weeks later, he gave his first concert at Liberty University in Virginia. Steve had never really had much to say in public before. But that night at Liberty, he started talking about how his brother had "lovingly" confronted him at a time when he needed it most. As he neared the end of the story, he looked down at the front row, and he saw men and women dabbing their eyes with handkerchiefs. *Strange*, he thought. *That's never happened before.*

When Steve finished the concert, Marijean looked at him and started to cry.

"I'm looking at a different man tonight," she said. "When I saw you up there, it wasn't the same person I've known."

Marijean was right. Her man had changed.

To the Present

Fast forward nearly fifteen years. These days, Steve Green is into *accountability*. He and his brother, David, who is his manager, meet once a year with a council of pastors to assess where they are heading. The pastors have full access to their financial records, and they also interview the Green brothers regarding their personal lives and goals for the upcoming year.

"It's a very meaningful time and a safeguard for us," says Steve. "Because David and I are brothers, we recognize the danger of doing whatever we think is right and deceiving ourselves. That's why we have a group of outside, unbiased individuals who give us counsel and advice. I even have the pastors review my lyrics to make sure the songs are biblically sound."

Except when he's performing in large stadium venues, he usually mingles with the audience following each concert. He patiently shakes hands, exchanges hugs, pats little heads, and *listens.*

"Even if I'm weary, it's still important to take the time to let people tell me things," says Steve. "I'm not just talking about flattery. Sometimes people have listened to my music, and they feel like they know me well enough to speak honestly and openly with me. I've been cautioned; I've been sobered; I've been encouraged; and I've been exhorted. I've had men come to me, grasp my hand firmly, look me in the eye, and say, "Steve, you're in a dangerous position. I pray that God will keep you pure and keep you and Marijean in love with each other."

Fortunately, Steve doesn't have to deal with women

GUARD YOUR HEART

written by Jon Mohr

What appears to be a harmless
  glance
Can turn to romance
And homes are divided
Feelings that should have never been
Awaken within
Tearing the heart in two
Listen, I beg of you!

Chorus:
Guard your heart, Guard your heart
Don't trade it for treasure
Don't give it away
Guard your heart, Guard your heart
As a payment for pleasure
It's a high price to pay
For a soul that remains sincere
With a conscience clear
Guard your heart
The human heart is easily swayed
And often betrayed
At the hands of emotion
We dare not leave the outcome to
  chance
We must choose in advance
Or live with the agony
Such needless tragedy.

throwing hotel keys on the stage. But the temptations are there.

"Because I travel a lot, I have the danger of impurity in hotel rooms with all the TV, and I suppose advances from women, although that's never happened to me. Probably it's because Marijean has traveled with me or I've talked about her in front of so many people. That's a safeguard.

"These are some of the reasons I've made myself accountable to Christian artists Michael Card, Wes King, and Phil Keaggy. If I've seen something that has caused me to stumble in a certain area, I contact them about it and ask them to pray for me. I know my own need for accountability because I know myself better than anyone else knows me." These experiences inspired him to sing "Guard Your Heart" (see sidebar).

Steve says it's very easy for people to buy into the image packaged by the record company. "But I've tried for the past ten years to dispel what I call the 'mystique,'" he says. "It's something that is easy for artists to hide behind. We often live just out of reach of the public, and we often try to hold on to that mystique because it draws crowds. But that's something I've not wanted to do because it's not true.

"Marijean and I are, quite simply, regular people who have a specific function within the body of Christ, and we are the most amazed that God would choose to use us. I know that I am one of the most unlikely candidates to be used by God, because of my eight-year period of running away from Him as a prodigal. I see my own frailties even now, even since God rescued me and turned my life around."

Mike Yorkey wrote the material on Steve Green.

5

Let's Have a Seder

· ·

■ **Last year, we were invited over to some friends for a Passover dinner. They had invited a Jewish friend—a fellow who had invited Christ into his life—to lead a seder. I knew nothing about this ancient Jewish ceremony, but I'd like to learn more. What can you tell me?**

A seder can be a new (but very old) way to celebrate Easter with your family. It's applicable to our faith because Jesus and His disciples shared the Passover meal the night before He died.

Stan Kellner, who works at Focus on the Family as a chaplain, grew up in a Jewish home on Boston's North Shore. Every springtime heralded the celebration of Stan's favorite eight-day holiday: Passover.

For nearly a week before the ceremony, his mother cleaned the house of all products that contained yeast or leaven. Then she'd scrub the pantry before storing the matzo meal and farfel flour she'd use in many of the Passover dishes, including the honeyed cakes Stan especially loved.

Their special dinner or *seder* came on the first night of Passover. Stan and his four siblings dressed in their best, and their dining room table would almost shimmer with a beautiful white cloth, fine china, and candles.

Stan loved the meal, which began with Mother singing the blessing over the candles. Then Father would hand out copies of the forty-eight-page text (called the "Haggadah") marked with all of their speaking parts—English on one side; Hebrew on the other. Since Stan was the youngest child for several years, he had the task of singing (in Hebrew, of course!) the four questions that would trigger the story of their nation's captivity in Egypt and the way God had led them out.

Stan loved the drama of the Exodus and the reminder through the stinging horseradish of how bitter slavery had been for the Jewish nation. Even as a youngster, he was impressed with the importance of passing the story from one generation to the next.

■ **You mentioned that Stan worked at Focus on the Family. So he must be a Christian. But how did Stan become one after being raised in a Jewish home?**

After six turbulent years in the hippie scene in the late sixties and early seventies, Stan wound up in the Air Force, where a buddy introduced him to Jesus, the Son of the living God. His first Bible study gave him a new appreciation of his heritage.

One week, the leader announced that they'd study the Passover. Stan thought, *Hey, I'm the Jewish one. How can you talk about that?* But as his friend explained the significance of each element, he was astonished at the link between Judaism and Christianity. Stan wanted to know more. So in 1975, after he was discharged from the service, he enrolled at Dallas Bible College. It was there that he met his wife, Nita.

Shortly after they were married in 1977, they heard a Jewish believer explain the seder to their church. As Stan watched him, he realized he could present Passover in the same manner.

■ **I would like to have my family celebrate this special occasion. How do we go about having a seder in our home?**

The following is a bare explanation. The ceremony takes about forty-five minutes, but you should know that the seders of Stan's youth lasted three or four hours.

Come to the Table
At each place setting, provide the following:
Parsley (2 sprigs)

Charoseth (1 tablespoon)—This is a mixture of chopped apples, nuts, honey, cinnamon, and a touch of wine or grape juice.

Grape Juice (4 servings, 3 ounces each)

Saltwater (1 bowl per 4-5 people)

Horseradish (1/2 teaspoon and as "biting" as possible)

Matzo (1/4 square, plain)

At the leader's place setting also provide:
1 bowl of saltwater

1 lamb bone (meatless and oven-roasted until browned)

3 whole squares of matzo and 4 napkins (the squares are placed between the napkins stacked on a plate)

1 roasted egg (boil for 10 minutes; then place under the oven broiler until shell is browned)

2 candles (white) and candlesticks (in the table center)

An extra setting for "Elijah": Same as the "per person" setting with the exception that only one glass of juice is poured and left next to the plate. This symbolizes the future appearance of Elijah, who will signify the coming of the Messiah.

The Passover Ceremony

► **The cleaning of leaven.** Even though each Jewish home is cleaned before Passover, a few crumbs of leavened bread are dropped on the floor just before the seder. You—the father—then sweep them up as a symbol that the house is ready.

► **The lighting of the candles.** The candles are lit by the mother, who recites, "Blessed are You, O Lord our God, King of the universe, who sanctifies us by Your commandments and has ordained that we kindle the Passover lights."

► **The first cup: The cup of sanctification.** The father lifts his cup and explains, "Sanctification means to be set apart. We are setting apart this ceremony as special to our Lord."

The Jews remember Exodus 6:6a, "I will bring you out

[set you apart] from under the burdens of the Egyptians." God performed miraculous deeds to free Israel from Egypt. As believers, we remember the death of Jesus to free us. (Everyone drinks.)

► **Washing of the hands.** Here the father washes in a basin as a reminder of the priests' need to wash before they could go before God on behalf of Israel.

As Jesus celebrated His last Passover with His disciples, John 13 records that He took a towel and washed their feet instead of washing His hands as a symbol of His rightful leadership. What a picture—a true leader is a servant.

► **Dipping the parsley.** Everyone dips his or her parsley, one sprig at a time, into the saltwater and then eats it.

The first dip refers to the tears shed in slavery by the Israelites. The second dip refers to the drowning of the Egyptian army in the Red Sea and the miraculous deliverance of the nation of Israel as a result (Ex. 14:13-31).

► **Breaking of the middle matzo.** The father then takes the middle square of the three whole matzos, breaks it in half, puts one half back and hides the other half under a napkin, on a shelf or anywhere he wants. Everyone closes his eyes while this is done. The children will look for the hidden piece later in the ceremony.

Jews do not have a solid answer as to the significance of the breaking of the middle matzo. Some say the three squares represent the three groups of Hebrews: priests, Levites, and Israelites. Others say it stands for the forefathers: Abraham, Isaac, and Jacob.

As believers, we see the Trinity—God the Father represented by the top piece; God the Son, Jesus Christ, the middle piece, broken and hidden away; God the Holy Spirit represented by the bottom piece. It is possible that Jewish followers of Jesus introduced this act into the ceremony shortly after He ascended into heaven as a way to forever feature Him in the Passover. Today, unbelieving Jews are including a clear picture of their Messiah, Jesus, in their celebration.

► **The four questions.** At this point, the youngest child and the father interact to explain why Passover is celebrated. After asking the first "stage-setting" question, the child will ask four detailed ones.

Child: "Why is this night different from all other nights?"

Father: "Once we were slaves of Pharaoh in Egypt, but now we are free, and we set aside this night each year to remember the great things God did for us."

Child: "On all other nights we eat either bread or matzo, but why, on this night, do we eat only matzo?"

Father: "Matzo reminds us of two things—we were delivered from slavery in Egypt, and we have a new life."

Child: "On all other nights we eat whatever kind of vegetables we want, but why, on this night, do we eat only a bitter one?"

Father: "We remember how bitter our ancestors' slavery was while they lived in Egypt."

Child: "On all other nights we do not dip our vegetables even once, but why, on this night, do we dip twice?"

Father: "We are reminded of tears and of a miraculous deliverance."

Child: "On all other nights we eat either sitting up straight or reclining, but why, on this night, do we all recline?"

Father: "Before we were slaves, but now we are able to recline to express the rest we enjoy as free people."

The Story of Passover

During this time, Exodus 12:1-13 is read with brief comments and with the elements held up at the appropriate moment.

► **The lamb bone.** The lamb was killed, its blood spread on the doorposts and lintel of the house to protect the home from the tenth plague, the slaying of the firstborn. God said He would pass over the house when He saw the blood.

► **The unleavened bread.** Unleavened bread is a necessary part of the Passover. It was not given time to rise since the Hebrews had to be ready to leave quickly.

► **The second cup: The cup of plagues.** God poured out ten plagues on Egypt, the last of which, the slaying of the firstborn, convinced Pharaoh to let Moses and the people of Israel leave the land.

After this explanation, the father invites the participants to reenact these plagues. He reads each plague aloud, they repeat it and then dip a finger into the grape juice, letting a drop fall onto the plate to symbolize the pouring out of the plagues.

"Blood." (dip) "Frogs." (dip) "Lice." (dip) "Flies." (dip) "Cattle Disease." (dip) "Boils." (dip) "Hail." (dip) "Locusts." (dip) "Darkness." (dip) "Slaying of the firstborn." (dip)

Believing fathers can add, "Now, let us lift our cups and drink, thanking God that He not only delivered the nation of Israel from the plagues, but that, through Jesus, He delivered us from the plague of sin, which is death that we all deserve."

▶ **The bitter herbs.** Have each person place a small portion of horseradish on a matzo and eat it. This symbolizes the bitterness of Israel's slavery. Believers also remember the bitterness Jesus endured on our behalf.

▶ **Eating of the *charoseth*.** Each person places a small portion of charoseth on matzo and eats it. This mixture symbolizes the mortar that was used to make bricks by the Israelites while in Egypt. The bittersweet labor is sweetened by the promise of redemption.

We also know that even though Jesus suffered bitterly on our behalf, it produces the sweetness of forgiveness of sins.

▶ **Eating the egg.** The father presents the roasted egg as a reminder of the temple's destruction in A.D. 70. The egg is dipped into the salt water—the symbol of tears—and then eaten.

▶ **Sharing the *charoseth*.** This part of the seder isn't in the traditional service but adds such meaning that many groups incorporate it. Here, each person places a portion of the sweet mixture on matzo and feeds it to the person on his right. As each feeds another, he says, "Shalom—Peace to you."

▶ **The eating of the meal.** At this point, the Jewish family eats a full meal. (Larger groups often present just the ceremony. Others start the evening with a potluck dinner.)

▶ **Eating of the *Afikomen*.** "Ah-fee-koe-men" is the only Greek word in the Passover and loosely translated means, "after dinner." At this point, the children hunt for the hidden matzo. Whoever finds the piece gets a token reward, maybe a coin or a piece of candy. When found, the *Afikomen* is broken and shared with the others.

▶ **The third cup: The cup of redemption.** Exodus 6:6c says, "I will redeem you." The word redemption means buying someone out of slavery. The sacrificial lamb offered on Passover was the price to deliver the nation of Israel. This third cup is what Jesus drank with His disciples as a symbol of His blood. (Everyone drinks.)

▶ **Searching for Elijah.** Here one of the children peeks out the door to see if Elijah is coming.

Father: "Is Elijah there?"

Child: "No, he is not here."

Father: "Maybe next year Elijah will come!"

The Jewish people knew, according to Malachi 3:1 and 4:5-6, that Elijah would prepare the way for the Messiah. They are looking for the Messiah year after year, not recognizing that He, Jesus, has already come.

▶ **The fourth cup: The cup of praise.** As everyone lifts this cup, the father quotes Exodus 6:7, "I will take you for My people." The Jewish nation looks forward to a golden age where everyone will be at peace. We, as believers in the Lord Jesus, eagerly wait for His return when He will take us home to heaven.

So, with the Passover ceremony finished, everyone drinks the fourth cup proclaiming, "Even so, come quickly, Lord Jesus."

This material is adapted from writings by Stan Kellner of Colorado Springs, who heads Sheresh Ministries. Each spring, he presides over Passover celebrations at local churches. Kellner can be contacted at Sheresh Ministries, P.O. Box 26415, Colorado Springs, CO 80936, or by calling (719) 532-1573. E-mail address is sheresh@aol.com.

6

It's the Percentage
That Counts

Editor's note: We thought we'd end this section on "Dads and Their God" by presenting this modern-day parable written by Cecil Shrock of Marshall, Arkansas.

Boyd wasn't exactly broke that morning as he stood beside the highway, thumb working in the pre-rush hour dawn. Fact is, he had exactly $5.35 left after eating a Grand Slam breakfast at Denny's. Boyd was trying to make his way from a little town in eastern Ohio to upstate New York, where his brother and his wife and two children lived on a small farm in a secluded valley of the Adirondacks.

While the cars whizzed past, he took stock of his financial situation. If he skipped lunch, he could probably spend the night at some Salvation Army center where he'd get a hot meal. That would buy him enough time to reach home territory by tomorrow night.

Once at his older brother's house, he could surely stay for a few days until he got some kind of work. He thought back to the automobile accident that had taken his parents' lives ten years earlier. *If only they were still around,* he thought. *They could help me get back on my feet.*

An hour or so went by as Boyd held his hand out in the morning chill. The sun was beginning to warm the spring air when a large car approached, occupied by only a driver. Boyd always made eye contact with passing motorists since that increased his odds of getting picked up. With a confident, friendly smile, Boyd looked the driver in the eye and waved his thumb. The Lexus braked and Boyd sprinted for the waiting vehicle.

"Good morning, sir," he said as he opened the front door of the brand-new car.

"Good morning," the driver replied. "Hop on in. The name's Sam Harrington." The Lexus smoothly picked up speed. "Where are you headed?"

Sam Harrington looked to be in his early seventies, a man who had spent his lifetime working with his hands.

"Upstate New York, back home," replied Boyd. "And my name is Boyd Newman."

"Your parents still living there?"

"No, sir. They've been dead for ten years. I have just one brother left and a few old friends there, I hope."

The man's voice seemed a little softer.

"You mentioned your parents died ten years ago. What happened?"

"They were hit head-on by a drunk driver on a two-lane road."

"That's mighty sad. What brings you out this way?"

"After my folks were killed, I headed west. I was working on a farm west of Chicago, but then the owner's son came back, took my job, and so I decided to return to my old home."

They made interesting small talk on various subjects as the car sped into Pennsylvania.

For some time, no more was said as the scenery sped by.

"I have no living relatives, either," said the driver. "My wife passed away last year. Our only son didn't return from the Vietnam war."

"I'm sorry, sir. That must have been very hard. I bet you miss him horribly."

The man didn't reply right away. Boyd thought he may have gotten too personal.

Fifty miles later, they resumed talking.

"What kind of work do you do, Mr. Harrington?"

"I'm in the manufacturing business," he answered. Then his face brightened. "Hey, how would you like to go to work for me in New

York? You look like a clean-cut young man of good intelligence. I own a factory in New York. You come work for me, and if you make good, I'll cut you in on the business."

"What do you mean by that?" asked Boyd.

"Well, I've been thinking a lot as we've been driving, and since I have no heirs to leave my possessions to, I'm prepared to give you all that is mine when I'm gone. How much money do you have right now?"

What's going on here? thought Boyd. *I'm just a hitchhiker, and now he's offering me his inheritance. I've heard of New York slickers. Since it's none of his business how much money I have, I'm going to tell him I have a dollar and see what he says next.*

"All I have is a dollar, Mister. You picked me up at a bad time to make a business offer."

"All right, you've got a dollar," replied the old man. "Let me tell you a little about myself. At present, I have $10 million in cash in the bank, numerous stocks and securities, a large factory in New York, and three homes in Long Island, Ft. Lauderdale, and Beaver Creek, Colorado. I suppose my net worth is around $25 million."

My jaw dropped to the floorboard.

"I'll make you an offer," he continued. "You put in all you have and I'll put in all I have, and we'll go 50-50 with the right of survivors. What do you say?"

"I'd be a fool not to accept an offer like that, sir, although I don't know why you make it."

"Because it's no fun living alone, and I have no one to whom to leave my wealth. If you play fair with me, I'll adopt you, and you can take the place of the son I lost. I'll be honest with you, and I expect you to be honest with me. Shall we shake on it?"

Mr. Harrington had a firm grip, to which Boyd responded with a strong hand squeeze.

Late that evening, they reached Mr. Harrington's Long Island estate. "This is Boyd Newman, perhaps my new partner," he said to the valet, after they parked in the long circular driveway. "Can you see that Mr. Newman is shown to his new quarters?"

Boyd was amazed to walk into a wing of the mansion with a large bedroom, adjacent study, bath, walk-in closet, and a balcony overlooking the ocean.

The next morning after breakfast, they drove to the factory in New York City.

"Good morning, Mr. Thompson," Mr. Harrington said to the plant manager. "I have a new man with me this morning. We're discussing a possible partnership. Can you show him around the factory while I attend to some urgent business? When you get back, I'll be ready to talk business with him."

It took several hours to go through the entire plant, and Boyd was amazed to see how much could be produced in half a shift.

"Well, what do you think of the layout?" asked Mr. Harrington. "Are you satisfied with our bargain? If so, I'll have the papers drawn up."

"How could I say otherwise, Mr. Harrington? Everything is beyond my wildest expectations."

"Very well, then. The papers will read like this:

This is a full partnership agreement between Mr. Sam Harrington and Mr. Boyd Newman. Each agrees to invest his total assets at the time of this agreement: Mr. Newman $1; Mr. Harrington, as stated in the latest financial report of his current earnings. Hereafter, the two parties will be in full 50-50 partnership with right of survivorship. Upon the death of either, all assets will become the property of the survivor.

"Does this sound like the agreement we talked about in the car?" asked Mr. Harrington. "If so, I'll instruct my attorney to finalize this agreement, which we sign tomorrow."

"Ah . . . yes, that would be fine," replied Boyd. A sinking feeling filled his stomach. Boyd knew that he hadn't been honest from the start. He had no reason to trust a stranger, but now he saw every evidence of good faith on the part of his benefactor. Perhaps it wasn't too late to admit that he had $5.35 in his pocket and not just $1. But he didn't want to admit that now—not at this time, not with so much money at stake. Besides, what difference did $5.35 make compared to all of Mr. Harrington's millions?

"Very well, then our contract is made," grinned Mr. Harrington. "We each put in all we have and go 50-50 from now on. Let's shake again!"

Boyd sheepishly stuck out his right hand, and something told him he would regret it. At first he had a guilty conscience over deceiving someone who had done so much for him, but he quickly ignored those thoughts. Gradually a feeling of superiority seeped into his conscience. A simple farm boy had been able to pull one over on a very successful businessman.

The next morning, Boyd strode into Mr. Harrington's office. "Well, here's the contract," said the wealthy man. "Fifty-fifty, just as we agreed upon."

This was Boyd's last opportunity to be honest with Mr. Harrington, but it was too hard to tell the truth. He just hoped he'd never get caught.

"That's right, Mr. Harrington."

A look of disappointment came over Mr. Harrington's face.

"Mr. Newman, know this: 'Be sure your sin will find you out.' How can I accept as a partner one I can never fully trust. You had $5.35 when you arrived at my estate, not $1. We found the money in your blue jeans when we washed them. I waited until the last moment, hoping my honesty and love for you would bring you to tell the truth.

"Good-bye, Mr. Newman."

Hasn't the Lord made us the same offer that Mr. Harrington made to Boyd Newman? What a pitiful offering we can present compared to the glory of God, and yet it's the percentage that counts, not the amount.

All to Jesus I surrender?

All to Him I freely give?

A LESSON IN CONTENTMENT

by Grace Merrill

My family and I buried Dad not too long ago—on his birthday. But the austere, bleak Minnesota cemetery, with its minus-thirty-degree wind chill, couldn't erase the warming in my heart for this man and the many lessons of life he had taught me.

One of those lessons penetrated my heart when I had flown from Colorado to Connecticut for a few final days with my dad. As I entered his room at the

continued next page

nursing home, he gestured to his half of the area and said with wonderment, "Just think . . . all this is mine!"

Startled, I looked around and saw a few pictures, his writing materials, a few clothes, and toiletries. In that moment, I took an important mental snapshot of what genuine contentment and gratefulness is.

He and Mom had made the climb from small living quarters to lovely parsonages and cozy homes—then back to an apartment, followed by an "assisted living" room, and finally, half of a room. Never had there been any complaint. Even at the end, there was still an amazement for God's goodness and provision.

Dad lived in the Scripture that says, "For I have learned to be content whatever the circumstances" (Phil. 4:11). And this was his last birthday gift to me.

6

Dads and Their
Finances

1

Saving Money Any Way You Can

. . . .

■ Our family has not seen much—if any—increase in real income this decade, and we have a sinking feeling that we will never get ahead. The pressure to live within our means is placing tremendous stress on our marriage. I want to put food on the table, but it seems as though we are one blown engine or one huge home repair away from going under. How can we turn the tide with our family finances?

You're not alone, that's for sure. Across the country, millions of families are looking for ways to save a few bucks on basic household expenses, such as food, clothing, housing, education, and health care. Often, saving $200 or $300 a month on disposable spending (food, clothes, restaurants, appliances, etc.) can be the difference between making it and falling further into debt.

Several years ago in *Focus on the Family* magazine, I (Mike Yorkey) described how my wife, Nicole, and I were consistently overspending. It was time to get a handle on our expenses. I sought several Christian CPAs for advice, and they told us to start a budget and stick to it.

■ **Did you make a budget? I don't think my wife and I have the willpower to stick to one.**

No, we didn't, but Nicole and I began tracking our expenses, which was illuminating. For the first time, we had a pretty good idea of where our money was *going*. We looked for ways to cut expenses, and we succeeded for the most part. As for the budget, we still don't have one, but neither do 95 percent of families in North America.

■ **Every month it's a struggle to pay all the bills, but I'm glad our family can support our local church and our Compassion child. Isn't this why we're close to the edge?**

It sure is. While dealing with the demands to pay for all the "basics," Christian families are committed to supporting their local church, which means a significant chunk of income—10 percent in many households—is "tithed." You mentioned that you also support missionaries, and other Christian families give generously to parachurch organizations. With all your sacrificial giving, it's little wonder that you live even closer to the edge.

But God will meet our needs, as He has promised in Malachi 3:10: " 'Bring the whole tithe into the storehouse, that there may be food in my house. Test me in this,' says the Lord Almighty, 'and see if I will not throw open the floodgates of heaven and pour out so much blessing that you will not have room enough for it.' "

Being God's children means we can go to Him with our finances. He knows *exactly* where we are and knows our needs before we do. Whenever you face an important buying decision, pray about it. Just as He can direct you to a good used car that won't break down every other month, He can also help you find a much-needed pair of soccer shoes at a garage sale.

■ **I have to admit that I'm a worrywart, however. I don't know how we do it sometimes, but it's a terrible strain on my wife and me to have $50 left in the checking account on payday.**

Although the Lord instructs us not to worry (Matt. 6:25-26), it's human nature to be concerned about making it to the end of the month without dipping into our savings accounts. If you're being careful about your spending—and not going to the plastic and getting trapped by credit card interest—you're getting the job done.

As nineteenth-century author Charles Dickens said during an end-of-the-year accounting: "Income: Twenty shillings. Expenses: 19.6. That equals happiness. Income: Twenty shillings. Expenses 20.6. That equals misery."

Finally, consider this point: Don't become obsessive-compulsive about saving every nickel. Yes, it's good stewardship to spend money wisely and stretch our paychecks as far as we can, but don't fret over leaving the 50-cent coupon for McDonald's at home. The key word is balance. God has given us financial resources, be they limited or plentiful. If we're not happy with a little money, then we won't be happy with a lot of money.

■ **Another problem is today's ad-saturated society. Everywhere we turn we are blitzed with "Sale of the Century!" advertisements. It seems as though we have to spend money to save money, and I fall into that trap all the time.**

Have you ever seen a Mitsubishi big-screen TV marked down from $2,499 to $1,899 and thought, *This is our big chance to save $600!* Don't forget that it's still going to cost you two grand to get that big-screen TV into the back of your minivan.

And the number of places where we can shop is extraordinary. Fifty years ago, many of our grandparents grew up in towns with one market, one hardware store, and one gas station. These days, huge one-stop supermarkets, expansive warehouse clubs, and brightly lit retail outlets have sprung up in the suburbs like mushrooms.

Our grandparents shopped at a Five & Dime; we can choose from Wal-Mart, Sears, Montgomery Wards, and yet another Wal-Mart. They had one clothing store; we have Kmart, Marshalls, Ross Dress for Less, and Target. They had once-a-season sales; we have coupons, rebates, and discount books. They had a Sears catalog; we have twenty-four-hour mail-order companies with 800-numbers. They paid cash; we have credit cards.

■ **With all these options, how do we keep our heads and spend wisely? What's a good deal and what's not?**

Since families can do little to save on housing and taxes, the best chance to reduce costs is on discretionary spending. This is where your wife can make a difference. In fact, searching out good deals on groceries and clothes—which takes time—can become a part-time job. Perhaps it can tip the scales toward Mom staying home to raise the kids rather than reentering the workforce.

■ **Where's a good place to start?**

Groceries, and that's why it's a war zone out there. Not only are supermarkets, grocery stores, and warehouse clubs locked in Mortal Kombat, but also value-conscious consumers feel like donning flak jackets every time they stride through the automatic doors.

For many, grocery shopping used to be a fairly mundane chore reserved for Saturday mornings. No longer. As families seek ways to cut corners, groceries come under scrutiny because of the hefty bite they chomp out of the family budget.

If you're a family of four, for instance, you're probably averaging $600 a month or $7,200 a year on groceries—maybe more. (Our definition of groceries is all food items, plus paper towels, toilet paper, diapers, aluminum foil, shoe polish, shampoo, dog food, etc.)

Let's say your family's take-home pay amounts to $2,000 a month. If groceries are $600, you're spending 33 percent of your income for groceries. Money can be saved here, and to accomplish that you should:

► Buy store brands
► Shop the loss leaders
► Stock up on sales
► Use coupons
► Frequent warehouse clubs

The *best* overall strategy is to "cherry pick" from all five of these options.

■ How do we save money at supermarkets?

Supermarkets' biggest strength is variety: You can choose from 147 kinds of cereal, 22 brands and types of peanut butter, and 25 brands of chocolate-chip cookies. Every day, supermarkets stock 30,000 different products, and at any one time have 1 million items on the shelves.

So where do you start? Actually, you should be well prepared to shop before you drive into the parking lot. That means going through your refrigerator and pantry and compiling a "tight" grocery list. But you also need to be flexible by buying what's on sale.

■ How do you find what's on sale?

Go through the supermarket flyers inserted into the Wednesday newspaper or mailed to your home. Take a look at each flyer's front page; that's where the loss leaders (items sold at a loss to lure customers) are bannered. Inside, you'll find in-store coupons or special "buy one, get one free" or "four cans for a dollar" ads.

As you push your cart through the store, take your time. When you're juggling coupons, reading price comparisons, and making snap judgments on which brand to buy, don't rush yourself. You're *earning* money every time you make the right choice.

■ My children want me to buy name brands—like Oreo cookies—because they see all the advertisements on TV. But when I see the Safeway brand of Oreo cookies for 33 percent less, those cookies certainly look the same to me. Should I buy the store brand?

Yes, you should, and more and more cost-conscious shoppers are snapping up "house brand" or private-label products these days. Private-labels now account for more than 20 percent of all grocery and consumer-product sales.

Think about it: Why should we buy Advil when Kroger's ibuprofen is exactly the same thing? Read the label: Each tablet contains ibuprofen USP 200 mg.

Supermarket chains, in an effort to fend off stiff competition from warehouse clubs, are heavily promoting store brands. Many place their house labels right next to the name-brand products and hang "Compare to the National Brand and Save!" stickers on the shelves.

That's a smart move by grocers: Store brands cost anywhere from 20 to 50 percent less than their name-brand cousins.

■ **But what about quality and taste? You're not going to tell me that Häagen-Dazs chocolate ice cream beats Lucerne Neapolitan.**

When *Consumer Reports* magazine conducted a taste test between name-brand and store labels, they judged the differences to be nil. Many of the magazine's conclusions stated: "No brand stood out. Shop by price."

You may disagree, and you'll have plenty of company. There can be considerable differences in quality and taste for certain products such as orange juice, chocolate chips, frozen entrees, ice cream, and canned vegetables. Some joke that store-brand green beans are made up of end pieces, and maybe the white cream filling of your store-brand chocolate cream-filled cookies doesn't taste like the real thing.

Despite the variations in taste, you should still buy store brands for the savings. Sure, the store-label canned corn might be a lesser grade, but you really have to be a gourmet—or fussy—to turn up your nose at smaller kernels of corn.

If you're still not convinced, look at the price comparison again. Can you justify a $40 difference in taste? Asked another way, would you rather spend that $40 on something else? All these reasons underscore why you should purchase the store brands as a rule, while making small adjustments for personal taste.

Calculated over a year, savings amount to $2,000 a year by purchasing store brands every week. It makes more sense to spend less money.

■ **You mentioned coupons earlier. I have to admit that I feel funny carrying my wife's coupon klatch and holding up the line while the checkout clerk scans my coupons. How much am I really saving?**

Folks who make couponing part of their supermarket strategy can save up to 20 percent, but it's probably more realistic to expect 10 percent savings.

Smart couponers have a three-tier strategy when they walk into a grocery store. The simplest coupon transaction is a **single play**, which happens when a consumer uses a standard "cents-off" or C/O

EATING OUT

Eating out is one of life's joys, although restaurant food is not a very good deal when compared to home cooking. But it's nice to be served, eat a delicious meal, and have somebody else do the cleanup.

Eating out, however, can blow a hole in the family budget, unless you keep these ideas in mind:

▶ **Make it an "occasion" to eat out.** Impromptu meals should be discouraged. You know the scenario: It's 6 P.M., and everyone's coming home tired and hungry, and dinner hasn't been started yet. The next thing you know, your family of four is sitting down at a nearby Italian joint, and 45 minutes later, you leave the restaurant with indigestion and a $34 bill.

Instead, cook something fast, like grilled cheese and ramen soup. Better yet, eat up your leftovers or take a pre-cooked meal out of the freezer and pop it into the microwave. As a last resort, you can order take-out pizza. Little Caesar's will feed a small family for around $8.50.

▶ **Take advantage of "early bird" specials.** If you can get the family out of the house by 5:30, you can save 25 percent in some restaurants. Most kids are hungry early, anyway.

▶ **Use coupons.** You'll usually find restaurant coupons in your local newspaper, but they are often for weeknights when restaurants are looking to stimulate business. And don't worry about what the help thinks of discount dining. Be sure to tip on what the regular bill would have been.

▶ **Do "date nights" at lunch time.** Eating out with your spouse is a lot cheaper during the day. Plus, you can save on baby-sitting costs if the kids are in school.

▶ **Purchase a "dining club" membership.** Nearly every city has a dining club that offers two-for-one entrees. Ask your parents to give you a membership for Christmas.

▶ **If you're dying to go out but the money isn't there, make it dessert.** Drop in after the main rush, though.

coupon. Example: a straight 50 cents off a box of Rice Krispies.

But good couponers look for double plays and triple plays. What's a **double play?** Let's say your supermarket is having a half-price sale on Ragu spaghetti sauce. The cost for two jars is $1.77. You pull two jars of Ragu off the shelf and take two Ragu coupons out of your file box. If you have two 50-cent C/Os, that's a double play. Final cost: 77 cents ($1.77 minus $1 in coupons).

But if you're shopping in a supermarket that is doubling coupons, you can go for a **triple play!** Again, you pull two jars of Ragu off the shelf for $1.77. Then, you take two Ragu coupons out of your file box. If they are 50-cent C/Os, each coupon is doubled to $1 each, or $2 total. Because you paid $1.77 for the two jars but received $2 at the check-out stand, the supermarket just paid you 23 cents to purchase two jars of Ragu. (Some stores, however, will not do this, saying they will not pay out beyond the discount of the coupon.)

■ **Here's my $64,000 question: Are warehouse clubs—one of those cavernous, bare-bones, stack-it-to-the-ceiling, blow-it-out-in-bulk stores—actually *cheaper* for groceries?**

The answer is yes. I (Mike) once made three comprehensive shopping trips over a six-month period, comparing a local warehouse club with two supermarket chains.

In general, the warehouse club was 15 to 48 percent cheaper on food and grocery items. My results mirrored a similar test conducted by *Consumer Reports* magazine. A CR staffer shopped a warehouse club and a supermarket in New Jersey, using a grocery list similar to mine. The warehouse club came in at $76.71 and the supermarket at $128.53—67 percent more!

Of course, you have to spend more up front to get your savings (since you're buying in larger quantities), and you need lots of storage space at home. Also, many warehouse clubs are not conveniently located, but you can buy high-quality, name-brand products for less than the supermarket store brand in most cases.

If it's convenient, do your main shopping at a warehouse club, buying in bulk as much as you can. Then shop the supermarkets once a week for fresh vegetables and items you can't purchase at a warehouse club. Stock up on the loss leaders, especially in the meat department, and if you can make a double or triple couponing play, go for it!

This material is adapted from Saving Money Any Way You Can, © *1994 by Mike Yorkey. Published by Servant Publications, Box 8617, Ann Arbor, MI 48107. Used by permission.*

AUTOMOBILES

If you're in the market for a new car (and have decided you can afford it), you need to do your research. Customers who pay the most are the ones who "drop by" the showroom to kick a few tires. After getting caught up in all the leather upholstery and "new car" smell, they ink a deal cut to the dealer's advantage.

Instead, be an informed customer. That means going to the library and reading about the car you want to buy. You should talk to neighbors, church friends, and coworkers about where to get the best price. And then you should call the *Consumer Reports New Car Price Service* (800-933-5555) and use the computerized report to figure out the cost of the dealer invoice.

With that information in hand, you walk onto the lot and try not to act too excited. After test-driving the car, the salesperson will often ask you what you want to pay. You open with an offer of $150 over invoice. Be patient, this dance may take a couple of hours.

That offer won't work for a popular car like the Ford Explorer, but if you're purchasing a Taurus, for instance, you can make that offer stick if you hang tough. According to my research, most deals end up at $400 to $500 over dealer invoice.

Leasing has become cheaper than financing a car purchase through a bank, thanks to "dealer incentives" from the Detroit automakers. Remember, however, that it's cheapest to pay cash in the long run, and leases are full of legal mumbo-jumbo written to the dealer's advantage.

As for used cars, you need to know what the car's worth. You find out by going to your bank or library and asking for the Blue Book or the National Association of Auto Dealer's used-car price book. The best prices come from private party transactions, but those deals are fraught with peril. Have a good mechanic standing by to give the car the once-over. Finally, remember that you're the buyer. You can walk out at any time if you don't feel comfortable with the deal.

HOME FURNISHINGS

Since new furniture is incredibly expensive, keeping an eye out for used furniture is a good idea. Estate sales are more expensive than garage sales, but the quality will be better. Scanning the newspaper classifieds for used furniture is a hit-or-miss proposition; it may take a few weeks to find what you want.

But for those with their hearts set on a new entertainment center, several mail-order furniture companies based in North Carolina can save you 20 to 50 percent on name-brand furnishings.

One of the largest is Edgar B (800-255-6589), and you can request a 126-page color catalog for $25. After ordering your new Drexel-Heritage entertainment center, be prepared to wait for three to six months for arrival by truck. Also, know what you want and order everything at once. Shipping costs will be lower if everything is shipped together. Caveat emptor: There's no return on big-ticket items.

Besides Edgar B, you can shop from Furnitureland (919-841-4328), Rose Furniture Co. (919-886-6050), or Hickory Furniture Mart (800-462-6278).

CLOTHING

Never pay retail. The clothing business is so competitive that there's always a sale going on. Clothes are sold in "cycles," which means that if you can buy out of season (purchasing a winter jacket in April, for instance), you'll save 50 to 75 percent. Also, outlet malls have sprung up outside of major cities like spring mushrooms, and they are great places to find name-brand clothing at a deep discount.

To buy clothes on sale, you have to:

► Shop the department stores "doorbuster" sales three or four times a year.

► Keep an eye out for sales at the off-price stores, such as Ross Dress for Less and Marshalls. Many of them are not advertised.

► Check out the clearance racks. Every store has them.

► Shop at warehouse clubs. Sure, you can't try on anything, but the prices are incredible. If you keep your receipt and the tags on, you'll have no problem returning something that doesn't fit.

► Know prices so when a deal comes along, you can pounce on it.

2

Avoiding a Credit Meltdown

■ My daughter Cynthia called from college to say that American Express had sent her an unsolicited application in the mail. The accompanying promotional material said that as a good college student, she was eligible for a credit card. What do I do? Should I get her a credit card?

While it's true that having a credit card can come in handy for ordering mail-order merchandise or holding a hotel reservation, you have to ask yourself: *Why does my daughter need a credit card?* The sad fact of the matter is that only 30 percent of Americans pay off their credit balance each month. So if your daughter is going to have a credit card to just go into debt, then the answer is no.

But this would be a great opportunity to teach Cynthia about the difference between credit and debt. In fact, you must take the responsibility to train your children in the proper use of credit cards because they won't receive this training from anyone outside the home. It's not taught in schools or churches, and certainly not by peer groups. The home is the place where kids must get sound, consistent teaching.

■ **What's the number-one point I want to get across?**

Tell Cynthia that one of the primary points she needs to understand is the difference between credit and debt. *Credit is having the right to borrow.* Credit deals with the potential borrower's integrity —her faithfulness and timeliness in paying the bills. Based on that integrity, a potential lender extends credit. That credit may require either the personal guarantee of the potential borrower, as with a "signature loan," or collateral—some type of security interest in something of value. This can be either the item purchased or another asset of the potential borrower.

Thus credit is not the same thing as debt, but it is used to go into debt. Debt results when the credit extended is utilized for the purchase of some product or service. The Christian who believes having credit cards is wrong should understand that having credit cards does not cause one to go into debt. It only means credit has been made available to him. An individual's misuse of those credit cards causes him to go into debt.

■ **But I grew up in a home where "being able to afford it" meant we could pay cash for whatever we were purchasing.**

What a difference time makes! Today "being able to afford it" has nothing to do with whether you have the resources to pay for it. It means strictly "being able to afford the monthly payments."

As such, every borrowing decision can be manipulated simply by extending the length of time of repayment in order to make it "affordable." Prior to World War II, home mortgages rarely went beyond ten years. Today, thirty years is the standard, and in some cases, it's possible to get a fifty-year mortgage. Fifty years may be longer than the home will last.

This change in the way we view debt is one of its major deceptions. Debt-related deceptions are highly effective because they make borrowing appear to be the wise and logical thing to do. For example, if you believe that "being able to afford it" means being able to afford the payments rather than being able to pay cash, you're certainly not equipped to resist the advertising that offers "easy payments." Nor will you consistently resist the advertising slogan proclaiming "No payments until next year!"

■ **My wife, Marcia, never gave much thought to how much she was spending with credit cards. She and her friends went to the mall with the babies and spent the day just walking around. She was always buying things ahead of time: a cute outfit our son could wear next summer; a toy on sale that we could put away for Christmas. There was never anything major put on the credit card; just clothes, meals, gas, birthday gifts.**

We used to pay off our credit card bills completely each year with our income tax refund. Thus we had a great credit rating, and every year the banks offered us a higher limit. Then, of course, there was the Sears card, Montgomery Ward, Lord & Taylor, Marshall Field, Lerner, Wiebolt, Amoco, Shell, and Texaco. Oh, yeah, we also had a line of credit on our checking account for $2,000.

My wife says, "It's great to know we can go out and get anything we need at anytime," but I have a sinking feeling in the pit of my stomach. Are we headed in the right direction?

No, and it's time to make a U-turn. But your case is hardly unusual for a married couple. More than 75 percent of Americans use credit cards, and there's no doubt these ubiquitous pieces of plastic are a tremendous convenience. But the headaches and heartaches that accompany a mounting stack of unpaid and unpayable bills easily outweigh all the advantages of credit.

Your situation is a classic illustration of how easy it is to fall into the credit card trap. With a billion credit card accounts for a U.S. population of 265 million, there are nearly four credit cards for every man, woman, and child in the United States.

■ **Yes, but you wouldn't believe how many credit card solicitations we receive in the mail each month. They arrive with great come-ons, like airline miles, discounts on Ford cars, and "free" gas.**

Credit card companies aren't foolish, and they don't extend credit in order to lose money. What they've found is that merely putting a credit card in your hand will lead you to spend *34 percent more* than if you didn't have that credit card. And because their losses will typically run no more than 5 percent of the outstanding balances, lenders can afford the risk of putting credit into the hands of those who are not creditworthy. Charging an average of 14–20 percent interest, they much more than make up their losses from the millions of cardholders who pay their bills faithfully.

■ How can I determine whether I have a problem with debt?

Take this little test and circle your answers:

1. I spend money in the expectation that my income will increase in the future. True   False

2. I take cash advances on one credit card to pay off bills on another. True   False

3. I spend more than 20 percent of my income on credit card bills. True   False

4. I often fail to keep an accurate record of my purchases. True   False

5. I have applied for more than five credit cards in the past twelve months. True   False

6. I regularly pay for groceries with a credit card. True   False

7. I often hide my credit card purchases from my family. True   False

8. Owning several credit cards makes me feel richer. True   False

9. I pay off my monthly credit bills but let others slide, such as doctor's bills and utility bills. True   False

10. I like to collect cash from friends in restaurants and then charge the tab on my credit card. True   False

12. I have trouble imagining my life without credit cards. True   False

Now score your responses. How many times did you answer true?

- ► 1-4 True. You can probably keep going. You don't splurge uncontrollably.
- ► 5-8 True. Slow down, you have entered the caution zone. It's time to draw up a budget, pay off your bills, and reeval-

uate your spending habits.

▶ 9-12 True. You have to stop! You might be wise to consult a credit counselor or financial planner for help in changing your spending habits.

■ **How do people typically get into trouble with credit card debt?**

They get into trouble by falling victim to one or more popular misconceptions about credit. Their fall is hastened by the way these misconceptions appeal to our natural desires or fears, and by the fact that lenders aggressively promote this form of borrowing because they find it so profitable.

Let's cover three of the most common misunderstandings:

1. You can't live without it.

This easily accepted notion accounts for a lot of credit card purchases. To a large extent, it also accounts for why people who already have "enough" credit cards will apply for another when they see advertisements using that pitch.

Credit cards are used exclusively, however, to buy temporal and depreciating items—nothing of any permanence. They're often used to pay for entertainment, which is certainly important to living a well-rounded life, but it's not the reason for our existence. People also use them, as one wag put it, "to buy things they don't need with money they don't have to impress people they don't know."

One way to avoid unnecessary use of credit cards is to never make an impulse purchase. Always wait at least a day to buy something you want. If after twenty-four hours and careful reflection you still want the item enough to make a second trip back for it, you're more likely to be making a good decision.

2. Having a credit card means you're creditworthy.

While credit card companies are concerned about creditworthiness, they're much more concerned about their profits. They're willing to take some significant losses while earning almost 20 percent in interest.

Don't assume that just because you have a credit card, you can afford to take on debt. The test you took earlier should have highlighted whether you have a problem with credit cards. It's really scary, when you think about it, how easy it is to get approved on a credit card application. In some cases, it requires little more than your name, address, and telephone number.

3. You have to have a credit rating.

There is no such thing as a credit rating. Various organizations compile credit reports on people who have used credit, but there's no single source to which anyone could go to get your credit rating. There's no scale that evaluates you in relationship to everyone else.

Credit reporting agencies collect data regarding your credit history, payments, delinquencies, amounts borrowed, and so forth, but no central place gives you a credit rating.

The reality is that if you choose to avoid the use of credit cards, then even if there were a credit rating, you wouldn't need it. A credit rating presumes there's risk associated with lending you money. But if you never borrow money this way, there's no risk, and therefore no need for a credit rating.

Establishing a good credit history is simple. Pay all your bills on time and establish some banking relationships: that is, maintain checking and savings accounts. You don't need to borrow in order to have a good credit report.

■ **Let's get realistic here and realize that in the 1990s, we need a credit card for car rentals or purchasing baseball tickets over the phone. What are your recommendations?**

Most of us have to use credit cards at least occasionally to function in our credit card society. However, we don't have to use them to go into debt. There are three ways to get the benefits of using credit cards without going into debt:

1. Begin with a spending plan.
2. Use a debit card rather than a charge card.
3. Always pay the full balance at the end of the month.

Regarding a spending plan: Unless you're operating according to that hated word—budget—you'll never have any real reason to control your spending. To use credit cards to fund your living expenses is to invite temptation into spending decisions. As stated earlier, researchers have shown that you'll spend 34 percent more using a credit card than if you don't.

The way to use credit cards legitimately is for convenience only—staying within your spending plan and paying the balance in full when the bill comes. If you haven't already done so, set up an annual spending plan.

The second recommendation is to use a debit card rather than a normal credit card. An amount charged to a debit card is immediately deducted from your bank or brokerage account balance. It's really no different from writing a check.

You can use a card that lets you earn interest on the total account balance until either a charge comes in or a check written against the account clears the bank. When you use the debit card, enter the item in your checkbook just as if you had written a check. Then deduct it from your available balance.

In place of the check number in the check register, write "VISA." Using such a card allows you all the convenience advantages of a credit card, but you never have a credit card bill to pay because, in effect, it's paid the moment you use it.

The third recommendation is to never allow a month to go by without paying off the full balance. If you're tempted not to pay the full amount because it will make a big dent in your available cash, you're not using the credit card properly. A credit card can be a great convenience, but it should never be used to go into debt. The cost of credit card debt, from a low 7.9 "teaser" rate to usury 21 percent interest, is always greater than the economic return of whatever the card was used to buy.

■ **What happens if I can't follow those recommendations and get into trouble?**

If you are having problems paying your credit cards, put them in a Tupperware container filled with water and place the container in your freezer. That way you can only use your credit cards in an emergency.

For those not so disciplined, you may have to cut them up. By the time the credit card companies send you unsolicited replacements, your spending patterns should be reset.

This material is adapted from The Debt Squeeze *by Ron Blue and published by Focus on the Family. Copyright © 1989, Ron Blue. Used by permission. Ron Blue is president of a financial advisory firm in the Atlanta area.*

3

Dealing with Tax Time

. . . .

■ **Every April 15, I have to write a big fat check to the Internal Revenue Service. I have to admit that I don't act in a Christlike manner when signing over my hard-earned money to the IRS. How can I improve my attitude?**

If there is one cash outflow that everyone is anxious to reduce, it is income taxes. Some time ago, Ron Blue, a Christian financial counselor, had a client in his office who earned a very good income, and yet he was adamant that he did not want to pay taxes. He did not agree with the way the government spent his money.

Ron was tempted to ask him whether he would like to give up his automobile—because the road system would not be maintained without taxes—or whether he could sleep at night with no military forces to protect him, and whether he would like not to have national parks to visit, and so on.

■ **Wait a minute! We all know that government taxes are too high, and giving them more tax revenue concentrates their power and promotes wasteful spending. So don't give me this civics lesson.**

Okay, you made your point. No one is proposing that we should pay more than we rightfully owe in taxes. There is a big difference, however, between tax avoidance and tax *evasion*. Tax evasion results in a jail sentence; tax avoidance results in lower taxes, but almost never does it result in no taxes. Tax avoidance is planning wisely and prudently to pay a fair share of taxes, but no more than what is rightfully owed.

■ Why is it that we detest paying taxes?

The answer is multifaceted, but the primary reason is that we get no perceived benefit from paying taxes. Only in this area of our finances do we feel that once the money is gone, it seems to be gone forever. For the salaried and those living on a fixed income, taxes take a disproportionate share of income compared to those who have the opportunity and ability to use various tax-planning tools and techniques.

■ Well, how can I reduce my taxes? Inquiring minds want to know.

It's easy to reduce your taxes—just reduce your income. It's a guaranteed way to reduce taxes, and there is no risk to it. The point is that if your taxes are going up, your income is also going up. Taxes need to be put into proper perspective, and the proper perspective is that income taxes are levied only when there is income earned.

The second guaranteed way to reduce taxes is to spend more money on deductible items, such as charitable contributions, medical bills, interest costs, professional fees, and the like. But know that there is no free tax deduction anywhere, at any time, for anything!

When you read or hear of persons who pay no taxes or who pay low taxes and have huge incomes, that may be true in the short-term because of their high deductions, but those deductions have to be paid for at some time.

■ **What should be my guiding principle for tax deductions?**

Here you go: Don't ever expect to get a free tax deduction and never make a financial decision on the basis of its tax deductibility.

It is easy for a tax accountant to make the client happy by having him overpay on withholdings and quarterly tax estimates during the year so that he always gets a refund. But that does not make good economic sense. In fact, getting a refund check is a sign of poor stewardship.

■ **If I'm going to try to do something to lower my taxes, when should I start planning to do that?**

The most popular time for tax planning is December, with the second most popular month being April. Both months, however, are too late to do any serious tax planning. Once December 31 has passed, nothing can be done (other than an IRA or pension plan investment) to reduce taxes for the previous year. Most people know this and become rather panicky in the month of December, wondering how they are going to reduce their taxes.

It's far preferable to do most income tax planning at least one year in advance with monitoring and the necessary adjustments made in the plan at least quarterly during the year. This means that the tax planning you do on December 31 would not be for the current year, but for the next year, so that you are always one year ahead.

■ **What are timing strategies? I read about those once.**

Timing strategies involve the timing of the recognition of income and the deduction of expenses. The general rule is that you should always push income into a future year and pull expenses into the current year. Why? Because even if it does not change the tax bracket one way or the other, the utilization of a timing strategy does delay the payment of taxes.

■ **What are some of the most commonly overlooked itemized deductions?**

The common ones are medical and dental expenses; state and local taxes, including property taxes; income taxes and all personal property taxes; certain interest paid; charitable contributions of either cash or property.

The overlooked deductions are:

► Expenses paid as a volunteer for charitable organizations;

► Points paid on a purchase of a personal residence;

► Giving away old clothes, furniture, etc., to charitable organizations.

Remember, tax planning is very important, but it is not a panacea for cash-flow problems. Every decision that causes a reduction in taxes has a corresponding cost associated with it. Never forget that there is no "free lunch," especially in the cafeteria of tax reductions.

This material is adapted from Master Your Money *by Christian financial counselor Ron Blue. Used by permission of Thomas Nelson Publishers, Nashville, Tennessee.*

4

How to Talk Finances with Your Wife

. . . .

■ **Money is an emotional subject for Chantel and me. One evening, she announced, "You're too tight with our money." "All you want to do is spend," I rebutted. Why can't most couples talk about finances without arguing?**

Money matters can be either the best area of communication in a marriage, or the worst. It's usually the worst.

■ **Why is that?**

Because money is an emotional subject. Too often it is a vehicle to attack a spouse's personality, and most purchases are made not on the basis of agreed-upon priorities, but on impulses.

■ **How can we talk more easily about money?**

You and Chantel should go away for an entire weekend alone. First, you should discuss your feelings on a number of general subjects—the house, the furniture, the cars, retirement, the children's education. Then you should work it all down to a practical level and prepare a budget. If you don't do this, your financial decisions will be based not on objectivity, but on emotions.

■ **I'm not sure Chantel and I could even *begin* such a discussion. What ground rules should we observe?**

Most obviously, don't belittle your wife. Since men historically have held the majority of finance-related jobs, many think their wives aren't qualified to talk about money. On the contrary, women can be excellent money managers.

Of course, if you can't talk about money without getting into an argument, you should seek a counselor who will help you work out your animosities. You need to get rid of any bitterness before trying to develop a budget.

■ **What is at the heart of financial responsibility for couples?**

If you have no money in the bank and you have to charge car repairs to a credit card at 18 percent interest, you are acting irresponsibly. On the other hand, if you are a doctor and you have set aside $500,000 in a retirement plan and keep adding $50,000 to it each year, you have an unreasonable craving for financial security.

Everyone should try to save something. That's basic to financial responsibility. But it's helpful to distinguish here between saving and hoarding. Saving means putting money aside for a future need. Hoarding means putting it aside because it makes you feel better. As we put money into savings, we need to ask ourselves, "Am I meeting a need or reacting to a fear?"

■ **Speaking of fear, bad economic news always seems to loom on the horizon. Although inflation has remained fairly steady in the nineties, analysts worry about the federal budget deficit. How worried should we be?**

The state of any economy is transient, and God wants us to be prudent: Save, invest, and set money aside for retirement and your children's college education. But to be consumed by fear of the future is unhealthy.

Let's admit, however, that some kinds of fear are healthy. If you are afraid of running across a highway with your eyes closed, that's good: God put the fear in you. Similarly, if you and your wife spend more than you make and get deeply in debt with no reserve, you should become apprehensive about the future. That fear tells you that you're acting unwisely.

■ What should we do to develop a savings plan?

You must ask yourselves, "Where is our real hope for the future? Is it in our savings? Is it in Social Security?" (If so, you have a *big* surprise coming!) Or is it really in Jesus Christ?"

For the couple who sincerely trusts in Christ, heed this warning: God will test that commitment. Sometimes He will either remove the surplus and see how we respond, or He will bring to our attention a large need to see if we will use part of our stored money to meet it. That kind of money is hardest to give away, because we feel like we've already spent it by setting it aside.

On the whole, we're not savers—we're consumers. If you "cashed out" the average sixty-five-year-old man—liquidated all his assets and liabilities—he'd be worth a mere $100.

Most families don't save anything, much less hoard. The typical couple in America, if the husband lost his job, could not last for even two weeks without government help.

The writer of Proverbs 30:8 puts it very well: "Keep falsehood and lies far from me; give me neither poverty nor riches, but give me only my daily bread."

■ How should we define success, and how can it be achieved?

Society defines success as a family, a nice house, a couple of cars, two weeks on a houseboat, three television sets, an IRA, and a college education for our kids. In God's eyes, those things are irrelevant. Even Christians have fallen into the success trap.

Suppose a young man graduated with honors from law school. Then he told his parents, "I want to go to South America and spend the rest of my life sharing the message of Jesus Christ. The job pays $18,000 a year, and I'm going to learn to live on that."

How many parents would be supportive of such a decision? Not many. They'd be aghast and think their son is a failure.

Should a man be considered a success if he achieves financial security but fails to offer his children proper guidance? Or if he has a miserable marriage and dies feeling he's wasted his life?

■ **What biblical guidelines should couples observe in financial planning?**

A key principle is: Would a financial crisis destroy your relationship with God? Would you cling to tangible resources rather than to God? That's what Jesus meant when He said, "No servant can serve two masters. Either he will hate the one and love the other, or he will be devoted to one and despise the other. You cannot serve both God and Money" (Luke 16:13).

Look at God's promise in Matthew 6:33. Seek *first* His kingdom, and all things will be added to you. In other words, don't deplete your energies seeking bigger homes and nicer cars. By seeking God's kingdom, you can be sure your every need will be met.

This material is adapted from an interview with Larry Burkett, a well-known Christian financial counselor, which originally appeared in "Financial Responsibility" by John Carvalho, Focus on the Family magazine, April 1986. Copyright © 1986, Focus on the Family. Used by permission.

5

Cash in on Savings

. . . .

■ **I've already made plans for spending my tax return check, but I'm promising myself that I'll do something smart with the cash this year. Sounds as though I got all my ducks in a row, doesn't it?**

Maybe until the month of June, when you get back on that dreaded paycheck-to-paycheck roller coaster. Just hope that your transmission doesn't go out.

But before you blow all that cash on a family vacation or a new computer, consider this: What if you *saved* your tax return this year? Or this: What if you called your company's payroll department tomorrow and took one more deduction?

By saving this year's tax return, you could start a nest egg to carry you and your family through life's inevitable emergencies. And if you increase the number of deductions you claim on your W-4 form at work, your paycheck immediately increases. By putting the extra cash into a savings plan, you will earn interest, instead of allowing the government to hold on to your money—and keep the interest.

Here is why you need a savings plan: The writer of Proverbs 6:6-8 encourages us to plan for the unexpected: "Go to the ant, you sluggard; consider its ways and be wise! It has no commander, no overseer or ruler, yet it stores its provisions in summer and gathers its food at harvest." The writer of Proverbs 21:20 also says, "In the house of the wise are stores of choice food and oil, but a foolish man devours all he has."

■ **So is Scripture saying that I have to think longer than just paycheck to paycheck?**

Right. Just when you think your job is secure or your health is excellent, a layoff or disabling injury can leave you reeling financially if you're not prepared for it. Having a savings account will allow you to "borrow" from yourself rather than from family members or the bank.

Also, you will someday have to replace your big-ticket items. If you don't save money for your next car, for example, you could be in debt every six years (that's how long most Americans keep their cars). You may end up paying interest for the rest of your life and never get out of debt.

■ **But how do I save money that I don't have?**

You may think that a savings account is just a dream. But no matter what your financial situation, you can create more income, sell your assets, or cut your present spending.

To earn more money, you will have to clock some overtime hours or moonlight by delivering Domino's pizza in the early evenings.

As for selling your assets, it can't provide you with an ongoing income, but it is a good way to start a savings account. You could, for example, hold a big garage sale or sell that speedboat in the backyard. As you take inventory of the items you could live without, you'll be surprised at how much cash is sitting right under your nose.

Finally, you can cut your spending. This is the most profitable option, since you'll see the money right away. If you earned $100 a week at a part-time job, you'd be lucky to see $65 of it. But if you cut your grocery bill by $200 a month, you will have 100 percent of that money for savings.

■ With all those options, where do I begin?

Make a list of where your income goes each month. Be very detailed and account for every cent if possible. Next, decide where you can cut back. Can you take your lunch to work instead of eating out? Is cable TV really necessary? What if you use public transportation or carpool to lessen your automotive costs? Remember: Every penny counts. Even if it's only $5 a week, you must begin saving *something*.

■ How big should my savings account eventually be?

Most financial planners recommend that you have three to six month's living expenses set aside. A nice round figure would be $10,000. The extra cushion will give you some peace of mind.

■ Are you nuts! Do you know how long it would take me to save $10,000?

Sure, the same amount of time it would take you to live from paycheck to paycheck a few years from now. With a little preparation and a few cutbacks, you can reach that $10,000 goal in almost no time.

Suppose you're starting today with nothing in the bank. If you put $10 a week in your money market account and let it earn an annual 6 percent interest, it will grow to $10,000 in 12.8 years. Not a bad deal for only $10 a week, though 12.8 years may seem like an eternity.

But what if you tightened your budget and saved $30 a week? You'd reach your $10,000 goal in just 5.4 years. And if you really got crazy and saved $50 a week, you'd be swimming in dough in less than four years.

The earlier you start saving, the better. Let's say Jack starts a paper route when he is eight years old and saves $600 his first year. He deposits the money into an individual retirement account (IRA) that earns 10 percent interest, then continues saving and depositing $600 each year until he is 18. At the end of ten years, Jack's savings total $6,600, which he doesn't plan to touch until he's sixty-five.

Pete doesn't have a paper route, but he starts a savings plan after college. At age twenty-five, he puts $2,000 into an IRA that earns 10 percent interest annually. He will continue to do this every year for forty years until he is sixty-five.

Whose fund do you think will be larger—Jack's IRA into which he put $6,600 or Pete's IRA, into which he put $80,000?

■ **It's gotta be Pete.**

No, Jack is the winner. His IRA will grow to $1,078,000, which is 162 times more than what he put in as a child. Pete will also do well with his investment, which will grow to $973,000. But Jack's earlier start, even with smaller amounts and deposits for fewer years, makes the difference. The "miracle" of compounding interest—interest earned on your principal *and* on your earned interest—will be on his side for more years.

The moral of this story is simple: Start saving today! The longer you wait to put money away, the less time compounding interest will have to work its magic. It's easy to put off saving until after you've gotten through an emergency, but the trouble is that an "emergency" will usually come up during every paycheck for the rest of your life. You must decide to save *no matter what.*

■ **Yes, but it's very hard not to get to the end of the month without dipping into savings to pay the bills.**

To avoid procrastination, have part of your paycheck automatically deposited into your savings account. It's easy, convenient, and encourages discipline. Plus, your savings may well be insured and available for withdrawal without penalty.

Also, take advantage of your employee savings plan—known as a 401(k) or a 403(b). Under such a plan, your employer deducts part of your pay before it is taxed and puts it into a retirement account. Some employers will even match every dollar of your money with $1 of theirs up to a certain amount. Though a 401(k) is primarily a retirement program from which you cannot withdraw early without a tax penalty, your tax savings and employer's dollars make it very attractive. In fact, with an employee-match program, where else can you double your money right off the bat?

■ **You've talked a lot about compounding interest. Can you explain it in plain English?**

In financial terminology, simple interest is interest paid on the principal *and* the earned interest. You should find a savings account or investment that offers compounding interest.

Let's say you deposit $1,000 in a one-year bank certificate of deposit (CD) that pays *simple* interest of 7 percent annually. After the first month, you will earn $5.83 of interest. But the bank won't give you that $5.83 until the end of the year: They'll hold on to it without paying you any interest. At the end of the year, you will have earned $70 in simple interest.

But let's say you deposited that same $1,000 into a CD with *compounding* interest. The first month, the bank pays you only on your principal, because you haven't earned any interest yet. But after the first month, they credit your account with $5.83. For the coming month, you'll earn interest on $1,005.83 instead of only on your original $1,000 of principal.

The second month, you'll earn $5.87 in interest, only 4 cents more than the previous month. By the end of the year, your total interest earned will be $72.29. That's $2.29 more than simple interest would have paid, and it came your way just by changing one item in the CD agreement.

■ **Do a few cents matter so much?**

For just $1,000 and for only one year, probably not. But when you consider how much you will have on deposit in a savings account over your lifetime, the difference can amount to thousands of dollars.

A word of caution: Savings accounts that compound daily are not always the best choice. A 7-percent CD with *quarterly* compounding, for example, has a better return than a 6-percent CD with *daily* compounding.

■ **Okay, we've been talking a lot of numbers here. Can you put a spiritual perspective on all this?**

In John 6, a group of people followed Jesus and His disciples onto a mountainside. When Jesus asked where they could get food to feed the crowd, the disciples responded in terms of what man could do: "Eight months' wages would not buy enough bread for each one to have a bite!"

Jesus, however, saw the situation in terms of what God could do. In what seemed like a hopeless situation—a hungry crowd, five small barley loaves, and two fishes—He said, "Have the people sit down."

When He said this, it's easy to imagine the disciples chatting among themselves in disbelief: "Wow! Did you hear that? There's no food, no place to get any, and no money to pay for it even if we knew where it was!" But that didn't matter to Christ: He knew His Father would provide.

Holding two small fishes and five loaves of bread, Jesus thanked God, then began distributing the food. With the touch of the Master's hand, the food multiplied many times. After everyone had eaten to satisfaction, there were twelve loaves of bread left! The disciples, who had doubted God before, stood in awe of His miracle.

Today, thousands of years after He fed that crowd, God is still working miracles. No matter how little money you have to begin a savings plan, start with what you have. As you remember to be a good steward of your money, He will bless your family and provide in ways you can't imagine. He expects His children to do all they can, then "sit down" and watch Him work. Are you sitting down?

This material is adapted from writings by Christian financial counselor Austin Pryor, author of Sound Mind Investing *(Moody Press). Pryor's* Sound Mind Investing *newsletter is terrific. For a free information packet, call (502) 426-7420. He lives in Louisville, Kentucky.*

6

God's Mutual Fund

. . . .

by Tom Pryor

When my pastor encouraged me to tithe 10 percent of my hard-earned income a few years ago, I was inherently skeptical. We were barely making it from paycheck to paycheck before I took that step of faith. Since then, that commitment has turned out to be the best "investment" I have ever made for my family's well-being and future.

I call it "God's Mutual Fund" when I sit down each week to write my tithe check to my church. I am pooling my family's resources with many other families in a mutual interest of exalting our Lord and Savior.

Here are my Top 10 Reasons to invest in God's Mutual Fund:

1. The investment yields an outstanding return (2 Cor. 9:10-11).

2. It has trustworthy fund managers, usually a group of wise elders.

3. The fund guarantees a return on our investment (Mal. 3:10).

4. We are pooling our resources with others who are of the same mind as us.

5. The funds are directed to worthy causes that evangelize

others and equip missionaries to have an impact on the world before Jesus returns.

6. The fund prospectus is rooted in proven facts—the Bible.

7. Everyone is eligible to participate in this fund. There are no qualifications to be met such as for an Individual Retirement Account or 401(k).

8. This is a "no-load" fund. Every dollar invested goes to work for you and your family.

9. The return on this investment cannot be taxed. The benefits accrue until eternity.

10. The risk is higher if we don't invest in this fund. In Leviticus 27:30, we learn that everything we have comes from the Lord.

God first loved me. I now love Him. He is my partner at home and at work. If you do not currently tithe, I strongly encourage you to review the Bible-based prospectus of God's Mutual Fund.

Remember Paul's admonition: "Whoever sows sparingly will also reap sparingly, and whoever sows generously will also reap generously" (2 Cor. 9:6).

Tom Pryor lives in Arlington, Texas.

7

Treasures in Heaven

. . . .

by Bob Welch

When my pastor spoke recently from the Book of Matthew about "not storing up for yourselves treasures on earth, where moth and rust destroy," I couldn't help but think back to an auction I'd once attended.

It was no ordinary auction. The public could bid on unclaimed items that people had left behind in safe-deposit boxes. These items were once deemed so important that people paid money to have them safeguarded in steel.

Diplomas, children's report cards, letters . . .

I remember how we shuffled along, past the coin collections, pocket watches, and jewelry to documents and small items sealed in plastic bags.

Boy Scout patches, receipts from a Waikiki hotel, a child's crayon drawing of a bunny rabbit . . .

It was all unclaimed property, waiting to be auctioned—the forgotten or overlooked possessions of owners now dead.

Rosaries, letters, train tickets . . .

Each bag was a mystery—the clues doing more to arouse curiosity than to provide answers. I read the immigration papers of Udolf

Matschiner, who arrived at Ellis Island in 1906. Did he find what he was looking for in America?

Two marbles, three stones, and a belt buckle . . .

Why these things? Did they represent some special memory, some special person?

Passports, telegrams, newspaper clippings . . .

A yellowed article from a 1959 Los Angeles newspaper was headlined "Vlahovich's Mother Sobs at Guilty Verdict." A mother's son had been convicted of murder. The mother wept, pleading with the judge to spare her son. "Take my blood," she screamed. "Kill me!" What happened? Did she watch her son die in San Quentin's electric chair?

Undeveloped film, birth certificates, marriage certificates . . .

The official business of life intermingled with the unofficial business of life—a lock of blond hair, a child's math paper, and a poem called "Grandmother's Attic," typed on a typewriter with a sticky e.

While up in Grandmother's attic today
In an old red trunk neatly folded away
Was a billowy dress of soft old gray
Of rose brocade were the panniers wide
With quilted patterns down the side
And way in the back against the wall
Of the little old trunk was an old silk shawl
Silver slippers, a fan from France
An invitation to a dance
Written across the program blue
Was "Agatha dear, may I dance with you?"

It was as if those of us at the auction had been allowed entry into hundreds of Grandmother's Attics, the attics of unknown people.

Diaries, photographs, the ink print of a newborn's feet . . .

In death's wake, most of the items spoke volumes about life. They also suggested a sense of finality, a realization that life on earth ends, and you can't take anything with you.

So what will we leave behind?

A six-by-twelve-inch box full of mementos can speak volumes about what we valued. But it's only a whisper compared to the legacy of our lives themselves.

Amid our he-who-dies-with-the-most-toys-wins world, perhaps

we should dare to leave . . .

An investment in what God so dearly loves—other people.

An example of a life guided not by the capricious winds of culture, but the rock-solid promises of Christ.

And an inspiration to our children to become all God has designed them to be.

"Store up for yourselves treasures in heaven, where moth and rust do not destroy, and where thieves do not break in and steal," my pastor concluded that Sunday morning. "For where your treasure is, there your heart will be also."

Ah, heaven. The ultimate safe-deposit box.

Bob Welch is features editor of the Register-Guard *newspaper in Eugene, Oregon.*

7

Dads and Their Work

1

Jobs vs. Family: Striking a Balance

. . . .

■ My friend George is a successful executive with a "Big 8" accounting firm. Only thirty-two years old, he's been promoted to partner after ten years in the trenches.

I have to say that he's dedicated to his job. He leaves home at 7 A.M. sharp for the hour-long commute. He often puts in eleven-, twelve-, even fourteen-hour days, arriving home after 9 P.M. He often goes to the office at least one day on weekends, sometimes two. His oft-voiced complaint is too much work and too little time to do it.

His three children are growing up without his notice; they barely know him. His wife feels like a single parent, trying to keep up with all the household chores, errands, carpools, and other parental duties. What hurts worst of all is that they haven't been to church together in ages. How can I help George see the light?

George's problem is even though he says he loves his family, the fact is that he's married to his job, not them. A hefty salary has seduced him, and the power and perks of corporate life has blinded him. His values are misplaced, and until he gets his priorities in line, don't be surprised if you hear that his wife checks out of the marriage some time in the future.

■ **I've heard George say that anyone who puts in an eight-hour day is "lazy."** I think he's actually afraid to leave the office before his boss leaves, and his boss rarely gets out of there before 8:30 P.M. His boss even sent a memo around stating, "I don't want to hear about weekends adding time to the schedule. God made weekends so we could catch up, not so we could fall further behind." Can you help me understand this life as a corporate manager?

Competition has grown more fierce in the workplace, and American companies are being driven to the wall. From New York to Los Angeles, companies are continuing to "downsize" operations—a euphemism for layoffs. The result is that the remaining employees must try to manage the same workload. Because of the erosion of our manufacturing base, firms are forced to offer intangibles—such as service—to compete in a world market. Competition in service means longer hours and greater efforts to meet or exceed the demands of the customer.

Tough-minded young professionals like George are rising fast because their high energy and aggressive nature are exactly what top management believes will give the firm the competitive edge. Bright, career-oriented women are also being promoted as never before. The face of management is changing. It's younger, tougher, leaner, and meaner.

■ **My goodness. Do you mean that everyone in upper management believes that anyone who puts in an honest eight-hour day is "lazy?"**

Some years back, David Ogilvy, writing in *Confessions of an Advertising Man*, made this statement: "If you stay home and tend your gardens and children, I will love you more as a human being, but don't expect to be the first person promoted in your group."

Consider the implications of this statement for the family! Management gurus really believe that those who want to get ahead must sacrifice the family on the altar of work. What's even worse is that a whole generation of white-collar workers are going through life never knowing what a forty-hour work week is like.

When *Fortune* magazine polled America's top corporate chiefs on the subject, their collective response was: "Stop whining and get back to work. You ain't seen nothing yet!" The CEOs believe American companies will have to push their managers *even harder* to keep up with global competition.

Little wonder that a Lou Harris poll found the workweek has increased from 40.6 hours to 46.6 over the last twenty years. For professional people, the number is even higher: fifty-two hours a week. Small-business and corporate executives put in fifty-seven hours a week.

■ **All this time must be coming at the expense of the family, like ours, right?**

You got it. Parents spend *40 percent* less time with their children than they did twenty-five years ago, according to an analysis by the Family Research Council. In the mid-sixties, an average parent spent about thirty hours a week with a child. Today, the average parent spends only seventeen hours.

This means no time for cheering a daughter's soccer game, hearing about Junior's fourth-grade teacher over dinner, or strolling through the neighborhood on a twilight walk.

■ **I know George can't keep this demanding schedule up—or anyone else trying to work sixty-hour weeks. Is anyone addressing the problem of burnout?**

Stress cracks are beginning to show through corporate America. Flesh and blood, after all, have limitations. Workaholism—whether it comes from within or is required—is not only creating havoc on the family, but also it's taking its toll on worker's health and mental well-being.

As burnout becomes more commonplace among management circles, companies are discovering that "survival of the fittest" promotion policies alienate—and lose—their best talent. More and more valued managers are bailing out and making midlife career changes to get out from underneath the relentless pressure to work twelve-hour days.

■ **Should Christian managers and employees abandon the search for excellence, as it is presently defined?**

Not at all. It's time American companies and workaholics hear a reminder about what our priorities should be. Meanwhile, we should be working smarter, doing things right the first time and, above all, getting our priorities in order.

■ **What are some strategies then?**

► **Pray about it.** Ask God to help you order your life according to His priorities. Examine what's important. If you're not committed to your family, you can't expect them to be committed to you.

► **Think ahead.** Ask yourself how your job will affect your family this year, as well as five years from now. Time does pass more quickly than we think, and we'll soon be facing the consequences of our present work decisions.

► **Have lunch with your wife more often.** If you have to miss family dinner, then invite your wife to lunch. Give her your undivided attention during that precious hour. This can have a wondrous effect on your marriage.

► **Block out a few minutes for yourself.** Set the alarm ten minutes earlier and aim for a gentler introduction to the day. Taking a short walk or spending extra time in the Word will do wonders for your blood pressure too.

► **If your family is suffering, consider changing jobs.** *No* job is worth sacrificing your wife or children. No career is more important than your relationship with those you love.

► **Ask permission to work at home.** More and more companies are allowing employees to pursue this option in this day and age of computers and fax modems. Find a Christian in the human resources department and explain your desire to work at home in order to spend more time with your family.

▶ **Negotiate with your boss.** Many superiors are simply unaware of the pressure they are putting on an employee's family by demanding overtime. Speak up! You may be surprised how reasonable your boss can be if you state your case.

As with most things, the modern world has turned divine values upside down. It's up to us—worker by worker—to get our lives and families back on the right track.

This material is from writings by Brian Knowles of Arcadia, California, and from William R. Mattox of Montclair, Virginia.

A LESSON FOR ALLISON

by William R. Mattox

I am not the kind of guy who normally takes part in feminist "consciousness-raising" efforts, but I participated in last year's "Take Your Daughter to Work Day" because I have an eight-year-old daughter whose self-esteem matters a great deal to me.

For the uninitiated, "Take Your Daughter to Work Day" is an annual event dreamed up by the Ms. Foundation in response to research showing that girls' self-esteem often plummets during the fragile preteen and early adolescent years. By exposing young girls to successful women in the workplace, organizers hope that girls will learn to think more highly of females in general and of themselves in particular.

So let me tell you about the great day I had with my daughter, Allison. In the morning, she attended a meeting chaired by a woman who often makes radio and television appearances. Later, she talked with a female colleague who has collaborated with me on several writing projects.

At lunch, Allison dined with a woman who has worked as a staffer in the U.S. Congress and the Canadian Parliament. And in the afternoon, she talked to a young woman who recently graduated from Johns Hopkins University and is now serving as a health-policy analyst.

I am sure all of this was very interesting to Allison, but the clincher came at the end of the day. As Allison and I sat down to talk about her experiences, I pointed out that some of the important tasks carried out by my female colleagues are tasks my wife, Jill, performed in jobs she held prior to motherhood. She used to do some writing and public speaking. She used to meet regularly with congressional leaders and senators. And she has a Phi Beta

continued next page

Kappa key from her college days.

After I reminded my daughter of these things, I looked her in the eye and said, "Allison, you must be a very special young girl. Mom could be using her talents and skills in all sorts of jobs in the workplace, but she has chosen instead to use them at home teaching you. Mom must love you very, very much and think that you are very, very important."

Somehow, I think that at that moment my daughter's self-esteem rose to a level heretofore unimagined by the organizers of "Take Your Daughter to Work Day." And for that, I owe a debt of gratitude to Jill, whose esteem-building job as a stay-at-home mom rarely receives the public esteem it deserves.

2

I've Got the Blues

....

■ **I feel tired all the time, and I have to admit it's getting harder and harder to get up in the morning and face the day. What can you say to inspire me?**

Rolf Benirschke, a placekicker with the San Diego Chargers in the 1980s, heard about a person who didn't give up when everyone said it would have been okay to do just that. This story happened in 1986 during one of the worst years in Charger history. The team started the season 1-6, and Don Coryell, the Charger coach, was handed his pink slip.

The new skipper of the sinking ship was Al Saunders, a receivers coach who didn't have any head coaching experience. The first game under Saunders was against the Dallas Cowboys, and Dallas soundly beat the Chargers, which meant they now had the worst record in the league at 1-7.

Their next game was against the team with the best record—the Denver Broncos, who had compiled a stellar 7-1 mark. Worse yet, San Diego had to play them at Mile High Stadium, where the Broncos win over 90 percent of the time. They were such underdogs that the Denver fans were expecting—no, demanding—an absolute massacre.

Before the game, the Charger team gathered for its usual pregame meal. The talk around the table was jocular and loose; no one was really talking about the Bronco game since their season was going nowhere.

Few looked up when Al Saunders, their new coach, stood up and asked, "Can I have your attention please?"

But all eyes turned toward him when he pulled a newspaper clipping out of his back pocket. "I want to tell you about a man who just ran the slowest marathon in history."

The players looked bewilderedly at one another. "What's this have to do with us?" asked one player.

"Yeah," piped in another, "I know we don't have much team speed, but come on, Coach."

Saunders took his time. He held up the clipping. "It says here that Bob Wieland just ran the New York Marathon in two days, two hours, and twenty-seven minutes."

■ **Did I hear you right? Did he say two *days*, two hours, and twenty-seven minutes?**

You heard right. Most people can walk a marathon in six or seven hours.

"Well, this man ran the New York Marathon without any legs," continued Saunders. "You see, he'd been in Vietnam, and he was in a foxhole when a grenade landed nearby. He jumped on it to save a buddy, but both his legs were blown off."

Saunders let that news sink in a little bit before continuing the story. "See this picture?" he asked. "It shows Bob Wieland crossing the finish line. He ran the marathon on the stumps of his legs by swinging his legless torso—a yard at a time—with his arms. And when he finally finished, the race director said to him, 'I thought you dropped out days ago. Why did you finish?'

"Wieland answered, 'Well, for two reasons. First of all, I've always wanted to run the New York Marathon. It's the greatest marathon in the world. And second of all, I believed I could do it. I'm a Christian, and this was a demonstration that faith in the Lord Jesus will always overcome the impossible. After I took those first few steps, I knew I was going to finish even if it took two days, two hours, and twenty-seven minutes."

Then Coach Saunders looked around the room and pointed to one of the players. "Do you believe we can win today?" he asked. Before he could answer, he looked at another player. "What about you? Do you think we can win?" And he looked at a third player. "You've heard the story. Do you think we can win?"

Saunders drove his point home. "I think we can win, and if you and you and you"—he was pointing to the three players now— "think we can win, then we'll beat the Denver Broncos today."

Saunders pulled his cap on tighter. "That's all I have to say. Buses leave in five minutes."

■ **What happened next?**

It became *really* quiet in that hotel conference room. Then a player whispered, "Do you think we can win?"

"Yeah, I do," replied the player. "What about you?"

"I think we can win today. I think we can beat the Broncos."

With that, the Charger players boarded the bus for the ride to Mile High Stadium. It was the quietest bus Rolf had ever been on in ten years of playing in the NFL.

When they pulled into the parking lot, the players could tell the Denver fans were up for this game. Everyone was dressed in orange sweatshirts, and they could see them standing next to their cars, having tailgate parties.

They had to walk through an orange gauntlet of rabid fans to get to the locker room. Many were fueled by adult beverages, and they screamed such niceties as "You're going to get your @#$% whipped today!" or "You guys suck."

With the taunts ringing in their ears, the players dressed for the game. Their quarterback would be Tom Flick, subbing for Dan Fouts, and Flick was coming off a terrible game against the Cowboys with five interceptions. But Tom and the rest of the players thought they were going to win.

All game long, the lowly Chargers played with dogged determination, and Flick didn't throw an interception as the Chargers beat the Broncos 9-3. They even intercepted a ball in the end zone to preserve the victory with no time left.

The Denver fans booed their Broncos unmercifully, firing garbage and other missiles at their players. But the San Diego guys were high-fiving and low-fiving one another, whooping it up. You would have thought they had just won the Super Bowl instead of their second game of the season.

■ Did the players whoop it up after the game?

Yes, they did. After a few minutes of bedlam in the locker room, Coach Saunders stood up and asked for some quiet.

"Stop for a minute and feel this feeling," he said. "This is what it feels like to accomplish something, particularly when everybody thinks you can't do it. You won because you believed you could, and you relied on one another to get it done."

That unexpected victory in Denver teaches a powerful lesson. We have to believe in ourselves—even when the odds are way against us. We have to persevere—even when other people don't think we can. We have to get up in the morning and work hard for our families—even when we are tired.

Because our families are counting on us.

This material is adapted from Rolf Benirschke's book, Alive & Kicking *(Firefly Press). The autobiography describes Benirschke's comeback from ulcerative colitis and ostomy surgery to become one of the most accurate kickers in NFL history. If you or someone you know is suffering from ulcerative colitis or Crohn's disease, then call toll-free (800) 560-9700 to request a copy.*

3

Adding Margins to Our Busy Lives

. . . .

■ **My workday is crammed, and it starts early in the morning, gobbling down breakfast and then rushing off with a cup of coffee in my lap—all the while struggling not to dump it into my lap as I drive. But when I get home, it seems like my second job is starting—helping Connie with dinner and laundry, doing homework with the boys, and keeping the house and yard up. My life is stretched so tightly that when an unexpected crisis surfaces, I snap like a rubber band. What can I do ?**

Create margin. Margin means establishing parameters that leave you energy at the end of the day, money at the end of the month, and sanity at the end of your child's adolescence. Marginless, on the other hand, is being thirty minutes late for your son's basketball game because you were twenty minutes late getting out of a meeting because you were ten minutes late getting back from lunch.

Marginless is carrying a load five pounds heavier than you need to lift; margin is asking a friend to carry half the burden.

Marginless is not having time to finish the book you're reading on stress; margin is having the time to read it twice.

Marginless is fatigue; margin is energy.

Marginless is red ink; margin is black ink.

Marginless is hurry; margin is calm.
Marginless is anxiety; margin is security.
Marginless is the disease of the nineties; margin is its cure.

■ **This "creating margin" idea intrigues me. Can you tell me more?**

Margin was easier to find in days past. Televisions were not blaring and phones weren't ringing. People seldom traveled long distances because they had no cars. Daily newspapers were unknown. The media could not broadcast events taking place in town. Churches and communities did not offer twenty simultaneous programs. With no electricity to extend daylight, few suffered sleep deprivation. The masses had not yet adopted time urgency, daily planners, and to-do lists.

Instead, people lived slower, more deliberate lives. They had time to help a neighbor. Their church and social activities drew them together often. People of the past might have been poor and deprived in some ways, but they had margin.

Today, conditions in Third World countries are heartrending. But if you were to spend any amount of time in an African country, for instance, you would be struck by how much margin people there have. They sit and talk, watch children play, walk without hurry, and sleep full nights. True, the people don't have the modern conveniences we enjoy. But missionaries will tell you that they wouldn't trade the slower pace there for anything.

■ **So how do I slow down?**

When flying from New York to San Francisco, we need more than three minutes to change planes in Denver. A much greater margin of error is needed. But if we make such allowances in our travels, why don't we do it in our living? Life is a journey, not a race. Do yourself a favor and slow down. Here are some ideas for restoring sanity to your day:

► **Expect the unexpected.** If you are chronically late, try adding an extra 20 percent time margin to your schedule.
► **Learn to say no.** Saying no is not just a good idea—some-

times it is an absolute necessity. If there are a hundred good things to do and you can do only ten of them, you will have to say no ninety times.

- ▶ **Turn off the TV.** The average adult would gain thirty hours a week.

- ▶ **Prune activities and commitments.** It is much harder to stop something than start it. Periodically, it is important to get the clippers and prune away activities that you are no longer interested in.

- ▶ **Practice simplicity and contentment.** We all consume lots of time buying and maintaining things. But if we had fewer possessions, wc would have less to take care of. Recognize that unnecessary possessions are stealers of divine time. Every day we are given opportunities that have eternal significance—to serve, to love, to obey, to pray. But we squander much of our time on things that very soon will leave us forever.

- ▶ **Short-term flurry versus long-term vision.** Americans are notoriously shortsighted. We live in a state of myopic mania that blurs our view of the future. The horizon is never visible in the middle of a dust storm. But we must have a vision that extends beyond tomorrow. Living only from week to week is like living a dot-to-dot life.

  It is good to have five-year plans, even ten-year plans. For many these plans will be vague, for others specific. Our goals should be flexible to allow for the new directions God so often asks of us. But each of us needs a direction and a vision to keep focused.

- ▶ **Enjoy anticipation, relish the memories.** Calendar congestion and time urgency have robbed us of the pleasure of anticipation. Without warning, the activity is upon us. We rush to meet it; then we rush to the next, and the next. In the same way, we lack the luxury of reminiscing. On we fly to the next activity.

  Have fun planning your family outings months in advance. And when the activity is over, remember. Tell stories. Frame a picture. Mount a fish. Make a special effort to remember funny happenings.

What about that box full of old photos in your attic or basement? Gather your kids around and spend an evening arranging them in albums or picking out the best ones for collages. You won't believe the fun you'll have!

► **Don't rush wisdom.** Seldom is true wisdom a product of speedy deliberation. If life's pace pushes you, push back. Take as much time as you need for clarity to develop.

► **Create buffer zones.** If you have a busy schedule with nonstop appointments, consider creating small buffer zones between some of the obligations, a kind of coffee break for the spirit. Even ten or fifteen minutes can allow you to catch up, make phone calls, close your eyes, pray, call your spouse, reorient your priorities, or defuse your tension.

► **Plan for free time.** If God were our appointment secretary, would He schedule every minute of the day? Of course not. Christ's lifestyle—His teaching, healing, serving, and loving—was usually spontaneous. If He chose spontaneous living, isn't that a signal to us?

► **Be available.** Margin exists for the needs of the kingdom, for the service of one another, for the building of community. It exists, just as we exist, for the purpose of being available to God.

This material is adapted from Margin *by Richard A. Swenson, M.D., associate professor of Clinical Health Services at the University of Wisconsin Medical School. Used by permission of NavPress. For copies of* Margin, *call toll-free (800) 366-7788.*

8

....

Dads and Their World

Trading Style for Substance

■ It seems that every election year, the political pundits talk about how a certain candidate is all style and no substance. Then I saw a television commercial touting a food product as a return to "home cookin'." And what was this new form of "home cookin'?" A TV dinner.

I'm getting sick and tired of all this. What's going on here?

Welcome to the age of style over substance, pomp over pithiness, charisma over content. This is a time when who we are has become less important than who people *think* we are; when euphemistic phrases can seemingly turn wrongs into rights; and when politicians are often judged more on their charisma than on their convictions. Bluntly, what you see ain't always what you get.

■ Oh, you mean like that German "singing" group Milli Vanilli that had its Grammy award withdrawn earlier this decade after it was discovered the duo had only lip-synched its songs?

Yes, from the triviality of TV dinners and lip-synching to the seriousness of abortion and infidelity, the American way often means selling beautifully packaged lies. And as it becomes increasingly difficult to separate the counterfeit from the real, we're increasingly reaching for our wallets. What's worse, we're starting to wrap ourselves in those same beautiful packages and forgetting it's the content that counts.

■ What do you mean?

This insane obsession with image works against the reality that God intends for us. It muddies an other-oriented Christian value system with the me-first murkiness of Madison Avenue. We subconsciously substitute real virtues such as honesty, humility, and forgiveness for cosmetic replacements such as designer clothes, bigger houses, and "perfect" bodies.

Our teenage children get pushed to conform at all cost. Mothers at home question their worth because they don't fit the briefcase-toting image of success. Our churches become more concerned with denominational pride than becoming a haven for the "poor in spirit."

Though the media have fueled the style-over-substance syndrome, the phenomenon is nothing new. In biblical times, the Pharisees were champions at creating the image that they were pure and holy. In fact, they were merely robe-clad forerunners of the dress-for-success movement—people whose outer appearance didn't necessarily reflect their inner selves. They loved to pray, give to the needy, and fast—all in front of others. Their motive was obvious: not to selflessly serve God and others, but to convince others that they were selflessly serving God and others.

■ Oh, you mean like the TV commercial a few years back when an actor urged us to buy a particular brand of pain relievers because while he wasn't a *real* doctor, "I play one on TV." Do people really fall for such rubbish?

Consider this: In the first five years of the "Marcus Welby" TV show, more than 250,000 people wrote letters to Robert Young, the star of the show, most of them asking for *medical advice*. We've become so anesthetized by image that it's becoming more difficult to choose the real from the fake.

Insignificant as it might seem, the home cookin' commercial is a perfect example of this intentional blurring of reality. The image is of a homespun meal: Huge helpings. Fresh-from-the-garden vegetables. The kind of dinner Grandma used to make on the family farm. But the image is more than a distortion of reality; it is a 180-degree lie.

In fact, people who probably live halfway across the country threw the food together on a conveyor belt. And what do we really get? Small portions in an aluminum tray that come to us not fresh from Grandma's oven, but from some not-so-fresh supermarket freezer.

The fact is, marketing executives would not be using the home cookin' image unless they knew we were gullible enough to fall for it. And we are. Is it any surprise that many of us also buy into deceptions with much more serious consequences?

■ **So how does all this relate to my faith? What are the dangers I should be looking out for?**

The same sales job employed by the TV dinner people is also employed by the pro-abortionists: *Let people believe they're getting one thing (personal rights) so they won't stop to consider another thing (an unborn baby's death).*

The goal is simple: If you emphasize home-cooking long enough, people will forget they're eating frozen food. If you emphasize loss of rights long enough, people will forget unborn infants are dying. If you use all the official rhetoric—"abortion rights," "choice," "reproductive freedom"—then, just as rock-hard biscuits can be passed off as Grandma's finest, so can abortion be passed off not only as ethically acceptable, but also downright dignified.

If pro-abortion forces honestly believed that a baby in its mother's womb were only a mass of tissue, why do they cry foul when antiabortionists use photographs of an unborn baby or show what happens during a partial-birth abortion? Because, in a very graphic way, such photographs and drawings bare a truth that cannot rationally be denied: *That it is a human life that is inside that womb.* Image can create a lie, but substance always reveals truth.

■ **Isn't that kind of like widening the playing field to convince yourself you're in bounds—even if you're not?**

That's what the International Olympic Committee did in 1988. At the time, the Olympic charter clearly stated that "the use of the [Olympic] emblem for advertising alcoholic beverages or tobacco is *strictly* prohibited" (italics added).

But a brewing company had put the five Olympic rings on its beer cans, a brewing company that, not incidentally, was spending millions of dollars to promote the Winter Games in Calgary. The committee deliberated, then announced its ruling: Since beer and wine weren't actually alcohol, it said, the company could leave the Olympic logo on its beer cans.

It's the same philosophy that more and more churches are using so parishioners—and pastors—can shirk accountability; instead of exhorting people to turn from practices that the Bible says are wrong, the churches simply rationalize that such practices are right. For such churches, truth isn't the Rock of All Ages, but twentieth-century Silly Putty, an elastic substance that can be stretched and stretched until it conforms to personal comfort zones.

■ **You mentioned earlier that another way our culture changes the rules is to change the language. Can you give some examples?**

Turn on the TV and you're apt to hear a trendy sociologist allude to "nonmonogamous" marriage. And what is she referring to? Adultery.

"Adultery" clearly sounds *wrong*. That's precisely why some sociologists have substituted the "nonmonogamous" term—because, they say, it carries no connotation of good or evil. Their switch represents yet another step into moral neutrality.

Through language, we cheapen that which is good and enrich that which is not. "Making love" is now euphemistically substituted for any act of sex, regardless of whether love played a part. What used to be "chastity" is now "neurotic inhibition." What used to be "self-indulgence" is now "self-fulfillment."

Such presweetened phrases represent the foundation of the

image-over-substance philosophy: Don't change your ways. Don't change your heart. And, above all, don't feel guilty. Instead, simply change the image of your actions.

■ So how do we combat the image-fiddling that's all around us?

Most importantly, by finding a role model to pattern our lives after. We need look no further than Jesus Himself. He needed no public relations firm. He simply lived His values, doing what He knew was right, obeying His Father, sacrificing for others. He was open. He was honest. He was holy. His virtues were reflected in the choices He made, the words He said, the promises He kept. Ours should too.

Said Jesus: "Woe to you, teachers of the law and Pharisees, you hypocrites! You clean the outside of the cup and dish, but inside they are full of greed and self-indulgence. Blind Pharisee! First clean the inside of the cup and dish, and then the outside also will be clean" (Matt. 23:25-26).

Jesus clearly saw the foolishness of the world. He refused to go with the cultural flow, choosing instead to follow His Father. "Watch out for false prophets," said Jesus. "They come to you in sheep's clothing, but inwardly they are ferocious wolves. By their fruit you will recognize them. Do people pick grapes from thornbushes, or figs from thistles? Likewise, every good tree bears good fruit, but a bad tree bears bad fruit" (7:15-17).

If seemingly righteous people can actually be unrighteous, seemingly ordinary people can actually be extraordinary. When you think of people of substance, don't necessarily think of CEOs or people featured on magazine covers or people with lots of money or people with lofty academic degrees.

Instead, think of a Sunday School teacher sitting at her kitchen table on a Saturday night, trying to make a scale model of Noah's ark with popsicle sticks. Think of the mother and father who get up at 5 A.M. every day to get their disabled son ready for school. Think of the single mom who cleans the church alone on Saturday nights.

Jesus didn't hang out with the chosen class. He interacted with lepers and the blind, prostitutes, and Samaritans. Likewise God used seemingly ordinary people who had weakness like you and me: Moses, a man with a speech problem, and Mary, a woman without notoriety. In choosing a king, God passed over the older sons of Jesse and chose the unlikely David.

"The Lord said to Samuel, 'Do not consider his appearance or his height, for I have rejected him. The Lord does not look at the things man looks at. Man looks at the outward appearance, but the Lord looks at the heart' " (1 Sam. 16:7).

No amount of image-makeover can change the real us any more than a paint job can fix a car needing an engine overhaul. Such changes come only from the heart. And, unlike the claims of image consultants, they don't happen in a weekend seminar. They happen through the power of the Holy Spirit and in a lifetime of commitment to God.

To buy the world's images instead of God's substance is to go through life eating TV dinner after TV dinner—only to discover too late that we never tasted genuine home cookin'.

This material is adapted from writings by Bob Welch of Eugene, Oregon.

2

Our Country's Heritage: Do Our Children Understand?

. . . .

■ I work in Washington, D.C., and driving home from work one night, I paused at a stoplight. To my right, a group of high school students were sprawled out on the lawn. A portable CD player blared heavy metal rock music.

The teens lay in the grass with their heads bopping to the music. They didn't have a care in the world. Their empty looks and designer jeans reminded me of a quip I heard about young people: "They have Calvin Kleins on their behinds and nothing in their minds."

I wondered if any of the kids had noticed a historical marker a few feet behind them. The plaque marked the site of a Civil War skirmish. The Virginia countryside is peppered with such markers, but the only people who stop and notice are tourists. How can young Americans grasp the price of freedom and the source of liberty?

You'd be surprised how little the average American knows about our country's origins, but then again, maybe you wouldn't. The same can be said for our schoolchildren.

Right on the spot of *terra firma* that you described, hundreds of men paid the ultimate price for a great cause: liberty, freedom, and the preservation of a nation. Many who died in that Civil War battle were young boys, some even younger than the youths who whiled the day away listening to rock music.

What did these teens know about Bull Run, Antietam, or Fort Sumter? Did any of them understand what Abraham Lincoln meant by "patriot graves bound together by mystic cords of memory"? It's doubtful.

■ Should I be angry at these kids?

You can't be. The blame sits squarely on the shoulders of their parents and teachers, many of whom pass that square daily on the way to work or to shop. Had any of them pointed out the significance of the area to their children? Probably not. We live in an age that's ignorant of the past and unworried about tomorrow.

■ Why is it important to teach my kids about our history?

Because it is the root that sustains us. Parents and children who don't feel any particular reverence for our historical heritage reflect the transparent values of our culture, which often seems to elevate commerce and instant gratification above all else.

As Washington and its suburbs continue to grow, the land is gobbled up for shopping centers and freeways. Who cares whether this land was where our great-great-grandfathers fought an epic battle? Who thinks twice about what this country would be like if we had lost the War for Independence or the War of 1812?

■ Didn't the Disney company want to build some huge amusement park in Virginia, right in the middle of some old Civil War battlefields?

Yes, the Disney folks had grandiose plans for a theme park in Virginia, but local preservationists and the nation's media spoke out against it, and Disney scrapped the idea.

Perhaps your town has witnessed zoning battles over historic lands. When we lose, we cut off ourselves and our children from our roots and the heroes who've sustained us, guaranteeing that our children's children will be deprived as well.

Unlike the hippies of the sixties, the teenagers you saw that day had not rejected the American experience. More accurately, no one had *taught* our national heritage to them. Since our culture has shirked its responsibility of teaching history to the young, our children are adrift.

■ **What's so important about learning history? I never did like it in high school.**

Because history has much it can teach us. When young people are more concerned about the pleasures available here and now, history takes a backseat. That's why it's up to parents and teachers to fill in the gap and instill a love for history and our country's heritage. No one else is going to do it. We should fear that much of the next generation is entering adulthood without understanding the nature of our liberty.

■ **How far have we gone toward losing a common culture?**

Consider these results from a national test given to over 8,000 students seventeen years old. On the history portion of the exam, the average student correctly answered 55 percent of the questions correctly. Students fared worse on the literature portion: 52 percent. In other words, most of our children flunked out when questioned about the history and literature of our civilization.

■ **Can you give me some specifics?**

For example, when the seventeen-year-olds were given the key passage of the Declaration of Independence—"We hold these truths to be self-evident, that all men are created equal, that they are endowed by their Creator with certain unalienable rights, that among these are Life, Liberty, and the pursuit of happiness"—fully one-third of them could not identify where the quote came from.

One-third didn't know the Declaration of Independence was

signed between 1750 and 1800, and two-thirds could not place the Civil War within the period 1850–1900. And one-half couldn't say within fifty years when World War I took place!

Questions about recent history fared no better. Barely half knew John F. Kennedy said, "And so, my fellow Americans, ask not what your country can do for you; ask what you can do for your country." Less than 50 percent of our seventeen-year-olds recognized the names of Winston Churchill and Joseph Stalin. Good grief!

■ **Where's a good place to start if I want to be sure my kids understand our heritage?**

Share some facts about our Founding Fathers, including our first President, George Washington. At the end of the Revolutionary War, Washington stated that our greatest blessing was "the pure and benign light of revelation."

When he took the oath of office as President on April 30, 1789, Washington added the words "I swear, so help me God." Every president since has repeated them.

Did you know that during Washington's administration the first Thanksgiving proclamation was issued? Or that Thomas Jefferson, who is often cited as the founder who wanted a strict separation of church and state, suggested that the Great Seal of the United States should depict Moses leading his people to the Promised Land?

Finally, Alexis de Tocqueville, a Frenchman who came to America in the early 1800s to determine the "secret" of our successful democracy, wrote, "Upon my arrival in the United States, the religious aspect of the country was the first thing that struck my attention. Religion in America . . . must be regarded as the foremost of political institutions of that country."

Our children need to know these basic facts. We need to teach them about Concord Bridge, Gettysburg, and Omaha Beach. They need to know how their liberty has been won and preserved through the years. And they also need to know that with freedom comes responsibility.

If we are not "One Nation Under God," then surely we will be but one more nation gone under. Our children need to be taken to the great historical monuments and read the tales of sacrifice so many have given. In this way, they can enjoy the fruits of liberty.

This material is adapted from writings by Gary Bauer, president of the Family Research Council in Washington, D.C., and a frequent "Focus on the Family" broadcast guest.

3

If You Could See Us Now, Pop Youngberg

. . . .

■ My parents divorced before I entered kindergarten, and then my father moved to the other side of the country and remarried. Consequently, I never knew him nor his family. Mom never got on well with her parents because her life was messed up. So I never knew my grandparents growing up.

In college, I became a Christian through Campus Crusade, and I found a godly woman who became my wife. We are trying to do what is right in raising our children.

Recently at church, they announced an "Adopt a Grandparent" program. Several of the "seasoned citizens" got up before the congregation and talked about how they were available to families without strong intergenerational ties. Their life experiences really impressed me, and I'm wondering if we should "adopt" a grandparent. What did I miss out on?

Unfortunately, a great deal, but it's never too late to learn from our elders. Although it's easy to dismiss the senior generation because they think the Internet is a new type of fishing gear, they have plenty of wisdom to pass along.

Bob Welch knew such a person. He recently visited a country

cemetery outside Carlton, Oregon, where his wife's grandfather, Pop Youngberg, was buried ten years ago.

Bob can clearly recall the memorial service on that cool afternoon. He remembers how strange it was that a man who was born in the days of horse and buggies was brought to rest in a baby-blue Cadillac hearse.

Pop Youngberg was probably the last of a vanishing breed. He was a man who held one job his entire life: farmer. A man who was married to the same woman for sixty years. A man who died in the same farmhouse where he had been born eighty-nine years earlier. A simple man who found meaning in tilling the earth below him, worshiping the God above him, and loving the family around him, including the granddaughter Bob married.

■ **Well, Pop must have been a wonderful man, but like I said, I never knew anyone in my family like him. He sounds like someone from the nineteenth century. But wouldn't Pop Youngberg be considered, well, "politically incorrect" these days?**

You're probably right, although when Bob wrote a newspaper column about Pop Youngberg, many people wrote and called to say what a wonderful man he must have been, and how they knew a Pop of their own.

But in the whole, Pop *would* be considered politically incorrect today. We're talking about a man who remained faithful to his wife, taught his children right from wrong, and kept his family together despite drought and Depression. But today, Pop would be guilty of promoting "family values," whose proponents, Hugh Downs once told his "20/20" TV audience, are fueled by the same intolerance that fueled Hitler and the Klan.

Pop Youngberg was a man who got tears in his eyes when he sang "Amazing Grace" at the tiny Baptist church he helped found in Carlton, but today he'd be considered a fool for worshiping some obsolete God when he should have been searching for his inner child, winning by intimidation, or awakening the warrior spirit within.

Pop was a man who made his grandchildren wind chimes for

Christmas and helped other farmers bale their hay when a storm was coming. He was a man who insisted that everyone hold hands before a meal and, when he had finished praying, would give the hands he was holding an encouraging squeeze. But today, Pop would be cast as a cultural villain, a white European male who wears a fur cap and eats meat loaf.

■ **I think we need more Pop Youngbergs, not fewer. Why would so many of the cultural elites put him down?**

Because we are living in a post-Christian era in which we've forgotten what it means to be righteous. In fact, we are living in an age when evil, if possible, has gotten even more evil. In 1995, a bomb blew up a federal building in Oklahoma City, killing 168 people. A mother in South Carolina drowned her two sons so they wouldn't interfere with her relationship with her boyfriend. And recently a St. Louis teacher died after being punched by a fourth-grader who didn't like his homework assignment.

You need more examples? Think about crack cocaine. Drive-by shootings. Assisted suicide. Fetal "harvesting." Partial-birth abortions. Video poker. Trashy talk shows. Greedy athletes. World Wide Web pornography. Runaway lawsuits. Shock radio. Sexual abuse. And grandparents who must raise their children's children because their sons or daughters are on drugs. All have mushroomed in the last decade.

The abnormal has become normal. Right and wrong have traded places. In 1992, the vice president of the United States suggested it would be better for children to be raised by two parents than one. He was verbally lynched. A year earlier, a famous basketball player, Magic Johnson, revealed he was HIV-positive after having sex with hundreds of women. He was hailed as a hero.

These days, your teenage daughter needs parental permission to get her ears pierced, but in many states, she could legally have an abortion without your permission—or your knowledge. And perhaps you live in a school district that enthusiastically passes out condoms, but watch out if your children try to hand out Christmas cards. Crazy, isn't it?

And yet some people, in the name of Christ, scorn their political leaders or take deadly revenge on abortion doctors. They act more like the Pharisee of Luke 18:11, who said, "God, I thank you that I am not like all other men—robbers, evildoers, adulterers . . . ." than like the repentant tax collector who said, "God, have mercy on me, a sinner" (v. 13).

What we've lost in this country is trust. We don't trust one another. We don't trust our government. We don't trust God.

What we trust in is ourselves, which Pop once said was a little like standing beneath a lone tree in a field during a lightning storm.

Gram Youngberg once told the story about the toothless old man who showed up asking Pop for free hay. He gladly obliged, she said, only to find out later that the man had money to pay the two farmers down the road for their hay.

EVERY SMOKE A WANTED SMOKE

When Joyceln Elders was U.S. Surgeon General during President Clinton's first term, Daniel P. Erb of Spokane, Washington, sent her this letter after Dr. Elders announced her stand against smoking:

Dear Dr. Elders:

There is no sense using scare tactics to persuade kids not to smoke. Young people are going to smoke no matter what we do. So we might as well accept that fact. We would be better off instructing all our young people that smoking is okay as long as they use a filter.

We should begin by holding classes that teach youngsters the proper way to fit a cigarette with a filter. We could use pencils as models and have all students practice placing a filter on a pencil.

I'm sure we'll get flack from parents who won't want their kids to smoke under any circumstances, whether they use a filter or not. We can circumvent these troublemakers by instructing all school health clinics to issue filtered cigarettes to any student who asks for them—regardless if they have permission from their parents.

Since kids are starting to smoke at earlier and earlier ages, we should start this education process in kindergarten so we can make sure every child has the proper information to experience this whenever he or she desires to do so. We might as well teach them how to smoke in the safest way possible.

We trust people, perhaps too much. But today, trust is the rarest of virtues, mirrored in the broken promises of spouses, politicians, even the head of United Way, who was convicted of embezzling from the charity he directed.

Today, people demand rights and ignore responsibilities. In the land of the free, 1.5 million Americans—almost the population of Philadelphia—live in prisons. In the home of the brave, men who exude great public courage are routinely uncovered as Wizards of Oz: all style, no substance.

The same Baby Boom generation that so fervently clamors for world peace is filled with people who can't even find peace with the person they once *chose* to spend a lifetime with. Dashing Hollywood actors promote noble causes, then get caught seeking sex in some red-light district.

Still, even when the public light is shined on them, people rarely humble themselves and admit their mistakes. AIDS cases have increased tremendously, but people still play around with sex as if it were a cheap, harmless toy. We've become like a bunch of your Herefords caught in quicksand: The harder we struggle on our own, the deeper we sink.

■ **Where is the hope so we can free ourselves from this cultural muck?**

Maybe it's in doing what the Coca-Cola folks did. Back in the mid-1980s, they introduced a new "improved" soft drink formula. It flopped. So Coke admitted they'd blown it, brought back the old formula, and everyone drank happily ever after. Today, we have "Coke Classic."

Oh, the intellectuals will say it's too simplistic, and the politically correct will scoff at it as a return to those intolerant days of family values. But maybe, as a nation, we should humble ourselves. Admit our mistakes. And while keeping the change that's been legitimately good, bring back the original formula.

Pop Youngberg was a Coke Classic kind of guy. He never talked much about faith or values or character or any of that stuff. He just lived it.

Every now and then, one of Bob Welch's sons, while playing baseball out back, will rip a line drive smack into the wind chime he made for them. It'll jolt Bob, as if to say: *Don't forget. Don't forget.* You shouldn't, either.

This material is adapted from writings by Bob Welch of Eugene, Oregon, and Daniel Erb of Spokane, Washington.

4

A Culture That's in Our Face

∙∙

■ I was a teenager in the seventies, an awful era of platform shoes, hip-hugger pants, white polyester (I mean the REAL polyester), and stringy, long hair. I can't believe I once wore a white suit like John Travolta did in *Saturday Night Fever,* nor can I believe that I actually *liked* disco, but I did. At the end of that decade, I vowed that if I ever saw platform shoes again I would use them as hammers.

But alas, here we are, shooting through the nineties, and what do I see prominently displayed at my local mall? Clothes from the seventies! Yes, the styles have been updated, but my stomach still turns when I see white polyester pants, bell bottoms, and . . . those awful platform shoes.

Who's deciding these fashion trends?

Well, in a sense, you are, or at least the consumer public. But it all goes to show you that no matter how much we try to escape the popular culture, the trends of the day hit us right in the face. Even *Stars Wars* has made a comeback! But if seeing a Darth Vader helmet or a white polyester suit in the shop window were our biggest worries today, then we wouldn't have much to worry about.

Let's face the truth here: We live in a sex-obsessed, violence-soaked, entitlement-demanding society, and our teenagers are exhibiting the starkest reflection of those traits.

While violent crime has dropped among the adult population, it has risen sharply among teens. Drug use, particularly marijuana, has climbed back up to dizzying levels not seen since the early eighties.

■ Can we really protect our kids from the popular culture that surrounds them? What is our role in helping our children learn to think in a Christian manner?

The Focus on the Family Youth Culture department has conducted focus groups with teens (who read Focus' *Brio* and *Breakaway* magazines) and their parents. These groups confirm what their youth mail has been telling them; namely, that teens' biggest concerns are music, TV, movies, and video games. Teens are not only asking for different entertainment choices, but they also want to learn skills that will help them turn down choices their non-Christian or even Christian friends may make.

Let's take a look at what you can do to help them make those right choices:

The Music Scene

Do you know what's going on in your teen's world? Do you know what he or she likes, and why? In order to help your child sort out the positive music from the negative, talk about album lyrics by discussing these questions:

1. Do the words of the song emphasize harmful consequences or actions?

2. Do the artist's words or actions promote immediate gratification?

3. Do the words encourage courage, self-control, and good judgment?

4. Do they emphasize secrecy?

5. Are the words or actions based primarily on feelings?

6. Finally, "Would Jesus listen to this?" (This question should also be applied to movies and TV shows.)

It won't work to tell your teen, "You can't listen to that music." Instead, suggest positive Christian alternatives (Rebecca St. James, Michael W. Smith, Steven Curtis Chapman, Point of Grace, DC

Talk, Sierra, Audio Adrenaline, and so on), even offering to buy their latest CDs.

Checking Out Movies

Be wary of ratings. Mainstream audiences may deem PG and PG-13 films acceptable, but discerning Christians will bristle at much of what's supposedly "age appropriate" material. That's why you should resist the temptation to drop off your children at the local cineplex. (Besides, they could easily slip into an R-rated flick.)

Better yet, arrange a date night with your teens. Viewing films together gives you the chance to talk about the content—and what the family standard is. Your best bet, however, is watching movie videos at home. To be on the safe side, preview them before letting your youngsters watch, if possible.

A Word about TV and Videos

Watching television requires no interaction—just someone willing to sit and stare. Numerous studies show that children who sit passively in front of the TV screen don't learn to concentrate, engage in creative play, or do task-oriented activities. This is particularly true of children exposed to many hours of television between the ages of one and five.

Of course, the VCR player has become an all-purpose baby-sitter and pacifier in many situations. Think about it. How do some teachers control their Sunday School classes? They plug in a video. How do some day-care centers occupy children in order to have peace and quiet? Play a video.

Psychiatrist Foster Cline, author of *Parenting with Love and Logic*, said that he would rather put televisions and videos away and have children string buttons or wrap tape around a chair—anything that makes them focus on a task.

Many parents of toddlers reason that if a child is watching a Bible story video, the time is somewhat productive. Cline believes that any video, good or bad, is a detriment to getting toddlers to concentrate or think creatively.

■ **Our son, Nicholas, just turned three. This is a boy who has watched nothing but *Winnie the Pooh* and *Psalty Praise* videos.**

When we stopped plugging in videos, Nick literally went through withdrawal symptoms the first few days. He asked to watch a video at least a hundred times. When he heard my no, he cried and got angry. You would have thought we were at the Betty Ford clinic!

Stay the course, Dad. By making the VCR player off-limits, you're forcing Nicholas to become creative with his time. Let him learn to entertain himself by riding his bike, bouncing a basketball, or playing with some blocks.

■ The national average for having the TV on in the home is something like seven hours a day. We're nowhere near that, but I have to say that we do watch a few hours of TV each day. What should we do about it?

Here is some good advice:

► Set either daily or weekly viewing limits for the family. Some families watch TV only on weekends. Others allow one hour daily after homework. Thirty minutes would be better.

► If you and your wife both work outside the home, consider purchasing TimeSlot, a TV time manager available through Synaptic Designs. Call (919) 829-3525 for more information.

► Arrange your furniture so the TV isn't the focal point of the room.

► If you see something objectionable on TV, discuss it immediately with your child, rather than waiting until the topic comes up naturally. It may never do so.

► Nothing is a substitute for previewing your child's favorite show and finding out what messages he or she is exposed to.

► Take an honest look at your own viewing habits. Are TV sports running from the time you get home from work until you go to bed? Even if you're turning in the big games as "background noise," what example are you setting for your family?

■ **My wife and I know there's a lot of trashy shows out there. How can we stay a step ahead of the popular culture?**

Start early. Cultural messages hit our children from the day they enter our world until the day they leave it. Teaching our children how to respond to music, television, videos, and other entertainment in an intelligent, savvy, and Christian manner begins the first time they hear or see something.

■ **What about children beyond the preschool years?**

The goal after age five for cultural discernment rests in your ability as a parent to use teachable moments to convey your values. When you pass a billboard that promotes smoking, use the opportunity to ask this question: "What is that billboard not showing?"

"I don't know."

"Well, could it be that if you smoke for twenty years you could get some kind of cancer?"

This has a twofold benefit. First, you let your child know that you are not ignoring real issues in the world and that you care to discuss them with him or her. Second, you develop critical thinking and discernment within your child.

The ages from eight to twelve are also a good time to attend movies and review music together so that your child has a good foundation before high school.

ZAP LIST
Popular Musicians Who Promote Violence and Promiscuity in Their Lyrics
Nine Inch Nails
Snoop Doggy Dogg
Salt-N-Pepa
Bone Thugs-N-Harmony
Dr. Dre
Silverchair
2Pac
Offspring
Warren G
Tha Dogg Pound
Nirvana
Naughty by Nature
Slayer
Pearl Jam
Too Short
Coolio
Pantera

ZAP LIST

Video Games That Promote Violence

Killing Time (3DO)

Mortal Kombat III (Midway arcade version)

Phantasmagoria (Sierra)

Rise of the Triad (Apogee)

Doom II (id)

Ecstatica (Sony/Psygnosis)

Night Trap (Digital Pictures)

Corpse Killer (Digital Pictures)

Killer Instinct (Nintendo)

Savage Warriors (Mindscape)

Daryl F. Gates Police Quest (Sierra)

Crime Patrol (American Laser Games)

Many boys are crazy about video games, which train players to maim, torture, and kill. A new game, "Duke Nukem 3D," places the player in a Hollywood red-light district inhabited by alien mobsters posing as Los Angeles police officers. The only humans seen are female strippers whom the player can brutalize and kill.

What do hours of playing these type of games produce in a child's behavior? Nothing of benefit! (There are Christian video games that are quite acceptable.)

■ So what's the key strategy?

Pray hard and pick your battles! There should be negotiable boundaries and nonnegotiable rules. Keep in mind that most children simply follow the crowd, but you want your son or daughter to exhibit leadership in the face of opposition. That leadership involves not accepting destructive messages that are sprinkled in seemingly good entertainment.

Training youngsters for leadership means engaging them in vigorous conversations that equip them to reason biblically. If you lay a strong foundation from toddlerhood, there is a better chance that your child will actually *want* to make good entertainment choices. We can and must counter the culture while living in its midst.

Now, about those platform shoes. . . .

This material is adapted from "In Your Face" by Amy Stephens, Focus on the Family *magazine, September 1996. Copyright © 1996, Focus on the Family. Amy Stephens, manager of the Focus on the Family Youth Culture department, says her favorite seventies groups were the Doobie Brothers and Steely Dan, but now she likes Jars of Clay.*

FAMILY-FRIENDLY FILMS

(Check them out for home video)

Toy Story	Searching for Bobby Fischer
Balto	Sense and Sensibility
Babe	Jane Eyre
Miracle on 34th Street	Shadowlands
Little Women	Hoosiers

5

E-Mail: The Write Stuff

. . . .

■ **I like surfing the Internet, but my wife complains that I spend too much time in front of the computer. What she doesn't realize is that I send and receive a lot of E-mail, and some of it even has ministry value. How can I convince her that I'm not just playing around with some new software?**

Tell her that you're tapping into one of the safest and best educational uses of the computer: E-mail, or electronic mail, where you can send and receive messages through your home computer, using a modem and phone line. It's like sending and getting regular mail in your mailbox, but *much faster!* This computer equipment also allows you to browse through the Internet, the global network of computers linking universities, corporations, and governments.

Your wife may not be aware of this burgeoning new technology that can bring the world to your fingertips. Although more than 35 million American homes have personal computers with modems, many of these families are missing out on the uses that can benefit their children's learning. And while much has been said about the dangers of kids in cyberspace, a major way to safeguard your family is to take the time to learn the workings of computers, modems, Internet software, and online services so you can monitor your child's use. That way, you can help your child use the computer as something more than a video game machine.

■ **What's a "good" use of E-mail? When I explain those benefits to my wife, she thinks it's a couple of guys passing notes to each other.**

Here's an example: When Richard and Penny Hook and their three children spent eighteen months in Beijing, China, they wrote and transmitted 190 E-mail messages to their parents, siblings, and friends back in the United States. Sitting in front of a computer screen, Richard and Penny related the extraordinary and the mundane—from passing through customs to exploring the Great Wall to trying to find a pharmacy.

When their once-in-a-lifetime trip was over, the Hooks bound all their E-mail messages (including 225 E-mail letters they received from Richard's family) into a special memory book called *China Letters.*

Today, the *China Letters* journal is a vivid reminder that the world is getting smaller. "Our families knew what was going on in each other's lives almost on a daily basis, even though we were thousands of miles apart," says Richard.

■ **What are some of the other benefits of having a computer and modem in the home?**

Well, the next time your children are assigned to report on the American Revolution, they can tap into the Library of Congress or a university library for a wealth of information. They can also E-mail a letter to the editor of a children's magazine they subscribe to, send thank-you letters to relatives, and develop a pen-pal friendship with a child or relative in another country.

When Oregon sixth-grader Andrew Tunnell's older brother spent last summer studying at a German university, they found E-mail an easy way to keep in touch. "Every other day we'd E-mail each other. My brother would tell me what castle he visited that day and some history about it." Not only did Andrew's typing and writing skills improve dramatically, but also he learned a lot of firsthand information about another country.

Children who learn to use the computer as a communications tool at home gain valuable language skills that help them achieve more in every subject. Since fluency and skill in writing are directly related to practice, online activities provide many reasons to write at home—the place most kids write the least. But *your* involvement as a parent is essential, both to your child's safety online and his learning how to tap into the best educational use of the technology.

■ **We have one home PC, of course, so how can I help my kids get the most out of their computer time?**

Keep these ideas in mind:

▶ **Set guidelines and ground rules.** Tom Lough of Simsbury, Connecticut, allowed his son, Kyser, to E-mail a friend he met at summer camp, but he set some house rules: Ask for permission each time you log on; don't ever leave the "Basic Services" area of the online service; anything dealing with adult language is off-limits; and don't ever give out our password. He and his son moved from joint sessions in which he helped Kyser log on, to Tom reading a book nearby and checking on Kyser periodically. He showed him how to get information on games and resources from the library for reports.

Tom instructed Kyser not to give out any personal information, such as their home address or telephone number. Since E-mail travels over phone lines and through many computers, strangers could read the messages.

▶ **Teach your children "netiquette."** Courtesy is just as important when writing E-mail letters as it is when talking in person. Discuss with your children these netiquette suggestions so they will practice politeness in print:

1. Answer your E-mail promptly and politely, and in most cases, briefly.

2. Address E-mail letters properly, using the person's correct title, such as "Dear Librarian" or "Dear Editor," and use such appropriate terms as "Sincerely, Kathy" or "Your friend, Brian."

3. Don't write in ALL CAPITAL LETTERS—it's just like SHOUTING!

4. Encourage your kids to use complete sentences and to end each sentence with a dot (keyboard term for a period).

■ **You mentioned earlier that the kids can do homework with help from the Internet. What are some activities that build literacy?**

There's a lot of fun stuff to do online that gives children great opportunities to learn:

- ▶ **Tap into libraries.** Meghan, a seventh grader, did all her research for her report on Thomas Jefferson by E-mail. She was even able to download some historical documents from the Library of Congress to add to her resources (address: lcweb@loc.gov).

- ▶ **Ask science and geography questions** by E-mailing National Geographic's World magazine (address: ngsforum @aol.com).

- ▶ **After reading and discussing an important national issue together,** E-mail your congressional leader with your opinion (address: comments@hr.house.giv).

- ▶ **Have an E-mail pen pal.** Your child can become connected with a pen pal in another country and learn about another culture and the differences in its schools, family, and lifestyle (address: dvandeve@nylink.org).

- ▶ **Create a family newsletter.** Let your child be the news reporter and even interview Granddad and other relatives. Then he or she can write it all up and E-mail it to the whole family with a click of the "send" key.

- ▶ **Discover educational opportunities.** Each online service (see related story) has sites where students can learn about everything from physics to a foreign language. For example, there are French- and German-only conferences where American students can practice those languages with students from France and Germany.

- ▶ **Use E-mail to stay involved with your child's education.** Most schools have computers and many have modems and are online, allowing students, teachers, and parents to stay in close touch. Ask your child's teacher if she or he has an online address, then correspond by E-mail to keep updated about what the class is studying. You can ask how your child is doing and how you can work with her or him on a problem area.

Many universities now supply students with computers and free Internet access. Therefore, you can also keep up with what's going on with your college kids. While Kathy's son was at the U.S. Naval Academy in Annapolis, Maryland, the two kept in daily touch via E-mail, which helped provide him with needed support from home.

You can read magazines that keep you informed and help you be a better parent. By getting on the information highway and using E-mail yourself, you'll quickly get over your fear of the online world, set a good example for your children, and at the same time effectively monitor your child's computer use.

Cheri Fuller, who lives in Oklahoma City, put her E-mail address in Focus on the Family *magazine when this material was originally published in 1996. She won't make that mistake again, she says.*

HOW DO I GET ONLINE?

The easiest way to take advantage of what online technology has to offer is to subscribe to one of the numerous Internet access servers or an online service. Check out any major computer magazine for more details. The three largest online services are:

► America Online. Call (800) 827-6364 for information and free software.

► CompuServe. Call (800) 848-8990.

► Prodigy. Call (800) 776-3449.

LET YOUR VOICE BE HEARD!

These days, you can write letters to your local newspaper by E-mail or by using "snail mail." Either way, you can weigh in with your opinions.

That's what Dianne Butts of Lamar, Colorado, did after reading Dr. Dobson's monthly newsletters describing the radical agenda of the U.N. Fourth World Conference on Women in Beijing, China. She heeded Dr. Dobson's challenge to "let your voice be heard."

After spending a couple of hours at the library studying the editorial pages of newspapers, she sat down at her computer and drafted a letter to the editor. She printed out four copies—sending each to a newspaper in her area. Within a couple of weeks, three of the four papers printed her letter!

A "letter to the editor" provides one way to speak out on an issue while reaching a wide audience. Here are some tips that will help you write letters to editors and improve your chances of getting published:

1. Pray first. Ask God to guide what you say and where you send it.

2. Know the word limit that the paper will print. Count the words in printed letters for a general guideline.

3. Study sample letters in your target publication to see how the authors made their points. How did they state their opinions? How did they call for action?

4. Focus on one issue per letter. For other issues, write another letter.

5. Be formal, not friendly. Stay respectful and polite. You don't need to scream from the page since you already have the reader's attention.

6. Don't be intimidated. Believe in the message that you want to convey. If you don't, others won't either.

7. Don't depend on the mainstream media for information or analysis—develop new sources. Subscribe to (or check your library for) alternative media sources, listen to talk radio, read Christian newspapers and magazines, and "surf the net" through an online service.

8. Allow your letter to sit for a day. Re-read and edit it.

9. Submit your letter to several newspapers and news magazines. With a few adjustments, you can often send your letter to political representatives, too.

10. Pray again. Ask God to use your letter to affect lives and to glorify Him. Pray also for the editors and their publications.

If your letter isn't printed, keep trying. Even if it's not printed, various editors will probably read it, which means your letter has reached an audience. Don't worry: God will use it for His glory.

The Ten Commandments of Great Nutrition

■ **Since I'm on my own when it comes to packing a lunch for work each day, I usually end up at the neighborhood Wendy's. I know fast food isn't doing my waistline any favors. How can I eat healthier in this day and age?**

Many people say it's impossible to eat well in today's junk-food world. The challenge, though daunting, is not as complicated as you'd think. These "Ten Commandments of Great Nutrition" emphasize what you should eat (rather than what to avoid), when you should eat, and why you should be eating certain foods.

Commandment I
Thou shalt never skip breakfast.

Think of your body as a campfire that dies down during the night. If it isn't stoked up with wood in the morning, the spark turns to ash. There's nothing left.

Your body awakens in a slowed-down state. If you don't eat breakfast to meet the body's demand for energy and boost the metabolic system, the body turns to its own muscle mass (not fat!) for energy and slows down even more, conserving itself for a potentially long, starved state.

Then when the evening gorge begins, most of that food will be stored as fat because the body isn't burning energy at a fast rate; the fire has gone out. The food you eat then is like dumping an armload of firewood on a dead fire.

Commandment II
Thou shalt eat every three to four hours and have a healthy snack handy.

Once you've begun your day with breakfast, the goal is to keep the system working for you. To prevent your blood-sugar level from dropping and to keep your metabolic rate high, you need food distributed evenly throughout the day. The blood sugar will normally crest and fall every three to four hours. As it begins to fall, so will your energy, along with your mood, your concentration, and your ability to handle stress. Going many hours between meals causes the body to slow down metabolically.

That means the next meal (healthy or not) will be perceived as overload; the nutrients will not be used optimally, and the lowered blood sugar will leave you sleepy and craving sweets. When you eat frequent, small meals, your body has a chance to metabolize those calories efficiently, burning them for energy instead of storing them as fat.

Several small meals a day deposit less fat than one or two large meals. You must keep your body fed with the right things at the right time to metabolize calories efficiently.

Commandment III
Thou shalt always eat a carbohydrate with a protein.

Eating evenly throughout the day is not the only important factor in keeping your metabolism burning high and your body working well. Every meal (and snack) should include both carbohydrates and proteins. Carbohydrates— fruits, fruit juices, and nonstarchy vegetables—are 100 percent pure energy and fuel for the body to burn.

Proteins (meats and dairy products) are the building blocks for the body, but if no carbohydrates are available, the body will burn proteins. Eat a carbohydrate with a protein to protect it from being wasted as a less efficient fuel source.

You need that protein for boosting the metabolism, building

body muscle, keeping body fluids in balance, and healing and fighting infections. But protein is so potent that you don't need much of it. Around six ounces of chicken provides all the protein you need in an entire day.

Commandment IV
Thou shalt double thy fiber.

Grandma used to say, "Eat your roughage." Now we are counseled to double our fiber. This can be done with wholesome foods prepared in a wholesome way—whole-grain breads and cereals, unprocessed oat and wheat bran, legumes, fresh fruits, and vegetables.

To increase your fiber intake:

► Use whole grains rather than the white, refined types. In the supermarket, look for labels such as 100 percent whole wheat, with the word "whole" first in the ingredient list.

► Eat vegetables and fruits with well-washed skins. Peel only those that have been waxed.

► Choose more raw or lightly cooked vegetables in as non-processed a form as possible. As vegetables are ground, mashed, pureed, or juiced, the fiber effectiveness decreases.

► Add a variety of legumes to your diet.

► Add unprocessed bran to your foods. Try eating it as a hot cereal or sprinkling it uncooked on your dry cereal.

Commandment V
Thou shalt trim the fat from thy diet.

Fat is a nutrient that the body needs in very limited amounts for lubrication and for transporting fat-soluble vitamins (A,D,E, and K). But when eaten in excess, fat:

► Increases your cholesterol level and your risk of heart disease and stroke.

► Increases your risk of cancer, particularly of the colon.

► Increases your risk of gall bladder disease.

► Elevates blood pressure, regardless of weight.

► And makes you fat!

As much as we need to eat carbohydrates and proteins at each meal, we don't need fat in the quantities we consume. One ounce of fat supplies twice the number of calories as one ounce of carbohydrate or protein, and research shows that fats in food are stored as fat on the body more readily than carbohydrates or proteins. Less fat in your diet means less fat on your body and less cholesterol in your blood.

Commandment VI
Thou shalt believe thy mother was right: Eat thy vegetables.

Vegetables and fruits are simple carbohydrates that provide a storehouse of vitamins, minerals, and other substances to protect against disease. They are also valuable no-fat, no-cholesterol sources of fiber and fluid.

Generally the more vivid the fruit or vegetable's color, the more essential nutrients it holds. That deep orange or red coloring in carrots, sweet potatoes, cantaloupes, apricots, peaches, and straw-berries signals their vitamin A content.

Dark green leafy vegetables such as greens, spinach, romaine lettuce, brussels sprouts, and broccoli are loaded with vitamin A as well as folic acid. Vitamin C is found in more than just citrus; it is also power-packed into strawberries, cantaloupes, tomatoes, green peppers, and broccoli. If they're loaded with color, they're loaded with nutrition!

Commandment VII
Thou shalt get thy vitamins and minerals from food, not pills.

Can good nutrition be put into a capsule? No! Do you need to take vitamin-mineral supplements? It depends on your lifestyle choices. Do you skip breakfast? Lunch, too, sometimes? Do you travel a lot? Eat out frequently? Drink alcohol? Have a high-stress career or home life? Drink coffee?

If you answered yes to many of these questions, your nutritional state is at high risk. If you were to continue this course, you would benefit from supplemental vitamins and minerals. However, sup-plements are not the only answer. You can remedy the situation by subtly rearranging your life to include balanced, wholesome meals, and snacks at regular intervals each day. Just learn what to grab and when to grab it!

Commandment VIII
Thou shalt drink at least eight glasses of water a day.

Increasing one's water intake to meet the body's needs can produce miraculous results. However, most people grew up drinking just about anything but water.

Water makes up 92 percent of our blood plasma, 80 percent of our muscle mass, 60 percent of our red blood cells, and 50 percent of everything else in our bodies. What an important ingredient to good health!

Although often ignored, water is as essential a nutrient as the other five: carbohydrates, proteins, fats, vitamins, and minerals. We can survive many days, even months, without food. But we can survive only three to five days without water.

How much water do you need? Eight to ten glasses each day. As you begin to meet this need by drinking more water, your natural thirst for it will increase. As you learn what water does for your body, your motivations for drinking it will grow. Drinking water is habit-forming; the more you drink, the more you want!

Commandment IX
Thou shalt consume a minimum of sugar, salt, caffeine, and alcohol.

Called by many names—honey, brown sugar, corn syrup, fructose—sugar is sugar. It causes dental cavities, obesity, and high triglycerides; it wreaks havoc with diabetes and hypoglycemia. Cut back on your daily use of sugar and eat fruit to satisfy your natural craving for a sweet taste. Sugar abuse is not worth robbing yourself of precious energy and stamina.

As for salt, most people consume five to twenty-five times more than they need, leading to hypertension and kidney disease. Caffeine, a relatively mild stimulant, promotes irritability, anxiety, and mood disturbances. As for alcohol, one of the most common and addictive drugs of our time, much medical research is implicating excess alcohol as a factor in many killer diseases.

Commandment X
Thou shalt never go on a fad diet.

Why is it so easy to gain weight and so hard to lose it? Why is it so hard to keep weight off? The solution begins with an acknowledgment: Weight is not the problem; it is only the symptom. One's eating patterns and perspectives about food are the problem. We eat, not to meet our bodies' physical needs for nourishment, but for other reasons, often emotional. Freedom comes only in dealing with the problem, not the symptoms.

The word "diet" can be a nasty four-letter word. It speaks defeat and depression and denotes temporary action. We go on diets only to go off them. Diets don't work; they modify behavior only temporarily.

It's time to break the diet mentality with a nutrition consciousness that works for life. You can feel better, have abundant energy from morning till night, and look more radiant and healthy. Now that you have a new plan of eating and the knowledge to undergird it, you never need to diet again!

This material is adapted from two books by Pamela Smith: Eat Well, Live Well *and* Food for Life. *Both books are published by Creation House. Used by permission. Pamela Smith, R.D., is a nationally known nutritionist, author, and culinary consultant.*

REDUCE THAT FAT!

Like any worthwhile goal, reducing your personal fat intake requires some effort and commitment. It's not easy learning new ways to season food without fat, ordering more healthy at restaurants, and discovering positive snack foods. But the benefits far exceed the effort. Here are some ideas to trim the fat when grocery shopping:

▶ **Switch from whole-milk dairy products to skim or 1 percent milk and nonfat plain yogurt.** Look for fat-free or lower-fat versions of such favorite cheeses as ricotta, mozzarella, cottage cheese, and cream cheese. Check the label to be sure they have fewer than five grams of fat per ounce.

▶ **At the deli, go for the leanest meats.** Select sliced turkey or chicken and lean ham. Limit use of high-fat, high-sodium sausages and processed meats, such as hot dogs, bacon, and salami.

▶ **Buy whole grain and freshly baked breads and rolls.** They have more flavor and do not need butter or margarine to taste good.

▶ **Use the new all-fruit jams on breads or toast, rather than fat spreads like butter or margarine.**

continued next page

▶ **Keep an abundant supply of fresh fruits and precut munchy vegetables on hand for snacking.** Buy light popcorn and low-fat crackers rather than chips and cookies. Substitute sorbet or frozen juice bars for ice cream. Nonfat frozen yogurts may also be used sparingly; although they contain no fat, they are higher in sugar than ice cream.

▶ **If you're in a restaurant, have any sauces, dressings, toppings, or spreads on the side.** Apply them in limited quantities. The typical restaurant meal contains the fat equivalent of twelve to fourteen pats of butter. Also, watch the portions. Most restaurants serve twice as much food as you need. Order "lite eaters" portions or take leftovers home for a great meal tomorrow.

7

Setting a New Course

. . . .

■ They were among the written prayer requests received at my church recently. "My husband says he knows it's wrong, but he's leaving me for his secretary," one woman had written. "He says he doesn't feel the love he once did for me."

"Please pray for our teenage son, who is having problems with drugs," said another.

"We have a beautiful home and plenty of money, but our family is falling apart. Help!"

My wife, Sally, and I went home feeling very low. While we have had our share of struggles, we keep putting one foot in front of the other. But we couldn't help but feel sad that so many families are hurting. What's happening out there?

The last few decades have not been easy years for North American families. If the sixties opened the door to drugs and rebellion, and the seventies marked the "Me Decade," then the yuppie years of the eighties continued the trend of materialism and self-indulgence. We're still trying to figure out what to call the nineties, but maybe a reprise of the "Gay Nineties" would be in order since same-sex marriage has become a cultural hot-button issue.

But the times have also buffeted the plain old regular

marriage—the kind between a man and a woman. In these choppy wakes, America is left with the highest divorce rate in the world, a record number of nonmarried couples living together, and an attitude among many that children aren't treasures, but trouble.

■ **Isn't a new era needed? I mean, I can't believe some people. Last Sunday I struck up a conversation with a thirty-three-year-old man in the park. He was taking a break from a long bike ride.**

"If I had a family, I couldn't do this," he told me. He and his wife divorced, he said, because of his passion for physical fitness. "I like to get up and have my freedom to go."

When he pedaled off, I just shook my head. Why can't guys like him see the light?

Because so many new parents grew up in homes split by divorce, meaning they must navigate without the role-model benefit of having seen a mother and father work in unison. This, then, must be a time of rededication for Christian families before the start of a new century. We need to take off worldly ways and put on godly ways.

We must herald the arrival of a new era: The We Decade. Families. Together. Not statistical families who share the same roof, but husbands and wives who love each other more than bicycle trips. And children who can turn to a parent, not some http://www.com address on the Internet when they need to talk.

■ **In order for renewal to occur, what has to happen?**

Several things. Let's take a closer look.

► **Fathers need to trade looking inward for looking upward.** We hear a lot about getting "in touch with ourselves" and confronting the "warrior child within." That's hogwash. The answer is not within us, but, in fact, the answer is from above, within Him. "The Lord is my rock and my fortress and my deliverer," wrote the psalmist. Families need to be built on that foundation. If not, they will continue to crumble.

► **Fathers need to trade secular information for biblical information.** We are headlong into the Information Age, in which knowledge is heralded as the byte-size savior. Sure, computer modems have given us access to libraries around the world. Sure, sophisticated polls and surveys measure society's every social hiccup. Sure, we can read self-help books by the hundreds.

What we need is not more information but the *right* information, which is found in the Scriptures. The writer of Proverbs 24:3 says, "By wisdom a house is built, and through understanding it is established."

► **Fathers need to trade quality time for quantity time.** As mentioned elsewhere in this book, the quality vs. quantity time argument has become a rather haggard cliché—and perhaps the quintessential rationalization of the day.

Let's face reality: Our children can't mold their needs around the 7-9 p.m. Thursday time slot you've penciled in for them, Dad. Yes, they need quality time—a great quantity of it.

► **Fathers need to trade trends for tradition.** To be traditional is to be out of step. *Leave It to Beaver,* though admittedly no documentary on family life in the fifties, has become a sort of cult joke. But you wonder if the father of the fifteen-year-old cocaine dealer would trade places with Ward Cleaver. You wonder if the divorced mother who puts her young son on a plane every other Friday so the boy can fly home to his father would trade places with June.

As the nineties come to a close, families have taken on an air of trendiness. Demi Moore poses *au naturel* and nine months pregnant on the cover of *Vanity Fair.* Madonna has a baby and says she wants to protect her daughter from the world. Rock singer Melissa Etheridge, a lesbian, starts a family with her lover.

There's a problem with these faddish families, however. Children aren't some sort of dolls to slap on a *People* magazine cover; they're gifts from God. We need to raise them as such and raise them in the traditions of biblical principles— not what the world sees as hip.

► **Fathers need to trade corporate ladders for family bridges.** Do you view success by your position on the company organization chart? Are you married to your job? Some people may wonder, especially if you're spending far more after-work hours at the office than at home.

Isn't it interesting—and sad—how we'll treat a client with gushing respect, then come home and greet our family with practiced indifference? Isn't it time we got our priorities straight? Isn't it time we put as much time into relationships as we do into reports?

Work *is* important; we should do our best, but shouldn't we give the family some overtime for a change?

► **Fathers need to trade style for substance.** Image became more important than substance. Our politicians certainly run for elective office that way, but some of us go so far as to equip our cars with fake car phones to show that we have "made it."

Since God has already validated our worth, we need to be real people with real needs. Otherwise, we'll be so busy trying to keep up with the Joneses that we won't have time to nurture our own family.

► **Fathers need to trade materialism for relationships.** The nineties have brought us computerized refrigerators, big-screen TVs, and portable compact disc players. The decade has also ushered in a rapid increase in one-parent families, child-therapy sessions, and parents who decided children just weren't worth the effort.

The Baby Boom generation had more potential mothers and fathers than ever before. Yet the percentage of couples without children doubled in the last two decades. Couples who complain that kids are too expensive are probably the same couples who drive expensive cars and take lavish golf vacations.

Children, not products, bring us our lasting satisfaction. In the final analysis, what's more important—that our house has 3,700 square feet and a big backyard or that the people inside are close to one another? That our kitchen is straight from *Architectural Digest* or that we make time to eat together? That we have a state-of-the-art intercom system or that we actually communicate love to one another?

▶ **Fathers need to trade the fast pace for the slow life.** In becoming hurried adults, we've created hurried children, robbing them of time to use their imaginations and simply be kids. Wrote *The Wall Street Journal:* "If Mark Twain penned *The Adventures of Tom Sawyer* today, his barefoot hero would be shuttling between tennis camp and piano lessons instead of dreaming up pranks with his pal Huck Finn."

▶ **Fathers need to trade convenience for commitment.** In the nineties, convenience has become a way of life. Domino's delivers, we can shop on the Internet, and first-run movies can be ordered on Pay-per-View. Call it instant gratification.

But have modern-day conveniences brought us closer together as a family? No, because relationships can't be popped into a microwave oven and zapped to life. Good families are the products of years of nurturing, seasons of sacrifice, months of sometimes mundane attention.

At the root of such nurturing is a commitment from fathers. Lack of spiritual leadership continues to plague many homes. Women still buy three-fourths of all books on the family. They make up the bulk of radio-program listeners for the "Focus on the Family" broadcast. Men too often allow the family to be run on automatic pilot, feigning concern for what's really lack of commitment.

It's interesting how some fathers will commit themselves religiously to daily workouts, long hours at the office, and weekend bicycle trips. But it's sad when they don't commit themselves to their children with similar zeal or the spouse with whom they once stood and vowed—for better or worse—a lifetime of commitment.

■ **This has been interesting reading, but I'm a Christian father trying to do my best. Is there anything I should be watching out for?**

Keep this thought in mind: Children, it's been said, are the one thing we can leave behind us to tell the world what we were like. What will your children say about you when you're gone?

This material is adapted from writings by Bob Welch of Eugene, Oregon, and Robin Wolaver, a mother of six from Hermitage, Tennessee.

QUIVERING QUIVERS

When I told friends last year that my wife was expecting our fifth child, it was amusing to sit back and watch their responses.

"Another baby?" exclaimed one of my coworkers, giving me a look that asked me if all my cups were in the cupboard.

"Was it planned?" gasped another friend, thinking I didn't have the slightest idea of how babies were produced. Another friend teased me by saying, "My, you and Jeannette have certainly been busy! Tee hee hee."

Well, have we lost our minds? Or is having "another baby" in 1990s America lost its cool?

It's definitely lost its cool. Although having kids is cool in itself, having too many kids is not cool. The unwritten rule these days says, "One or two kids is okay; three is pushing it a bit; four or five is stepping over the line; and six or more means you should have your head examined."

You got it! Another comment we heard was, "How will you afford college education? Surely you realize that you should not have more children if you won't be able to send them to college." What should we say to that?

It should be your view that your family will have the opportunity of living forever in close fellowship with Almighty God Himself, who has promised to provide for every need and to perfect His highest purpose in your lives. And He can do that with or without a college degree in each of your kids' pockets!

Everywhere we go, we feel this pressure from friends. It's not very pleasant.

That's unfortunate—and a sad commentary on our times—because we

continued next page

devalue the joy that children bring to our lives. Many, many couples have fore-gone bearing additional children for fear of inadequate finances or having to make changes in their lifestyle. Society has reinforced that message, as you've noticed, by streamlining itself for the small family. Restaurants, automobiles, houses, bedrooms, and kitchens are all designed with Mom, Dad, and 1.7 kids in mind.

The pressures come from others, too. If your church refuses the presence of young babies at the women's retreat, that effectively means young mothers are expelled for the next fifteen years. The organizers have not considered that someone might be called to bear more than two children and desire to nurse those children longer than a token period of time.

Where did we get this idea that two children are the way to go?

If you came of age in the 1970s, you probably heard about the so-called "replacement theory," the idea that a couple should have just enough kids to replace themselves. But the American fertility rate has dropped below the replacement rate, and the only reason this country is growing is because of immigration. Isn't it time for the people of God to examine family size more closely?

—Robin Wolaver

9

· ·

Dads and Difficult Problems

1

Why Gambling Is a Bad Bet

■ **Driving down the Harbor Freeway in Los Angeles, I heard the following reggae-tinged jingle on my radio:**
Sweet dreams, may millions find you. . . ."
It was a pitch to play California's state lottery. I can remember going to church when I was a kid and listening to the preacher rail against the "evils of gambling," but now my state government is doing the best it can to separate me from my money. What's happening out there?

Throughout history, state-supported gambling has been an alluring quick-fix approach to raising tax revenue. Despite steady opposition, legal gambling has become widely accepted.

Gambling is enjoying unprecedented growth. Casino gambling is expanding; floating gaming parlors are back on the Mississippi; sports betting is increasingly accepted, and lotto fever has seized the entire nation in its grip.

Let's be direct: State governments are in the gambling business, and their pitches are becoming more direct with each day. "Everyone benefits from the lottery," claims a TV spot for "Money Match" in Virginia. An Illinois commercial urges residents to dip into their savings to buy Powerball tickets. Every holiday season, promotions remind viewers that lotto tickets make "perfect Christmas gifts."

After listening to such enticing ads, it's little wonder that millions of Americans believe lotteries are the best invention since programmable VCRs. Each day, slick million-dollar advertising campaigns purchased by state lottery commissions bombard TV audiences with claims that lotteries offer something for everyone: lower taxes, increased state revenues, and good, clean entertainment.

■ **The way I figure it, the California Lottery Commission wants me to believe that its lottery offers the quickest route to happiness and long-term financial security. So why not dream a little and take my best shot at becoming filthy rich?**

Because the sorry truth is that the odds are astronomical—around 14 million to one. Frankly, it's more likely that lightning will literally strike you than you winning a million-dollar jackpot from the state.

Casino gambling isn't any better. Sooner or later, the "house" will take your money. Have you ever heard of anyone making a living playing games of chance or betting on horse racing?

■ **But the news media play up the mega-dollar lotto winners all the time!**

What you don't hear about are the lines of down-on-their-luck families spending their last dollars on lottery tickets; the compulsive gamblers stealing from their employers to support their habits; and the lotteries actually generating small amounts of revenue.

Even big winners can't take it all with them. The state makes sure it gets its share of the payout, and long-lost "friends" and relatives will have their hands out as well. Besides, since jackpots are paid out in increments, inflation makes each year's payment worth less than that of the year before.

■ **But aren't lotteries a form of "painless taxation?"**

Those words ring hollow. Looking past the glitter, lotteries do not deliver on their pecuniary promises. In fact, after nearly thirty-five years of modern-day lotteries in America, five hard realities can be described:

- ► lotteries raise little tax revenue
- ► lotteries create few jobs
- ► lotteries hurt the poor
- ► lotteries encourage certain types of crime
- ► and lotteries create compulsive gamblers

■ When we voted to approve lotteries, we were told that lotteries were as "American as apple pie."

You were probably also told how the Continental Congress authorized a lottery to finance the Revolutionary War; how Harvard, Yale, Dartmouth, and other universities raised money through lotteries; and why three great Americans—George Washington, Thomas Jefferson, and Benjamin Franklin—supported lotteries.

Yet by 1900, every state had outlawed lotteries, many by state constitutional amendments because of widespread corruption and crime.

Lotteries began to make a comeback in 1964, when New Hampshire became the first state in modern times to reinstate a legalized lottery. New Hampshire voters forgot the lessons of history and saw the lottery as an easy way to avoid instituting new taxes. Nearly all states quickly jumped on the bandwagon; today, forty-one states and the District of Columbia have legalized lotteries.

■ You mentioned that lotteries generate little tax revenue. Why is that?

Lottery supporters love to point out the sums of money brought into the state's tax coffers, and it's probably close to $10 billion these days. That's a lot of money, but this figure shrinks rapidly when put in the following perspectives:

- ► **Lotteries are *not* a major source of state revenue.** In past years, lotteries provided only 1.9 percent of total state revenue, according to U.S. Census Bureau statistics. By comparison, states earned 29 percent of their revenue from sales tax, 22 percent from income taxes, and 24 percent from federal aid. No one has yet seen their state taxes go down because of the lottery.

▶ **Lottery revenues gyrate wildly, making them an unstable source of state revenue.** Over the years, some states have showed *decreases* in lottery revenues. Why? Because people tire of lottery games, and state governments must come up with new gambling innovations to boost sagging sales.

In Illinois, the revenue statistics for the lottery resemble a carnival roller coaster. When a new game is brought on board, interest climbs for a year or so. But as soon as the novelty wears off, income takes a dive. Illinois will try its luck with riverboat gambling, which has seen some initial success in neighboring Iowa. Since there is but one river between the two, competition is bound to be fierce. Gambling simply does not produce reliable, constant revenues for the state.

■ **But gambling revenues go to public schools, construct senior citizen centers, and buy open space. Aren't these worthy causes?**

They also say that gambling is an easy way to raise much-needed state revenues that can be dedicated to roads, hospitals, and health services. But these arguments just don't hold up.

First of all, dedicating gambling revenues to some noble cause—such as education—only conceals the moral question of how the money will be raised. A state could generate more money for education by legalizing heroin or prostitution, but the ends hardly justify the means.

Second, dedicating gambling revenues to education does not necessarily mean that public schools will get more money. California is one of the states that dedicates its lottery revenues to public education, but state funding of education has *dropped* $600 million—the exact amount raised by the state lottery.

State legislators, mindful that education will receive a certain amount of money from gambling, are merely shifting tax monies around like so many shell covers.

Legislators who want more money for education—or other noble causes, like toxic waste cleanup—should publicly convince their constituents of the wisdom of paying more taxes to support that goal. Appealing through legalized gambling is not the solution.

■ You're probably going to blow a hole in this argument, but don't lotteries create new jobs?

The only kind of employment created by lotteries—besides a relatively small management staff—are low-paying jobs for selling lottery tickets.

But lotteries may not create *any* jobs, said the late Dr. Walter Heller, once a leading economist for the Kennedy Administration and a professor of economics at the University of Minnesota. Dr. Heller also pointed out that people spend money on lotteries that otherwise would have been spent on other products or services in the marketplace.

The bottom line is that states simply do not create wealth—or jobs—with a lottery.

■ I've read that lotteries hurt the poor the worst. Can you explain why?

Since the ad campaigns for lotteries target their appeals to the have-nots, the lottery hurts the poor—and their innocent families—the most. In addition, the economically disadvantaged are hurt because a lottery is a regressive form of taxation: It is not based on one's ability to pay. Quite simply, poor people purchase lottery tickets for the same amount as rich people.

The lottery's marketing blitz, filled with get-rich-quick inducements, appeal more to the poor and middle class than the rich. Studies show that the poor play certain lottery games (such as the three-digit daily numbers games) out of proportion to their percentage of the population.

For example, one Michigan study revealed that lower-income

groups contributed only 2.16 percent of earned income statewide, yet purchased 6.01 percent of state lottery tickets. Another survey in California found that the poor wagered 2.1 percent of their income on the lottery, compared to 0.3 percent for the wealthy.

Lottery supporters hotly deny these charges. They object to lotteries being labeled a regressive tax because lotto sales are voluntary—a form of entertainment provided by the state. But by implementing a full-force advertising campaign, the state does influence its citizens to buy lottery tickets. Moreover, many states leave the impression that playing the lottery is a civic duty.

■ **But one good argument I've heard is that state-legalized gambling is a way to keep organized crime out. Why isn't that true?**

Lotteries, like other forms of legalized gambling, encourage at least two types of crime—illegal gambling and white collar crime.

As strange as it may seem, legal gambling begets illegal gambling. Organized crime can step in and offer their customers a better deal because illegal winnings aren't taxed; bookies will sometimes offer credit (impossible with legal games); and bookies frequently offer other types of gambling that the government does not, such as sports betting.

Lotteries encourage white-collar crime because legalized gambling can fuel compulsive behavior. These types of gamblers inevitably lose their money because the house odds are stacked against them. Some resort to embezzlement or thievery in order to support their habit. Bad checks are written and productive work time is missed. No one subtracts these costs to society.

THE BIBLE AND GAMBLING

The Bible does not explicitly condemn gambling, but gambling does violate several major themes in Scripture:

▶ Gambling encourages greed (Luke 12:15; 1 Tim. 6:10; Heb. 13:5).

▶ Gambling encourages materialism and discontent (Ps. 62:10; 1 Tim. 6:9).

▶ Gambling discourages honest labor (Prov. 13:11; 28:19).

▶ Gambling encourages "get rich quick" thinking (Prov. 28:20).

▶ Gambling encourages reckless investment of God-given resources (Matt. 25:14-30).

■ Don't lotteries create compulsive gamblers, too?

A Delaware study reported that as many as 86 percent of compulsive gamblers commit felonies. The American Insurance Institute estimates that as much as 40 percent of the nation's white-collar crime comes from compulsive gamblers. Perhaps that is why New Jersey now labels its lottery ticket terminals with the telephone number of the State Council on Compulsive Gambling.

In another instance, a Seattle woman reportedly used up her savings to buy lottery tickets, purchasing hundreds at a time. When her bank accounts emptied, she sold her jewelry collection, then stole $5,000 in silverware and a $2,000 ring from her housekeeping clients to maintain her gambling habit. She was later arrested while trying to pawn the objects for money. She was treated for compulsive gambling.

Lottery supporters admit that these stories are sad, but claim that compulsive gamblers are born that way and that they will gamble excessively whether the vice is legal or not.

Experts disagree. They say that gamblers are made and not born. They believe legalized gambling encourages those on the edge to cross over the line. A study commissioned by the U.S. Congress said, "A government that wishes merely to legitimize existing illegal wagering must recognize the clear danger that legalization may lead to unexpected and ungovernable increases in the size of the gambling clientele."

At least six states have begun operating compulsive gambling treatment programs—paid for

COFFEE, TEA, OR SLOT MACHINES?

Gambling fever has even reached the friendly skies. Such airlines as Swissair, British Airways, Singapore Airlines, and Alitalia are installing video screens that allow passengers to play poker, blackjack, or the slots.

In case you're wondering if any U.S. airlines are installing the same video gambling screens on board, the answer is no—for now. A 1994 federal law prohibits gambling on all flights originating from or going to the United States.

But can you imagine what could happen at 39,000 feet when Joe Sixpack loses several hundred bucks and begins acting like a sore loser? It seems some foreign airlines will be gambling with air safety.

by lotto game proceeds. Even more ironic is the number of bills introduced in Congress over the years that would establish a national lottery. Whether titled, "The National Revenue Sharing Lottery Act," "The National Social Security Lottery Act," or "The National Lottery and Deficit Reduction Act," the bills' sponsors ignore the growing evidence that gambling is indeed a bad bet.

This material is adapted from writings by Jordan Lorence, an attorney living near Washington, D.C., and the Minnesota Family Council in Minneapolis, Minnesota.

2

When Alcoholism Hits Home

. . . .

■ **I have a neighbor friend who drinks too much, but I've never been able to broach the subject with him. We were standing in his front yard a few days ago, and out of the blue he said, "You want to know why I drink? I drink because of that wife of mine. She's thirty pounds overweight and looks nothing like the day we got married."**

I didn't know what to say. Do alcoholics really think this way?

Alcoholics drink not because their wives are frumpy or their children are slow in algebra or their checkbook balance is too low—they drink because they are in the grips of a compulsive disease. Yet many alcoholics are quick to blame their families for the problem, and they can be very convincing. Meanwhile, sons, daughters, and spouses often accept the accusation that it is their fault.

■ **I'm sure that guy's wife thinks if she could lose a few pounds then her husband wouldn't drink so much. Am I right?**

It's very likely that she feels like she's the cause of his alcoholism, and consequently, the entire family is being torn apart. As everyone alters their lives to accommodate the drinker's habit, their own needs get pushed aside. They learn quickly that the alcoholism is not something they can talk about; it is a private shame.

This drama is enacted in countless homes. At an early age, Kate endured the trauma common to so many. Now in her thirties, she remembers vividly an evening when she was just nine years old. She was playing cards with her father and her big brother, laughing and having fun.

Her dad was smiling, too, and talking—perhaps a bit too loudly. Then her brother, who had begun to show increasing irritation at his father, suddenly threw his cards on the table and left the room. Kate's father, turning a flushed face to her, spoke in a strange and frightening way.

"The remarks were sexual," she recalls, "and they never should have been heard by someone as young as I was. I felt disgusted and scared, and I went to find my mother. But when I got to her bedroom door, I was afraid to go in."

Should she wake her mother? If she did, what would she tell her? It sounded terrible to say that her father was drunk. She decided that it wouldn't sound too bad if she said Dad was "half drunk."

"Here I was, scared to death because my dad was downstairs, absolutely stoned," she recalls. "I still can't believe what came out of my mouth. I rushed in and cried, 'Mom, come quick—Dad is one-quarter drunk!' She laughs at the incident now, but it remains a bitter memory.

■ What did her mom do?

Kate's mother sat up and, without a word, hurried downstairs. Later, as Kate curled up in her own bed, she worried about what she had said—what she had done. No one came to ask her if she was still afraid. No one ever explained that what had happened was not her fault.

"People need to be told that it is *not* their responsibility if someone else decides to drink," says marriage and family counselor Steve Powell, who lives in the Los Angeles area. Powell works with patients and their families in an in-hospital treatment program for alcoholism. He says that a lingering sense of guilt and embarrassment traps families into assuming more and more responsibility for all their loved one's actions.

■ **What would be an example of this?**

For instance, if an alcoholic drives home drunk and parks the car on the neighbors' front lawn, members of his family—particularly if they are Christians—typically spring into action:

The wife helps him out of the car and into the house, where he vomits on the rug. The daughter cleans up the mess while the son parks the car. By this time, the wife has managed to put her husband to bed. Then she apologizes to the neighbors ("John has been under a lot of stress at work lately . . .").

On Sunday, Mom and the children are at church, praying that God will help Dad stop drinking. The family members are compassionate, loving, and Christian—and they are doing everything wrong.

■ **What do the experts advise in this situation?**

Alcoholism treatment experts advise families not to help the alcoholic unless his personal safety is threatened. Steve Powell says that once it is clear that no harm has come to the alcoholic, nothing should be done: "Don't clean him up. Don't put him to bed. Don't move the car. Don't apologize for him."

■ **What's wrong with helping?**

Basically that kind of "help" dulls the natural consequences of a person's alcoholism. What is needed is tough love—the kind of love that will keep someone from throwing his life away.

If an alcoholic sobers up on the neighbors' lawn, he is surrounded by evidence that he has a serious problem. He may consider getting help before he dies—or kills someone else—in a car accident.

■ **What will the alcoholic probably do if his family decides to let him take responsibility for his actions?**

He very well may become enraged. "You have betrayed me!" he may sputter. "I needed you, and you let me down!"

Such a hard message is difficult for loved ones to hear. Compounding the problem are well-meaning pastors who don't fully understand alcoholism and often counsel family members to keep meeting the alcoholic's expectations.

What is needed are biblical models for love that include confrontation. Dr. George Patterson, director of psychological services at a Southern California alcoholism treatment program, says that he tries to help Christian families understand this important but uncomfortable approach.

"Respectful love and painful honesty are not mutually exclusive," Patterson emphasizes. He notes that while most people know how to be honest, they don't know how to "speak the truth in love." Learning that skill can be the key to changing the family pattern.

■ **What if the alcoholic doesn't want to hear me?**

An "intervention" may be necessary—a carefully planned confrontation between the alcoholic and his family and friends. During a four-to-six-week period, a counselor meets with the family members to help them recognize how the alcoholism has affected them and continues to damage their loved one, physically and emotionally. During these sessions, each family member prepares a list of specific instances during which he or she was hurt, embarrassed, or upset by the alcoholic's behavior. Angry, hurtful words must be replaced by bare, factual statements. Finally, the time for the actual confrontation is set.

Several guidelines are commonly recommended for staging such a confrontation:

▶ **The intervention must be scheduled at a time when the alcoholic is sober.**

▶ **It is best held in a doctor's or counselor's office.** The encounter should not be attempted without professional help.

▶ **Incidents should be read aloud calmly from an approved script with factual details and dates included.** This is how Joan reminded her husband: "Jim, the doctors thought I had cancer. The symptoms looked bad, and I was afraid. On June 12, however, you were not sober enough to drive to the doctor's office with me. I had no one to share my fear as I drove there. And when I got the results, I had no one to share my relief."

Joan's daughter read: "Dad, you were drunk on June 21. It was my wedding day. It should have been a perfect memory, but you weren't sober enough to stand in the reception line."

► **The alcoholic is then asked to take action,** often by entering a hospital treatment program or by participating in daily Alcoholics Anonymous (or a similar group's) meetings.

By the end of the intervention, the subject is miserable. Scene after scene of his destructive life has been flashed before him by those who care about him: his family, his pastor, perhaps, or his best friend or employer.

■ **In other words, the people who have been spending years keeping the problem quiet haven't been doing the alcoholic any favors.**

Exactly. Most alcoholics have to "hit bottom" before they agree to enter treatment. But an intervention raises the bottom they have to hit. It feels just as hard, just as intense, but this way they hit bottom before they lose their job and their family. And they have an alternative of hope: treatment.

Accepting that option, however, is difficult. For years, the alcoholic has believed he could stop drinking by mustering up enough "willpower." But that alone cannot free someone who is locked into a physiological addiction. Determined, strong-willed personalities with this compulsive disease have no more control over their drinking than weaker-willed alcoholics.

■ **What if the alcoholic refuses treatment?**

Well, at least his intervening family has taken an important step toward restoration: The truth has been told. The family can stop shouldering the blame for their loved one's condition, and they can stop participating in his sickness.

This article is adapted from writings by Joanne Ross Feldmeth, executive director of Child S.H.A.R.E. (Shelter Homes: A Rescue Effort) in Los Angeles.

3

Combating the Darkness

. . . .

An exclusive interview on pornography with
Dr. James Dobson

Editor's note: In 1997, Dr. James Dobson accepted an appointment to the National Gambling Impact and Policy Commission, but the Focus on the Family president is no stranger to government commissions. In the mid-1980s, he spent fourteen difficult months serving on the U.S. Attorney General's Commission on Pornography. In these questions and answers, Dr. Dobson talks about the dangers of pornography.

■ **Why was the Attorney General's Commission on Pornography created?**

Dr. Dobson: It was done at the request of President Ronald Reagan, who expressed concern over the explosion of pornography that had occurred since the first Commission on Pornography brought out its report in 1970. He asked that a second commission be established to study again the effects of pornography on individuals, on families, and on society at large.

I was there at the White House that day as he made this proposal, not knowing that I would be asked to participate in this effort. When Attorney General Edwin Meese responded to the President's mandate, he appointed an eleven-member commission. My name was on the list.

■ **Why was the second commission necessary?**

Dr. Dobson: For two reasons. First, the pornography industry today bears little resemblance to what it was in 1967 when the first commission launched its investigation. Sexually explicit materials that were illegal then and only available under the counter are not even published today. They are so tame that there is no market for them.

■ **What were the conclusions of that first commission?**

Dr. Dobson: Essentially, it said that pornography had a beneficial impact on society. It saw porn as a marital aid and as a source of information about sex. It also believed that pornography would have a so-called "cathartic effect" on the sexual tension evident in the culture. That is, by allowing people to have free access to sexually explicit material, their passions would be reduced and the desire to commit acts of sexual violence would be lessened. It was anticipated that incidences of rape and molestation of children would be reduced by removing governmental restraint on pornography. Unfortunately, the commission was wrong. Dead wrong!

■ **What is the scope of pornography and who is producing it?**

Dr. Dobson: Eighty percent of all pornography sold in the U.S. is produced in Los Angeles County and is then shipped illegally to the rest of the country. Eighty-five percent of this multi-billion-dollar industry is controlled by organized crime (the Mafia). Those who try to barge in on their business are either killed or mutilated. One persistent distributor was tied against a wall and a truck was driven into his legs. The Mob simply does not tolerate competition!

■ **How did your commission go about the task of assessing the problem of pornography?**

Dr. Dobson: We conducted a rigorous, year-long investigation that left us exhausted and emotionally depleted. Serving on this commission was the most difficult and unpleasant responsibility I have undertaken in my adult life. We held lengthy hearings in six U.S. cities, during which we heard testimony from victims of pornography, police officers, FBI agents, social scientists, and even from the producers of hard-core materials.

So many people wanted to testify that the hearings sometimes lasted as long as twelve hours a day with minimal breaks. Hundreds of pounds of documents and reports were sent for our consideration between meetings, which intensified as we approached the final report. But by far, the most distressing assignment was the material we were asked to review. Some of it was so shocking that members of the public fled from the auditoriums when it was displayed. Obviously, it was a very long year for me.

■ **Within the limits of propriety, how would you describe the nature of the pornography industry today?**

Dr. Dobson: It is *extremely* important for Christians to know what is being sold by pornographers, although I can't adequately describe it in a family book like this. If our people understood the debauchery of this business, they would be far more motivated to work for its control.

You see, most people believe that mainstream pornography is represented by the centerfolds in today's men's magazines. In fact, that is precisely what the ACLU and the sex industry wants us to think. But if one were to go into the sex shops on Times Square or in most other large cities in the country, he would find very little so-called normal heterosexual activity.

Instead, he would encounter a heavy emphasis on violent homosexual and lesbian activity, on excrement, mutilation, sadomasochism, urination, defecation, cutting of the genitals, enemas, oral and anal sex, instrumentation for the torture of women, and depictions of sex between humans and animals. Amazingly, there is a huge market for materials of this nature.

■ How did you handle the pressures associated with this responsibility?

Dr. Dobson: I have a very steady personality, but at times during this assignment I hung on to my emotions pretty tightly. Having been a faculty member at a large medical school and serving on the attending staff at a major children's hospital for seventeen years, I thought I had seen and heard just about everything.

I have stood in an operating room while a team of surgeons massaged a woman's heart after her husband blasted her at point-blank range with a shotgun. She never regained consciousness. I've seen children with pitiful deformities that tore at my heart. I've witnessed cancer in its final stages and all of the tragedies that arrive in hospital emergency facilities on busy weekends.

Like other professionals, I've learned to control my emotions. Nevertheless, nothing in my training or experience fully prepared me for my confrontation with pornography. I learned that purchasers of this material, like vultures, prefer their meat rancid and raw.

■ What aspect of what you saw most troubled you?

Dr. Dobson: The child pornography distressed me more than anything I've witnessed in my years. Though categorically illegal since 1983, a thriving cottage industry still exists in this country. Fathers, stepfathers, uncles, teachers, and neighbors find ways to secure photographs of children in their care. Then they sell or trade the pictures to fellow pedophiles.

Those pictures are often sold eventually to publishers in Holland, who print them in slick magazines and export them back to America. I will never forget a particular set of photographs shown to us at our first hearing in Washington, D.C. These pictures were taken of a cute, nine-year-old boy who had fallen into the hands of a molester. In the first photo, the blond lad was fully clothed and smiling at the camera. But in the second, he was nude, dead, and had a butcher knife protruding from his chest. My knees buckled and tears came to my eyes as hundreds of other photographs of children were presented.

■ **You were very critical of the way the mainstream press reported on the pornography commission, blaming it for censorship. Explain that.**

Dr. Dobson: There was not a single secular publisher in America who would print the commission's report, nor would any television network report the facts. CBS sent correspondent Bob Schieffer to my office to videotape a 45-minute interview for use during Dan Rather's evening news program. When edited, I was seen for exactly six seconds of irrelevancy between two full statements of objections by Hugh Hefner of *Playboy* magazine.

Similar interviews with *Time* magazine, the *Washington Post*, and *USA Today* went unreported. *People* magazine also requested an interview. The reporter and I spoke for an hour after she assured me that my time would not be wasted. The following week, *People* carried a lengthy cover story on the subject of pornography, but not a single comment of mine was included!

■ **Why do you think your remarks were ignored?**

Dr. Dobson: Because they apparently wanted to perpetuate the myth that pornography is limited to relatively mild material in men's magazines, surrounded by good literature and fashion features. They wave the banner of censorship while carefully editing the information given to the American people.

■ **What effect does pornography have on society at large?**

Dr. Dobson: So-called adult bookstores are often centers of disease and homosexual activity. Again, the average citizen is not aware that the primary source of revenue in adult bookstores is derived from video and film booths. Patrons enter these three-by-three-foot cubicles and deposit a coin in the slot. They are then treated to about ninety seconds of a pornographic movie.

If they want to see more, they must continue to pump coins

into the machine. The booths I witnessed in New York's Times Square were even more graphic, involving live sex acts on stage. These booths are also used for private or homosexual gratification and become filthy beyond imagination. Given the current concern about sexually transmitted diseases and especially AIDS, it is incredible that local health departments have not attempted to regulate such businesses.

States that will not allow restaurant owners, hairdressers, counselors, or acupuncturists to operate without licenses have permitted these wretched cesspools to escape governmental scrutiny. To every public health officer in the country I would ask: "Why?"

■ **What about the children who stumble onto their father's sexually explicit materials? How common is that, and what effect does it have when it occurs?**

Dr. Dobson: It would be extremely naive for us to assume that the river of obscenity that has inundated the American landscape has not invaded the world of children. There are more stores selling pornographic videos than there are McDonald's restaurants.

Latchkey kids by the millions are watching porn on cable TV and reading their parents' adult magazines. For 50 cents, they can purchase their own pornographic newspapers from vendor machines on the street. At an age when elementary kids should be reading *Tom Sawyer* and viewing traditional entertainment in the spirit of Walt Disney, they are learning perverted facts that neither their minds nor their bodies are equipped to handle.

■ **Talk briefly about pornography and the fathers reading this interview. What is its impact?**

Dr. Dobson: Raising healthy children is the primary occupation of fathers, and anything that invades the childhood and twists the minds of boys and girls must be seen as abhorrent to the fathers who gave them birth.

Furthermore, what is at stake here is the future of the family itself. We are sexual creatures, and the physical attraction between males and females provides the basis for every dimension of marriage and parenthood. Thus, *anything* that interjects itself into that relationship must be embraced with great caution.

Until we *know* that pornography is not addictive and progressive . . . until we are *certain* that the passion of fantasy does not destroy the passion of reality . . . until we are *sure* that obsessive use of obscene materials will not lead to perversions and conflict between husbands and wives . . . then we dare not adorn them with the crown of respectability.

This material is adapted from an interview that originally appeared in Focus on the Family *magazine. Used by permission.*

4

Ted Bundy:
A Fatal Addiction

. . . .

Editor's note: In early 1989, Ted Bundy, the convicted mass murderer who was scheduled to die in the electric chair, wanted to grant his last interview to Dr. James Dobson.

Bundy was aware of Dr. Dobson's crusade against pornography, and he wanted to share his final thoughts about the subject with someone who would not censor his comments. It was the only interview granted by Bundy, who admitted to killing more than twenty women in four states.

On a moment's notice, Dr. Dobson flew to Florida State Prison in Starke, Florida, where the following conversation was recorded on video-tape. Bundy was executed a few hours later.

Although some proponents of pornography have tried to discredit Bundy's final words, they stand on their own as a validation of what Dr. Dobson and others have been saying about the addictive, progressive, and destructive nature of hard-core pornography.

Dr. Dobson: Ted, you are scheduled to be executed tomorrow morning at seven o'clock. What is going through your mind?

Bundy: Well, I won't kid you to say that it's something that I feel I'm in control of, or something that I've come to terms with, because I haven't. It's a moment-by-moment thing. What's going through my mind now is to use the minutes and hours that I have left as fruitfully as possible, and see what happens. Right now, I'm feeling calm and in large part because I'm here with you.

Dr. Dobson: First of all, you were raised in what you consider to have been a healthy home.

Bundy: Absolutely.

Dr. Dobson: You were not physically abused; you were not sexually abused; you were not emotionally abused.

Bundy: No. No way. That's part of the tragedy of this whole situation, because I grew up in a wonderful home with two dedicated and loving parents. I'm one of five brothers and a sister. [It was] a home where we as children were the focus of my parents' lives, where we regularly attended church. [I had] two Christian parents who did not drink; they did not smoke; there was no gambling; there was no physical abuse or fighting in the home. I'm not saying this was "Leave It to Beaver."

Dr. Dobson: It wasn't a perfect home.

Bundy: No, I don't know that such a home even exists, but it was a fine, solid, Christian home, and I hope no one will try to take the easy way out and blame or otherwise accuse my family of contributing to this because I know, and I'm trying to tell you as honestly as I know how, what happened. I think this is the message I want to get across.

As a young boy of twelve or thirteen, I encountered outside the home . . . in the local grocery store and the local drugstores softcore pornography. As young boys do, we explored the backroads and side ways and by ways of our neighborhood, and often times people would dump garbage and whatever they were cleaning out of the house. From time to time we'd come across pornographic books of a harder nature . . . more graphic you might say, [of] a more explicit nature . . . and this also included detective magazines.

Dr. Dobson: And those that involved violence then.

Bundy: Yes, and this is something I think I want to emphasize as the most damaging kinds of pornography. Again, I'm talking from personal experience—hard, real, personal experience. The most damaging kinds of pornography are those that involve violence and sexual violence, because the wedding of those two forces, as I know only too well, brings about behavior that is just too terrible to describe.

Dr. Dobson: Now I really want to understand that. You had gone about as far as you could go in your own fantasy life with printed material, and then there was this urge to take that little step or big step over to a physical event.

Bundy: Right. And it happened in stages, gradually. It doesn't necessarily, not to me at least, happen overnight. My experience with pornography that deals on a violent level with sexuality is that once you become addicted to it—and I look at this as a kind of addiction—I would keep looking for more potent, more explicit, more graphic kinds of materials. Until you reach the point where the pornography only goes so far. You reach that jumping-off point where you begin to wonder if maybe actually doing it will give you that which is beyond just reading about it or looking at it.

Dr. Dobson: One of the most important [questions] as you come down to perhaps your final hours: Are you thinking about all those victims out there and their families who are wounded? You know years later their lives have not returned to normal. They will never return to normal.

Bundy: Absolutely.

Dr. Dobson: Are you carrying that load, that weight? Is there remorse?

Bundy: Again, I know that people will accuse me of being self-serving, but we're beyond that now. I mean, I'm just telling you how I feel. But through God's help, I have been able to come to the point where I—much too late, but better late than never—feel the hurt and the pain that I am responsible for. Yes, absolutely.

In the past few days, I and a number of investigators have been talking about unsolved cases—murders that I was involved in. And it's hard to talk about all these years later because it revives in me all those terrible feelings and those thoughts that I have steadfastly and diligently dealt with—I think successfully, with the love of God. And yet, it's reopened that. I felt the pain, and I've felt the horror again of all that. . . .

Dr. Dobson: Ted, as you would imagine, there is tremendous cynicism about you on the outside, and I suppose for good reason. I'm not sure that there is anything that you could say that people would believe. And yet, you told me last night, and I have heard this through our mutual friend, John Tanner, that you have accepted the forgiveness of Jesus Christ, and are a follower and a believer in Him. Do you draw strength from that as you approach these final hours?

Bundy: I do. I can't say that being in the valley of the shadow of death is something that I've become all that accustomed to, and that I'm strong and nothing's bothering me. Listen, it's no fun. It gets kind of lonely, and yet, I have to remind myself that every one of us will go through this someday in one way or another. . . .

Dr. Dobson: It is appointed unto man.

Bundy: . . . and countless millions who have walked this earth before us have. So this is just an experience which we all share. Here I am.

This material is adapted from Fatal Addiction, *copyright © 1989, Focus on the Family, and from writings by Rolf Zettersten, now publisher of Thomas Nelson Publishing. Used by permission.*

WAS TED BUNDY SAVED?

As Christians, we believe that God's love and grace are sufficient to redeem every sinner. But would the Lord forgive a murderer?

From a theological perspective, the response is an unequivocal "yes." We are all familiar with biblical accounts of people like the Apostle Paul and the thief on the cross who were saved in spite of treacherous pasts.

From a human perspective, however, it is difficult for us to understand how God could forgive a murderer like Ted Bundy. He killed not just once, but more than twenty times. Among his victims were young, innocent girls who endured unspeakable tortures before he took their lives in cold blood. He had been, without question, one of the most depraved, wicked, and violent criminals in our lifetime.

So it is with understanding why some people may pause a moment before acknowledging that even a Ted Bundy could have entered into fellowship with Jesus Christ by repenting of his sins.

Yet, to those who knew him in his final years, Ted Bundy's confession of faith dramatically changed his life. According to John Tanner, who led Bundy to the Lord and discipled him during 200 hours of personal contact over several years, Bundy's conversion was real.

In the 1980s, Tanner wrote Dr. Dobson and related the story of Bundy's new faith. "I am convinced that the Lord is going to use Ted for His purposes," Tanner predicted.

That opportunity came on the eve of Bundy's execution when Dr. Dobson learned that the condemned man wanted to grant his final interview to Dr. Dobson. Bundy knew of Dr. Dobson's work against hard-core pornography and violent obscenity, and he wanted to leave society with a warning about its addictive, progressive nature.

As Dr. Dobson approached the interview with Bundy, he was skeptical about the killer's conversion. But after two meetings involving thorough questions and prayer, Dr. Dobson came away with a sense that Bundy's Christian testimony was indeed genuine.

Their interview also suggests that Bundy did, in fact, know the Savior. Ultimately, only God knew this man's heart and only God can judge his life.

Fortunately, our Christian faith does not depend on whether Bundy's conversion was genuine. But his public confession reminds us of the lesson that God's love is powerful enough to forgive any sin and every sinner.

—Rolf Zettersten

5

Homosexual Rights: What's Wrong?

Editor's note: Homosexuals, who argue loudly for public acceptance of their behavior, are seeking public approval for their lifestyles. As part of their strategy, homosexuals are pressuring schools to adopt sexually explicit AIDS brochures and demanding that cities and companies grant them benefits typically reserved for heterosexual marriages. They are also seeking the legal right to marry.

If you are wondering what the Christian response should be to homosexual activism, these questions and answers will help. They are the arguments homosexuals and their sympathizers most often use.

■ **I don't personally approve of homosexual practices, but aren't homosexuals entitled to the same civil rights as all other Americans?**

Homosexuals already have the same rights as other Americans. They want special privileges.

■ **But homosexuals aren't looking for special privileges. They want protection and tolerance.**

If you want to create a distinction in the law, you're looking for special privileges. Homosexuals will not settle for tolerance. They want public endorsement. For example, the Gay Teachers Association's Bill of Rights calls for the affirmation of "the beauty and legitimacy of our lifestyle."

Homosexual leaders demand that schools offer sex education courses "to encourage students to explore alternative lifestyles," that school libraries be stocked with books extolling homosexuals, that books disparaging homosexuality be banned, that schools establish homosexual clubs, and that counseling services take a positive view of homosexuality.

■ We grant special status to other minorities. Why not homosexuals?

Homosexuals enjoy the rights ascribed to all Americans and do not warrant minority legal status. Homosexuals are not like other minorities. Race, nation of origin, and gender are innate, immutable, and do not necessarily affect one's lifestyle or moral behavior. Homosexuality, on the other hand, is not an inborn trait. Researchers think it's learned behavior. Evidence for this comes from several sources:

1. No one has found a single replicable genetic, hormonal, or chemical difference between homosexuals and heterosexuals (Marmor, J., ed., *Homosexual Behavior: A Modern Reappraisal*, Basic Books, 1980).

2. Those raised in nonreligious homes have a 450 percent higher chance of choosing homosexuality (Institute for the Scientific Investigation of Sexuality, *What Causes Homosexuality and Can It Be Cured?* ISIS, 1984).

3. A number of homosexuals do change their behavior. If homosexuality were innate, change would not be possible.

Most psychologists still believe homosexuality is learned, and even if there is a predisposition to homosexuality, it should not be encouraged. Alcoholics and child abusers may be biologically predisposed to their behavior, but we still hold them responsible.

■ **But don't homosexuals engage in sexual behaviors like the rest of the population, just with the same sex?**

Studies done in the mid-1980s found that the average homosexual has between 20 to 106 different partners per year—300 to 500 in a lifetime. AIDS is dampening gays' sexual activity, but the change has been minimal.

■ **Shouldn't a person do what he or she wants as long as it's in the privacy of a bedroom?**

Bedroom behavior has always been a concern of the community and society. There are laws against incest, child abuse, and wife-beating. A man can go to jail for raping his wife. Even marriages are regulated and licensed by the state. Besides, much homosexual behavior occurs in parks, bathhouses, cars, and other public places, not just in bedrooms.

■ **Doesn't the U.S. Constitution protect homosexuals' right to privacy?**

"To hold that the act of homosexual sodomy is somehow protected as a fundamental right would be to cast aside millennia of moral teaching," wrote former Chief Justice Warren Berger.

The Supreme Court ruled in 1986 in *Bowers v. Hardwick* that the Constitution does not provide a right for homosexuals to engage in sodomy. Twenty-four states still outlaw sodomy, with penalties ranging from a minimum fine of $200 to a maximum sentence of 20 years.

Every right carries with it a responsibility. All rights are balanced by competing rights. No one has the right to inject a harmful drug into his body, because as a society we've decided that the price we pay for such an action more than outweighs the right of the individual.

Likewise, the right of gay men to sodomize each other has a financial and social impact on the rest of society that negates the idea that the right to such privacy is supreme.

■ **If 10 percent of Americans are homosexual, shouldn't we treat them as simply an "alternative lifestyle"?**

If you repeat a lie often enough, it can take on the force of truth. Alfred Kinsey found that 10 percent of Americans were "more or less" exclusively homosexual for about three years of their lives; only about 4 percent were exclusively homosexual for life. Yet many scientists criticized Kinsey's study, saying his interviews didn't represent mainstream Americans. For example, present and former prison inmates, mostly sex offenders, made up as much as 25 percent of Kinsey's male sample group.

The University of Chicago reported in February 1990 that only 1 percent of Americans identify themselves as homosexual. Less than 1 percent reported having homosexual sex in the past year. A 1989 study in *Science* magazine said that 1.6 to 2 percent of the American population had engaged in male-to-male sexual activities within the previous twelve months. More recent studies have backed up these findings.

■ **Homosexuals really don't harm anyone else, do they?**

Because homosexuals couple with so many partners, they spread sexually transmitted diseases like wildfire. They represent just 1 or 2 percent of American society, but have 50 percent of syphilis cases and 60 percent of AIDS cases. Between one-half and three-fourths of homosexual men have had hepatitis B, a rate that is twenty to fifty times greater than among heterosexual males. Hepatitis A, amebiasis, shigellosis, and giardiasis are so common among homosexuals that doctors call these diseases "gay bowel syndrome."

During the first ten years that homosexual rights laws were in effect in San Francisco, the city's venereal disease rate rose to twenty-two times the national average. Hepatitis A increased 100 percent; infectious hepatitis B, 300 percent; and amoebic colon infections, 2,500 percent.

■ **Why shouldn't everyone have the right to choose their own lifestyle?**

Just because someone chooses a certain lifestyle doesn't mean society must ratify their behavior. A Ku Klux Klansman has the right to dress up in a white sheet, but that doesn't mean we extend social approval to his behavior.

There are people in our society who find sexual satisfaction from engaging in intercourse with animals—bestiality—and there are others who find pleasure by inflicting pain—sadomasochism. Would anyone suggest that these groups deserve special protection because they happen to follow bizarre sexual practices? What about people who cannot be sexually satisfied without molesting children?

■ **It is cruel and dishonest to compare homosexuality to bestiality and to suggest that all homosexuals molest children. Many homosexuals are decent, loving people who neither commit bestiality nor recruit schoolchildren. There is no single homosexual "lifestyle."**

It is true that the homosexual community is diverse. There are vast differences in fashion and sharp disagreement over politics and activist strategy. But the fact is that human physiology, psychiatry, history, and morality all argue strongly against all forms of homosexual behavior.

■ **Currently, there is a huge debate regarding same-sex marriage. Why should the state deny homosexual couples the same rights as married couples?**

Strong traditional families have been the bedrock of Western society. Families bring children into the world and nurture them to adulthood. Without them, government would bear an overwhelming burden, providing services to infants and children. Homosexual "domestic partnerships" are transitory, do not reproduce, and do not train others in sound morals.

■ **Why shouldn't homosexual couples be allowed to adopt children?**

Families that are allowed to adopt children have many qualities:

They are good role models, have a stable long-term marriage, and adequate income. Homosexual couples merely have the income.

The norm of homosexual promiscuity does not provide stability in the home. Also, much research shows that a child benefits from having both a father and mother.

■ **Homophobes, who fear gays, beat and sometimes kill them. Societies must be educated in order to understand that gays are no different from other people, and gay and lesbian pride marches are one way of doing that. Why do you oppose such an effort?**

Violence against homosexuals is reprehensible. It is against the law to assault any individual, regardless of his/her sexual preference. We don't need gay pride marches, we need better law enforcement.

■ **Our communities let other ethnic groups celebrate their ethnicity in public places. Why shouldn't we let homosexuals celebrate their lifestyles in public places?**

Communities do not let prostitutes, pedophiles, voyeurs, adulterers, and those who sexually prefer animals to publicly celebrate their lifestyles. Why should homosexuals get special privileges?

■ **You're just being homophobic.**

At one time, "homophobia" meant an "unnatural fear." Now homosexuals and their sympathizers in the media use the word to describe just about anyone who does not endorse homosexuality. It is a "hate crime" to speak out against homosexual privileges or to refuse to endorse homosexual lifestyles.

Most pro-family activists do not fear homosexuals; they simply disapprove of their behavior.

■ **Many great historical figures were gay.**

Men and women have been bedeviled with sins against nature

throughout the ages. A number of historical figures have made contributions to society in spite of their infidelities and afflictions.

■ You misinterpret the Bible when you say that God condemns homosexual behavior.

The writer of Leviticus 18:22, 24-25, says, "Do not lie with a man as one lies with a woman; that is detestable. . . . Do not defile yourselves in any of these ways, because this is how the nations that I am going to drive out before you became defiled. Even the land was defiled; so I punished it for its sin, and the land vomited out its inhabitants."

Paul wrote in Romans 1:26-27: "Because of this, God gave them over to shameful lusts. Even their women exchanged natural relations for unnatural ones. In the same way the men also abandoned natural relations with women and were inflamed with lust for one another. Men committed indecent acts with other men, and received in themselves the due penalty for their perversion."

The Bible couldn't be more explicit.

This material is adapted from writings by John Eldredge and Brad Payton of the Focus on the Family public policy department. David Davis lives with his family in Boone, North Carolina.

ONCE GAY, ALWAYS GAY?

My early childhood was filled with scenes of my father coming home drunk and smashing furniture. Mother, my older brothers and sisters, and I would stay with a neighbor until he was sober again. When I was eight, he nearly died from a brain aneurysm and spent the next six years in a VA hospital. That ended any hope of developing a relationship with him.

About this time, I was the constant companion of two brothers my age in our Atlanta neighborhood, and we began to experiment sexually with each other. Even though my family didn't go to church, my conscience still bothered me. I was too young to understand what was happening, but our activity introduced me to homosexual behavior.

My mother worked to support the family and was out of the home a lot. Since she worried that I didn't have a father-figure, she sent me to live with my

continued next page

older sister and her husband stationed in the Panama Canal Zone. I was excited about that, but my brother-in-law had a drinking problem, too. One night he even slapped my sister and choked her in front of me and their two-year-old son.

I was really frightened. Then he suddenly threw her aside and left the house.

I had two emotional reactions. First, I decided never to trust adults. Second, I hated myself for being male, thinking that the same anger I saw in my father and my brother-in-law was also in me. I returned home shortly after that incident.

When puberty hit, I had strong homosexual desires, but I didn't act on them since I had started attending church. I prayed all through high school and my first year of college that God would take away the urges, and when He didn't, I couldn't reconcile Christianity and homosexuality. So I left the church—and college—and took off for San Francisco's homosexual community. It was 1975, and I was nineteen years old.

When I joined the gay bar scene, I wanted to settle into one relationship. But since that didn't fill the void in my heart, I turned to drugs and alcohol. I stayed in California for six months, then traveled to other major cities. Eventually, I moved to rural Georgia and took a job in a convenience store, trying to put the past behind me. There a local pastor invited me to church, where, on separate occasions, two men asked me out. These guys were both married and, supposedly, upstanding Christians. That made me feel justified in my lifestyle. *At least,* I thought, *I've lived more honestly.*

By 1978, my alcohol and drug abuse was getting worse. So I began looking for answers in the Bible. Even though I didn't understand most of the passages, reading it gave me peace and a longing to find people who really believed its message.

A few months later, I left Georgia and eventually wound up in Boone, North Carolina. I arrived with a backpack and $60. I rented a room for a week, not expecting to stay, but I found a job immediately. After several lonely months, I went to a concert put on by a local church. The man who greeted me at the door shook my hand, looked me in the eye, and welcomed me. I thought, *This man knows the love of Christ.*

That night I was moved not only by the words of the songs, but also by the spirit of the people. When I returned to my room, I flushed away my marijuana, and said, "Okay, God, I want to be clean, and I want to know You. What next?"

The following Sunday, I set out for that little church and was heartily welcomed again. For the next two weeks, I went to every service Watauga

continued next page

Christian Center offered, and I listened—and watched—carefully. After a while, I even went to the pastor and apprehensively told him about my homosexuality. To my surprise, he didn't condemn me but answered my questions about the Lord. He also helped me see that my homosexuality was *learned* behavior, and that I could choose to leave it.

Then he helped me make a commitment to Jesus Christ, the only One who could fill my heart's need. The months that followed were the beginning of a wonderful adventure in learning loving acceptance from the congregation. I also began understanding that men in the church need encouragement to befriend those who struggle with homosexuality. I know now that the emotional makeup of homosexual behavior is rooted in self-hatred and the overwhelming sense of being different from heterosexual men, and therefore, not being able to relate to them.

But while I was confident when helping others understand homosexuality, I worried about dating women, since I didn't have a clue how to go about it. I prayed, "Lord, I can't do this. So would You please bring the one You want to be my wife to me. And make it *real* clear who she is."

Freida, a second-year teacher, and I worked in a nursing-home ministry and became acquainted. After much prayer, I asked her to date me. Four months later we were married, and we've now been married nearly eighteen years.

We have five wonderful children ranging in age from eight to fifteen who daily remind me of the joy I would have missed if I had continued believing the lie that homosexual men cannot change. Praise God, we can! I'm proof of that.

- by David Davies

6

Unplugging the New Age

. . . .

■ **I've heard New Age promoters say people need look no further than themselves for life's answers. How should Christians respond?**

This is a difficult question because the New Age is all around us. For instance, a middle-aged businessman learns in a management seminar that to be more productive, he must get in touch with his "innermost being." A teenage boy tells his parents their values are fine for them, but he must discover his own. Millions watch an ABC-TV miniseries of Shirley MacLaine floating out of her body high above the Andes and talking with "channelers" who conjure up the spirits of people long dead.

■ **I saw that movie of the week with Shirley MacLaine years ago. But it seems like I haven't heard much about the New Age movement recently. What's it all about?**

The New Age is a hodge podge of spirit worship, Hindu mysticism, and avant-garde psychology. In a society whose shared Christian roots are shriveling, this phenomenon is finding room to flourish.

Although the trend is called "New Age," its essence lies in ancient Hinduism, which holds that everyone—and everything—is part of God, part of a divine "oneness" within. Thus people need look no further than themselves for life's answers.

New Age guru Swami Muktananda, who is very influential in today's pop psychology, writes: "Kneel to your own self. Honor and worship your own being. God dwells in you as you." Adds Shirley MacLaine, "We already know everything. The knowingness of our divinity is the highest intelligence."

The view that everything and everyone is part of God is called pantheism, and it is worlds removed from the biblical view that God is separate and distinct from His creation. The belief that man is part of God is a sin that can be traced back to Creation itself: "When you eat of it, your eyes will be opened, and you will be like God, knowing good and evil," the serpent told Eve as he lured her to the forbidden fruit.

■ How do these nonbiblical ideas pose a threat to the family? If so, where does it surface?

First, although New Age influences seem to be everywhere, some are less harmful than others. When Luke Skywalker of *Star Wars* tapped into the "Force," a sort of universal power within himself, the lasting effect on kids seemed slight. But other children's movies pose more problems.

In the film *Dark Crystal* (produced by the late Jim Henson, the Muppets' creator and available in video), good does not overcome evil. The lovable Mystics do not win over the evil Skecsees. They fuse into one unified group of beings when the missing chard is restored to the magic crystal.

Writer Douglas Groothuis says of the plot: "All is one; ultimate reality is beyond good and evil. This is the essential teaching of much of Eastern religion." When a plot like this crops up unexpectedly in a children's movie, alert parents should point out the differences between what the movie teaches and what real people actually believe.

■ What inroads are New Age ideas making into the education arena?

New Age concepts have made frightening—but so far sporadic—inroads into schools. Values clarification is an example. It teaches children to discover and clarify their own values (because they have divinity within), and not have values imposed by others. The promoters of values clarification say it is appropriate in a pluralistic society, since it does not impose a particular belief system upon children (except, of course, the belief that anyone's values are as good as anyone else's, and there are no absolute values).

Another concept heard in some school districts is meditation—not on God or His Word—but on Transcendental Meditation, a barely disguised form of Hindu religious worship. TM was instituted in the New Jersey public schools at one time, financed by federal funds. A federal court declared it a constitutional violation and removed it, but TM is not dead.

Jack Canfield and Paula Klimek, pioneers of "transpersonal" education (education that allows for the spiritual—but not Christian—needs of children) promote to fellow educators the benefits of meditation. They tell teachers to call it "centering" or "relaxation exercises."

Elliott Miller of the Christian Research Institute says "visualization" is still another New Age educational concept. It instructs children to imagine themselves filled with pure light (their essential goodness).

■ Just how widely are these New Age concepts taught?

Thankfully, New Age teachings have not permeated the nation's classrooms to any large degree. But they certainly are more prevalent on the West Coast than elsewhere. Parents should be on the alert whenever they hear their children or teachers using terms such as "centering," "visualization," "the inner self," and "transpersonal" learning.

If parents detect genuine New Age influences in school (and not merely buzzwords used unknowingly), they are obliged to respond politely but firmly. You have the constitutional right not to have your children taught religious concepts with which you disagree. And New Age concepts are deeply religious, though often disguised.

It is usually fruitless for parents to argue that New Age ideas are "Satanic" or "unbiblical." If these arguments had any meaning for school officials, they wouldn't have permitted New Age concepts in the first place. It is better to stand on constitutional ground. The U.S. Supreme Court has said religious concepts need deal only in "ultimate realities" such as man's nature and his place in the universe.

■ What about the workplace? Do I have anything to worry about?

New Age concepts are present in the workplace. Robert Burrows of the Spiritual Counterfeits Project (SCP) reports on a Stanford Business School professor who leads his students through a meditation: "He tells them to let go of judgments, obstructing thoughts, past perceptions, whatever keeps them from tapping that 'reservoir of magnificence' within them."

Many large companies have employed "consciousness-raising" or "human-potential" techniques to improve employee productivity. These have a New Age religious basis, that the self is the source of goodness. This foundation is almost always denied, disguised, or ignored, however, to make the teaching palatable.

According to Miller, thousands of health-care professionals have learned "therapeutic touch" from New York University Nursing School Professor Dolores Krieger. Practitioners of this technique, which is based upon a Hindu religious doctrine, move their hands around a patient's body, trying to tap "universal life energy" and channel it for the patient's benefit.

■ How does one detect New Age concepts, since they are frequently shorn of overt religious references?

Be "worldview" conscious. Know clearly what your own view of God and humankind is, and you will be better prepared to respond when a suspicious concept or activity presents itself.

Ask questions about meaning. What is explicitly stated or implied about the nature of God, the nature of humanity, and the relationship between them? This process will aid parents as they prepare to respond.

It is also important not to respond wrongly, as some Christian books have done. Some books have depicted the New Age movement as a worldwide conspiracy, but without real evidence. Conspiracy theories are plentiful, but they seldom pan out, and usually they produce more unhelpful hysteria than constructive response.

■ **Why is the New Age movement growing? It seems like this is the biggest bogus religion out there.**

Some have found Christian worship dry and boring. Others automatically drift to whatever seems new and trendy.

Cult expert Brooks Alexander says of channeling: "Spirit contact fits neatly into the jiffy-solution mentality of our day. It's quick; it's morally undemanding. And above all, it provides a strong and immediate experience of the beyond to substitute for our alienation from God."

The movement underscores the truth that people want and need spiritual direction in their lives. A *Wall Street Journal* reporter who investigated channeling said as much: "Most [who flock to channeling] just want advice on personal problems from a higher being. Any higher being."

Trouble is, the advice is deadly. Brooks Alexander says, "The thrust of most spirit messages is to deny the reality of death and its function as judgment. The Bible implies that judgment is a spur to conscience, which convicts us of sin and leads us to our need of repentance and redemption."

Someone once said that people who stand for nothing will fall for anything. This has never been more true than with the New Age movement. The best protection fathers can provide their families is a strong grounding in the truth of God's Word upon which they can stand firm in any age.

7

The Significance of a "Significant Other"

. . . .

■ I called my younger brother and said I had heard that he had moved into a condo with his girlfriend.

"Don't hassle me," said my brother Dave. "I already know what you think."

"Why do you say that?" I asked.

"Because I know you're going to tell me that it's a major sin or something," said Dave. "I know you'll judge me, and I don't need that hassle right now. It was hard enough to make the decision without worrying about a guilt trip from my brother."

But we both knew what he was doing: My younger brother was living—and sleeping—with his girlfriend, all without "benefit of clergy."

This is a dicey family situation. Any thoughts on how I should handle it?

As you talked long distance—you and your younger brother, you may have been wondering how you could really connect with him. After all, these are gut issues, and you wanted your brother to understand why you felt it was wrong—this decision to move in with his girlfriend.

Realize that it may be tough sledding at the outset. Since your brother is not a Christian and doesn't understand the concept of sin, it won't do much good to tell him what the Bible says about sex outside of marriage. He'll just blow you off.

■ **You're right; I know he would. Besides, how could I judge my brother when I had my own mistakes to account for? Even though it wasn't my place to judge, I told him that I believed that living together was wrong. He didn't accept my statement, however. What could be another tack I could take?**

As you talk with your brother, gently remind him that his living arrangement is unfair to everyone involved. It's unfair to her. It's unfair to you and the rest of your family.

■ **What do you mean?**

This will be tricky, because you're going to have to get across the concept of deprived relationships. That means your brother must understand that marriage confers a new association, not just upon the couple, but upon other family members as well. You become "family"—with all the legal weight that society can muster around that designation. Cohabitation confers nothing. Even contrived labels such as "significant other" have no meaning. They are merely hollow attempts to establish a relationship—a relationship with a here-today-and-gone-tomorrow commitment.

When your brother moved in with this young woman—set up house, changed the phone message from "I" to "we," and embarked upon this pseudo-marriage, he cheated everyone concerned. He cheated your parents of a daughter and her parents of a son; he cheated his nieces and nephews of an aunt, and he cheated you of a sister-in-law. Worse, he cheated both himself and his girlfriend of the dignity associated with marriage and all that word implies: union, commitment, fidelity, honor, respect, family.

A couple who "lives together" can buy a sofa and some chairs, combine their kitchen utensils and linens, and "create" a home. They usually view their arrangement as a "trial marriage" at best or a "something to do" at worst. They'll usually tell you they are just testing the waters. Give it a few months, then decide. But things rarely work out that way.

In the meantime, you're holding your affections in reserve. Why begin to care for someone who may not be around next year? But if she does stick around, it's human nature to care about her. The nieces and nephews, being children and less circumspect, may fall madly in love with your brother's girlfriend. Slowly, inevitably, she may feel like "one of the family."

■ **That's what happened after my brother and girlfriend moved in together. Sometimes at family gatherings, they seemed quite happy; other times, they acted tense and upset. But I couldn't inquire, I couldn't probe; I couldn't even wonder. How do people testing the waters struggle to stay afloat on their own?**

They don't. Breakups occur much more often than in married couples, but that makes sense, since there is no legal commitment, no communal property to haggle over—or is there?

Don't be surprised if in a few months that you hear on the QT that she has quietly moved out while your brother was on a fishing trip. Because their relationship won't last. It can't.

Sooner or later, the woman (in nearly all the cases) will begin wondering where the "relationship" is heading. For the altar? If so, when? If not, why stick around? She may finally see the light and understand that besides paying half the rent, she is probably doing all the cooking, cleaning, and laundry washing. But that's par for the course for couples who live together.

■ **Well, that's what finally happened to my brother. She moved out, and that was that. But I wanted to ask my brother, *If you weren't ready to get married, why did you move in together in the first place?* But I couldn't upbraid a grown man. He'd tested the waters, found them unsuitable, and bailed. It's his life, his business. Meanwhile, I couldn't even say good-bye to the person I had begun to regard as my sister-in-law.**

They say that when a couple gets married, it's not just two people who walk down the aisle. Like it or not, parents, siblings, nieces, nephews—every family member—are inextricably yoked the moment the couple's vows are exchanged.

It's the same with living together. When two people test the waters of marriage without the formality of ceremony and certificate, like it or not, others accompany them into the surf. And when it's all over—when the furniture, kitchen utensils, and linens get redistributed, and the phone message is changed again from "we" to "I"—everybody involved huddles together on the sand, cold, wet, and shivering. It's hard to get warm again.

This material is adapted from writings by Elaine Minamide of Escondido, California.

8

Will I Go to Heaven, Son?

. . . .

■ **I was not raised in a Christian home, but fortunately a Campus Crusade worker led me to Christ in my junior year of college. These days, I'm concerned about my father—where he is spiritually. Mom became a believer before she died, but Dad is holding out. What can you say to encourage me?**

Greg Johnson had a father who was a great guy, but after three marriages, an alcoholic past, a brief foray into drugs (including times when Greg and his father smoked dope together), and a career as a professional gambler in Reno, his heart seemed pretty distant from anything spiritual. Ralph had politely tolerated Greg's faith for years, but he just wasn't interested when it came to hearing anything that made him examine his life.

Greg remembers a time when he was twenty-six years old and his father was in his mid-forties. They went out to play golf on a day that hackers live for: no wind, about seventy degrees, and a few silvery-white billows dotting the blue Oregon sky.

Greg had been trying to get in eighteen holes with his dad for months. Finally they connected on a weekday about 10 A.M. at Emerald Valley Golf Course in Creswell, Oregon—a regulation course that had always been one of their favorites. No one behind them, clear sailing ahead, riding with his dad in an electric cart—that he paid for! *Was this heaven?*

When Greg rolled up and parked their golf cart after the round, he had other things on his mind besides what the penciled-in scores told about their four hours of bliss.

Greg had been a Christian for about eight years and had decided it was time to talk seriously with his dad about his faith . . . or lack thereof. For some reason, however, that day seemed different.

As they headed for the clubhouse for a sandwich and a cold one (Coke, of course, since his dad was on the wagon), Greg was talking to God feverishly.

How do I bring it up without turning him off? What if he asks a question I can't answer? What if he rejects, ignores, or laughs at what I say?

■ **Those are the same questions I have. How did Greg start the conversation?**

As Greg thought about how he should begin, he decided to begin with a personal question. He said, "Dad, how's life been treating you?"

"Funny you should ask," Ralph slowly replied, looking Greg in the eye. "I've been doing a lot of thinking about that for some reason. I'm in the autumn of my life, Greg, and I don't always like what I see."

Greg's heart rate immediately doubled. *Could this be the day, Lord?*

"What do you mean by that, Dad?" Greg knew what he meant. Everything in his life pointed to that fact he had just admitted, but Greg wasn't ready for that type of honesty. He needed a few minutes to map out a quick strategy in his brain.

"I just mean that as a man gets older and has a chance to look over his life, there are certain things he regrets. He wonders if his remaining years will just be a continuation, or if they'll get better."

Greg asked a few more questions, then Ralph asked him one in particular that he'll never forget.

"Greg, do you really think I'm going to hell?"

Greg knew what he really was asking because of the way he asked it: *I haven't killed anyone. God sends only bad people to hell. I've done more good than bad in life, therefore, He'll let me in, right?*

■ **That's the type of question that I'm afraid my dad will ask. How did Greg handle this hot potato?**

Once in the past, Greg had explained to him that God didn't grade on a curve, that it was either pass or fail, but he needed something more descriptive.

"Dad, remember seven, the hole with the big gully filled with murky water in front of the green?"

"You mean the one you hit three balls into before finally limping one over to the other side?"

"No, that was twelve. The one with the bridge we drove over."

"Oh, yeah."

"Anyway, let's pretend God is on the green and you're on the other side. Your goal is to get to that green, but unless there's a bridge you'll never make it. Dad, that's the way it is between earth and heaven. If you live your life on the fairway side of the gully, never taking the bridge across, that's where you spend eternity. Eight years ago I realized the gully was my sin; I needed a bridge. The Bible says the bridge is what Jesus Christ did on the cross. It was the hardest thing I ever did, but I took that walk across."

"I see. So if I use Jesus as my bridge to God, that's the only way I can get to heaven."

"That's what the Bible says, Dad."

"Hmmmmm."

Greg felt he had finally broken through. His father seemed to understand.

■ **Did Ralph accept Christ's finished work on the cross for him that day?**

No, he didn't.

Instead, Ralph spent the next ten years living pretty much as he did the previous forty-five. His theme song in life truly was, "My Way."

Greg continued to pray and look for opportunities to share his faith with him, but because they saw each other only a couple of times a year, few chances came.

■ **You see, that's my dilemma. I see my father only a couple of times a year, and each time we visit, it's a reminder that he still hasn't given his life to the Lord.**

If you were to ask 100 men who didn't grow up in Christian homes what the toughest thing in life is, a high percentage would say, "Watching family members who don't know Christ try to live their lives without Him." A close second would be, "Trying to share my faith with unsaved relatives, especially my dad."

Since there are no pat answers, you won't receive any here. But Greg has learned a few things through the years that you may want to consider as you seek to share your faith in Christ to an unsaved father.

1. Pray for the Un-prayed for

Until Greg's dad married and inherited a church-going mother-in-law, he had little or no Christian influence in his life. Oh, perhaps a Christian teacher or two in his growing-up years took his name to the throne, but for the most part Ralph was left spiritually unprotected during the most significant years of his life. When hard times hit, he went to the bottle.

What did Greg do after he became a Christian? Since he was too scared to verbally share his faith with him, he prayed.

2. You're Still Their Kid

Our parents watch us grow up. Since they remember us "before" we became Christians, it's going to be difficult for them to see what we see. They're going to have to watch us in action, usually for years, before they're even interested in hearing our words.

If you're not aware of this fact, you'll be tempted to give up after a few years, often with decreased fervor in your prayers for them. But put yourself in their heads, and don't stop praying.

3. Send Reading Material

Whenever Ralph had honest questions, Greg would always try to give him a complete answer, but then he would ask permission to send him something to read. His father always said "Sure."

Ralph would bring up questions like "What about those who never hear of Christ?" and "How could God allow all those wars and the Holocaust?" If you get those questions, give your father Josh McDowell's book *Evidence That Demands a Verdict*. If he says that Christianity just doesn't make sense, send him *Mere Christianity* by C.S. Lewis.

Sending literature gives God a chance to speak through someone besides yourself.

4. Letters, Cards, and Phone Calls

Unless you're answering a specific question, fight the urge to preach when you send something through the mail or talk on the phone. Instead, simply express words of love and appreciation for who they are.

Greg's love for his dad—in short notes or long-distance phone calls—was always a big theme. He was laying a foundation in two arenas: relational and theological. Remember that people rarely like what you say unless they like you.

5. Serve and Pursue

Greg's dad had his first heart attack at age thirty-two. So it seemed he always needed help with the heavy stuff. Whether it was help moving from one house to the next or doing little things around his home, Greg tried to be the first to volunteer. Being inconvenienced and going out of his way always made a positive statement. And it was another way to make time to be with him.

It was August 15, 1987—Ralph's fifty-fifth birthday—and he'd flown to Portland, Oregon, to see some friends for a few weeks. Greg and his family were living in Seattle at the time, about a three-and-a-half hour drive. Greg was extremely busy with work. They spoke on the phone, and then Ralph said he'd love to see Greg and the kids. Greg paused on the phone, then asked him if he had lunch free the next day. Surprised, Ralph said he did. Greg told him they'd get in the station wagon and drive down. "Where would you like to eat?"

Greg took a vacation day off from work, and he and his wife, Elaine, piled their two toddlers into the car and drove to Portland for lunch. They met at a small Mongolian restaurant in downtown Portland and had a great time together. When they were through, Greg paid, and they said their good-byes.

Greg hugged him . . . hard, and they got back on Interstate 5 for the trip home. As he wiped away his tears crossing the bridge from Portland to Vancouver, Washington, he said to his wife, "I bet that's the last time I see him alive." He was almost right.

■ **What happened?**

Two weeks later, Ralph suffered a massive heart attack at his home in Reno. He was in a coma, and the doctor who had seen him for many years gave Greg absolutely no hope he'd recover. "There's just been too much damage over the years," he said. "We'll keep him alive as long as we can."

Greg jumped on a plane and got to the hospital about midnight. No matter how many TV shows or movies you watch, there's still something heart-wrenching about seeing your father hooked up to machines helping him breathe and eat. Greg prayed like he never had before—and he told Elaine to enlist the prayers of everyone they knew to do the same. He didn't know if God had reached him in some way before his heart quit working, but Greg wanted one more chance to find out.

For a week he stayed at his house, going through old photographs and letters he had stashed away. Dad remained in a coma, but he hung on. He'd visit twice a day, put his hand on his heart and pray, read Scripture out loud, and talk to him about the Lord. The doctors told him comas can last a long time, and they didn't know how much longer he could hang on.

Since his family needed him back home, Greg made the tough choice to return. He arranged an early afternoon flight back to Seattle. In what he knew would be his last visit, Greg arrived and went through his same routine. Suddenly, Ralph opened his eyes.

Greg was ecstatic! Though his father couldn't talk through all of the tubes, he blinked his eyes, one for yes and two for no. They "conversed" for about fifteen minutes, with Greg filling him in on what had happened.

Then Greg broached the subject he knew he had to broach.

"Dad, has the Lord been talking to you in there?" he asked, while gripping his hand.

One blink.

Then Greg quickly paraphrased the story Jesus told about the group of laborers who was hired early in the day, another group was hired at noon, and another just one hour before quitting time. They all received the same pay.

"Pop, God is not so petty as to shut you out just because you've lived fifty-five years away from Him. We've talked about all of this before. You know I've staked my life on the fact that Jesus Christ was crucified for my sins, then rose again to prove He was really God."

One blink.

"Dad, I'm going to say a prayer. If it really reflects what you want—and you don't have to pray this to please me—then you say it in your heart, okay?"

One blink.

For thirteen years, Greg had been laying a foundation in his dad's life. The relationship was strong, he'd heard all of the facts, and God had been gracious enough to give him one more chance.

When Greg was done leading him through the Sinner's Prayer, he asked, "Dad, did you mean that prayer?"

One blink.

"Do you have any doubts you're going to heaven?"

Two blinks.

For the next two hours, the tears came easily. Down the hospital corridor, in the cab, at the terminal, and looking out the airplane window at the hospital below. *Goodbye, Dad. I'll meet you on the first tee when I get to heaven.*

Greg was told that his father went back into a coma later that afternoon. He died five days later. Although no one knows if there's golf in heaven (let's hope so!), Greg knows he'll see his dad again.

Greg Johnson, former editor of Breakaway *magazine, lives in Colorado Springs, Colorado.*

9

Single Dads: When You Need a Mentor

Editor's note: This chapter is directed to single-parent fathers. Dr. Tony Evans of the Urban Alternative recognizes the importance of mentoring and recommends it for parents raising kids alone. In this chapter, he answers several commonly asked questions about mentoring.

■ **I have heard many people recommend mentoring as a way to help raise my daughter. What exactly is mentoring?**

Mentoring occurs when someone becomes a positive, nurturing role model for another person. The goal is to equip the father being mentored to manage his future in the day-to-day issues as well as the spiritual.

In the Bible, mentoring is called discipleship. Jesus was a mentor to His disciples. He taught them basic principles about money management and giving. He conducted culture sensitivity training with them. He challenged and motivated them to believe in themselves. He steered their life perspectives from temporal concerns to eternal matters. Jesus mentored the disciples in both the spiritual and the daily concerns to make them effective for God in their future ministries.

■ Is mentoring the same for everyone?

Mentoring can take many shapes and forms. It can occur one-on-one or with an organization or family unit that mentors more than one individual. It can also take place when one person mentors a group of individuals.

Mentoring can occur over a long period or for only enough time to accomplish a certain task like tutoring a child in a school subject. It can be done face-to-face as in teaching or indirectly when a child wants to pattern his life after a celebrity.

Because of different needs and varying spiritual levels, gifts, and callings, no cookie-cutter mentoring programs exist. Each is specific to the individuals they address.

■ I'm a single-parent dad. How important is mentoring in the single-parent home?

Usually, it's single-parent moms who need a male mentor for their children. They need someone to do activities with their children and answer questions only a man can understand. If the male mentor is married, her children will be able to observe a healthy marriage and interaction between husband and wife.

In your situation as a single-parent father, you could use a mentor for your daughter and also a mentor for yourself. A mature Christian can offer godly direction and accountability. Most of all, mentors can remind you that you are not alone and someone cares about you.

God never intended for any Christian to be a lone ranger. God's goal in establishing the church body was to create a place where people could develop committed relationships to enhance their spiritual growth. In Ecclesiastes 4:9 we read, "Two are better than one, because they have a good return for their work."

God developed the Christian two-parent family as the ideal structure for raising healthy children. He knew it took more than one to accomplish this task. But when a family unit does not fit the preferred scenario, another solution for the problem is needed. Mentoring provides such an answer.

■ How do I start and maintain a successful mentoring relationship for my child?

Many have found mentoring to work well in their homes by following guidelines similar to the ones below.

1. Define what you want from a mentor. Ask yourself questions that will help you decide what type of mentor to look for and what to tell the mentor about your expectations. (Remember that no one person may be everything you need him or her to be for your child, because of time restraints and other commitments.)

► Do you simply want someone to spend time with your child and involve your child in activities? This would require only short-term mentoring and may be your best choice if you cannot find someone who will commit to a long-term relationship. Youth clubs, sports, or other recreational activities at your community center might be good choices. Make sure the leader of such activities is the same sex as your child.

► Do you want someone to nurture your child's spiritual development? This could involve a short- or long-term commitment. If a person can't commit to full-time involvement, at least your child can become a part of nurturing church activities.

► Do you want someone to help your child with a particular task? You might contact an elderly person or a teenager who is considering a summer internship.

► Has your son become a problem, and does he need another male figure to help steer him with a stern hand? Ask a family to mentor him so he can observe a stable family environment where the father takes responsibility for his role, with his wife as a partner. He may also need to get involved in a group where there are other kids of the same age.

► What are the areas in which your children are struggling the most? Do they have difficulty trusting God? Do they crave masculine attention from a missing father? Are they sensitive to rejection? Is your daughter searching for a father figure in older men? Has your son become the "macho man" to hide his insecurity? Do they struggle with self-esteem?

2. Match an individual to your needs.

► Begin with the friends you have. Approach a godly man or woman in your church or at your job. Explain your situation and ask if he or she might be interested in spending a minimum of one hour a week with your child.

► If your friend is unavailable, ask for names of others who might be interested.

► Join a Big Brother organization, knowing you will have to add a spiritual emphasis on your own.

► Since coaches are usually role models, allow your child to join a sport, and ask the coach to spend time talking to him or her when possible.

► Ask an athlete if he or she would spend time with your child to help him or her learn a sport.

► Notice whom your child admires from afar—celebrities, athletes, or businesspeople. Discover as many positive attributes as you can about those people and discuss them with your child. Create goals to help your child take on similar characteristics.

► Involve the missing parent as a mentor in as many ways as possible.

► Talk to the child's teacher or group leader. Ask if he or she will spend some extra time with your child.

► Investigate what extracurricular activities are led by biblically or ethically motivated individuals in your neighborhood. A strong leader may impact your child.

► Challenge your church to start a mentoring program.

If you still don't know anyone who wants to become a mentor, ask your church to announce the need to the congregation and have them call the church. Leave information on how you can be contacted.

Once you have established a mentoring program for your child, talk with the mentor, group leader, or family to find out what they see your child needs and what they suggest. Let the relationship flourish naturally. Allow your child and the mentor to create variety in their friendship. With your approval on activities and your insight on what and what not to emphasize, the relationship should grow.

■ **What encouragement can you give me, as a single parent, to "finish well" with my children?**

While mentors are good, single parents should not underestimate the power of their own influence on their sons and daughters. Many mothers have raised sons to be quality men; dads have brought up daughters to be remarkable, godly women. And if you don't have another mentor for your child, know that God will make His grace abound toward you by being your child's mentor Himself.

God reaches out to every parent with love, provision, and hope. Since single parents have the same God as two-parent families do, they don't have to settle for second best. And God uses His people to help them accomplish the task—mentors from the hand of God.

This material is adapted from writings by Dr. Tony Evans, president of The Urban Alternative, host of a national radio program, and senior pastor of Oak Cliff Bible Fellowship in Dallas, Texas. For more information on how your church can start a mentoring program, contact The Urban Alternative, P.O. Box 4000, Dallas, TX 75208 or call (214) 943-3868.

10

How Loving Is a Living Will?

. . . .

■ **What is a living will? Although I'm hoping the Lord gives me many more years, I have been thinking about my mortality lately.**

Back in the 1980s, the name of Nancy Cruzan became a symbol of death's nightmare. A severely disabled girl in a persistent vegetative state. Feeding tubes. Patient rights. Messy court battles. A long, lingering death by starvation.

In its historic 1990 "right to die" decision, based on the *Cruzan vs. Webster* case, the Supreme Court held that competent adults have a constitutionally protected right to refuse or have withdrawn any and all medical treatment, provided they show "clear and compelling" evidence of their wishes. As a result, patients can sign an advance directive, commonly called a living will, which legally expresses the medical circumstances under which a person is "willing" to die.

■ **When Richard Nixon and Jacqueline Kennedy Onassis died a couple of years ago, there was much publicity about their refusals of "futile" treatment. Is this what you mean?**

Their deaths certainly renewed the public's interest in living wills. And since most health-care facilities receive federal funds requiring them to inform patients upon admission of their right to an advance directive, it is likely that living wills have fueled the trend for more patients to die by choice in nursing homes or at home. In Missouri, for instance, an estimated 16 percent more stay out of hospital beds altogether by refusing medical treatment.

■ **My perception of such a document is that it will be a prescription for a no-muss, no-fuss passing. Is that true?**

Depending on the document, the doctor, the diagnosis, and the decisions to be made, an advance directive may *not* be the answer to eliminating the sting of death's medical dilemmas.

If you are a senior citizen or have elderly parents, end-of-life care decisions need to be made before reaching the hospital admission station.

■ **How can I determine the best "treatment" for my family?**

It will be difficult. Even the best living will does not provide the flexibility or detail required to appropriately direct end-of-life decisions. They are difficult to write, let alone understand, and cover the variety of medical options available. (Most books on the subject say "see an attorney" before signing.)

Medical journals are chock-full of articles like "Confronting the Near Irrelevance of Advance Directives," which challenge the validity and usefulness of living wills. Emergency room personnel are encouraged to ignore one if there is any doubt at all that the document is valid. Ignored, perhaps, until long after you may have been resuscitated, ventilated, and exasperated.

For example, there was a Colorado Springs woman who was dying of cancer and had also battled diabetes for over ten years. Toward the end of her life, Lorraine slipped into a diabetic coma and was revived. Afterward, she often lamented to friends and family that she had been "brought back."

Despite a long history of diabetes, Lorraine's advance directive had not specifically covered what to do in case of a diabetic coma. And though she was spiritually ready to leave her physical body, the hospital staff was required to assist her recovery since her advance directive was not clear enough.

■ So that means you have to spell out exactly what you want?

Even if the advance directive is written well, it still might not be honored. In other words, where there's a will, there might not always be a way. A health provider who disagrees with a patient's advance directive is not required to follow it, although some states require that the patient be transferred to a doctor who will.

On the flip side of the medical chart, living wills can be too binding. While it's nice to try to tidy up the paperwork neat as a nurse's corner, death isn't a dress rehearsal. It's important for the patient to be allowed some leeway on such a once-in-a-lifetime decision.

Gregory Rutecki, M.D., works with kidney disease patients and has studied their acceptance of end-of-life medical care decisions and living wills. Some of his patients like to review or change their advance directives as many as four times per year. Up to 40 percent wouldn't mind if a designated decision maker had some leeway in adhering to an advance directive. Patients need and want support in making such important choices. Dr. Rutecki advises, "You can't have patients check off a list of features they want as you would at a car dealer. It's just too complicated."

Physicians may second-guess your intentions, wondering if you knew what you were signing. Since advance directives come into effect only after you're incapacitated, there's no way to hash out such details. And the physician must do the best he or she can in good faith. At least one study cited by the University of Minnesota's Biomedical Ethics Center suggests that physicians consistently underestimate when patients would want aggressive treatment.

■ Do family members lose all control and legal rights once the living will comes into effect?

According to the International Anti-Euthanasia Task Force, advance directives are designed to protect the legal rights of physicians, *not* patients and their families. Since most doctors and nurses would act in good faith, this should not be a problem. However, living wills can be interpreted to allow an attending physician or other health-care worker to terminate treatment *they* would consider burdensome or futile.

In 1993, Phyllis Robb reported that her seventy-three-year-old mother had signed an advance directive just before admitting herself to a transitional care facility following successful hip replacement surgery. Without consulting the alert and active patient, a staff person wrote on the chart "no code, patient's request," which means "don't give help in case of a heart attack."

Eleven days later, the patient went into cardiac arrest. According to Robb, "The staff did not call a doctor or attempt to treat her in any way. . . . They stayed by her bedside for twenty minutes while she died." No one called Phyllis, who would have demanded that her active, alert mother be given a chance to live and recover. Even though Robb's mother was not facing a terminal illness, she was allowed to die.

Another potential danger awaits those in the care of a physician with a different set of life values. By signing a living will, you may *intend* to let God's physical laws take their course and slip into death—but you may instead be on the slippery slope toward euthanasia.

■ It's very difficult to talk to my parents about end-of-life decision-making. What do I need to know?

With a little planning, you and your family don't have to take the confusion surrounding end-of-life medical decisions lying down. By obtaining a Durable Power of Medical Attorney (DPMA), your parents can avoid many of the hassles and uncertainties of living wills and end-of-life choices.

The benefits of having someone act as their proxy and health-care advocate far exceeds the scope of an advance directive. A DPMA protects them even if they aren't terminal. A DPMA empowers you to act on their behalf when they are unable to do so (under anesthesia, heavy medication, or unconscious) and make decisions based on facts, discussions with their physicians, and any options available at that moment. Please don't make the medical personnel decide which son, daughter, aunt, uncle, sister, or brother really knows what they want. Make it legal.

■ **What if my parents have fears of "being a burden" to the family?**

Tell them their fears are unwarranted, and a well-informed physician can direct the family to support groups and other resources to help them cope.

By discussing death with a counselor who shares biblical values, God's love and hope for eternal life can be reinforced. We are all "fearfully and wonderfully made" as the psalmist said; even in the last days of life we should cherish each moment.

Much of the pain suffered by end-of-life patients is mental or spiritual, not physical. The you-die-then-you-rot mentality of our society can tempt us to keep our eyes on the present world. A person who looks forward to an afterlife with God can rest peacefully, knowing that he or she is moments away from being in His presence.

This material is adapted from "How Loving Is a Living Will?" by Marianne K. Hering, Focus on the Family *magazine, July 1995. Copyright © 1995, Focus on the Family. Marianne Hering is the former editor of Focus on the Family* Clubhouse *magazine.*

LIVE AND LET LIVE

Over fifty years ago, as Britain's King George V lay dying, his doctor, Lord Dawson of Penn, injected him with two overdoses of morphine and cocaine to spare the king and his family any royal pain—and to make the press deadline for the next morning's *Times.*

Shortly after the affair was revealed, this poem circulated throughout Britain:

Lord Dawson of Penn
Has killed many men.
That is why we sing
"God save the King."

It happened to King George V; it can happen to you. If your doctor doesn't share your values on the sanctity of life, or if you want help communicating your views to medical personnel, here are a few resources to protect your medical rights:

► **Protective Medical Decisions Document (PMDD).** The International Anti-Euthanasia Task Force has designed a Durable Power of

continued next page

Medical Attorney regarding health-care decisions that protects the patient's rights and does not confer immunity to physicians. To receive more information and a sample copy of the PMDD, send $4 for the Living Will Fact Sheet and the PMDD to IAETF—Dept. LP, P.O. Box 760, Steubenville, OH 43952.

► **Will to Live.** The National Right to Life is compiling documents for each state that will protect the rights of the patient to receive life-sustaining treatment. Information about the Will to Live and your state's laws may be obtained by sending a letter of inquiry and a self-addressed, stamped envelope to National Right to Life, Will to Live Project, Suite 500, 419 Seventh Street, NW Washington, DC 20004.

► **Americans United for Life *Insights*.** For a well-documented but easy-to-read outline of court battles surrounding "right to die" decisions and a list of common misconceptions about living wills, a Durable Power of Attorney, and euthanasia, send a $4 donation and a request for the February 1992 issue of *AUL Insights* to Americans United for Life, Public Affairs Assistant, 343 South Dearborn Street, Suite 1804, Chicago, IL 60604.

► **The Loving Will:** This document is designed to ensure that food and water will be provided as long as the patient can assimilate them. It also states that the life of a child in the womb be favored in the event that saving both mother and baby cannot be reconciled. For information send a letter of inquiry and $7.50 to The Loving Will, American Life League, National Headquarters, P.O. Box 1350, Stafford, VA 22555.

BEFORE YOU SIGN ON THE DOTTED LINE

The terms in a living will are extremely difficult to interpret and can leave you vulnerable to the views of an attending physician who may not regard life as sanctified. living wills were first developed and written by pro-euthanasia groups and can be loaded with "right-to-die" buzz words, such as:

► meaningful life
► quality of life
► demeaning pain and/or suffering
► easy death
► prisoner of medical technology
► heroic
► ethically extraordinary
► burdensome
► nonbeneficial

Also, avoid any documents requiring treatment to be terminated if the patient remains in a persistent vegetative state for a certain number of days. This is too risky. Recovery of PVS and other "burdensome" patients is too common to assume the individual's condition will not improve. A designated surrogate decision can consider all the options and use good judgment when making a complex end-of-life decision.

Epilogue

Reader's note: I (Mike Yorkey) would like to end this book by printing one of my favorite articles in Focus on the Family *magazine by award-winning author Max Lucado. I think "Dearest Jenna" expresses the fears many fathers have while capturing the tenderness of our hearts.*

Dearest Jenna
by Max Lucado

I just put you to bed. Like every night, I rocked, and you resisted. I sat in the chair with you and your pillow on my lap. You lay belly-down with arms spread. You turned your head from side to side, attempting to ward off the arriving slumber. But finally you surrendered; your legs stopped their twisting, and your arms relaxed. Your body went limp, and your eyelids slid shut.

As you slept on my lap, I sat in the darkness. I stroked your golden curls and ran my fingers across your chubby cheeks. You were so innocent, so full of life—even in sleep.

I thought of tonight's big event. I couldn't get it off my mind. Tonight, for the first time, you walked! Oh, you'd taken little steps before, but always with caution and timidity. You would gingerly step one or two paces and then squat or fall. We had practiced with you many evenings.

"Go to Mommy," I'd say and off you'd go, holding my hand until you could almost touch hers, then you'd solo for one or two, or even three steps and then tumble into her arms.

But tonight, you were something to behold. You let go of my hand, spread your arms ever so slightly to get your balance, and you took off . . . eight, nine, ten, even twelve steps to Mommy. Then you looked at me. You turned your palms up, like you do when you want me to carry you, and started in my direction. You hesitated a few times. But then you got your courage and balance and came bounding to me. Oh, how we clapped and rejoiced!

Life has a way of whispering to us when sacred moments are occurring. And life whispered tonight.

As you released my hand and stepped alone, an emotion surged within me—an emotion I didn't identify until I held you sleeping in my lap.

What was I feeling? This may surprise you, but the emotion was fear. I was afraid.

You see, Jenna, until tonight, you depended on your mother and me for everything. Everywhere you wanted to go, we took you. Anything you wanted to do, we did with you. But tonight marked your "stepping out." Soon you won't want to be carried. Soon you will squirm from our arms and proudly walk alone.

I thought, *If she had known what she was doing, would she have done it? Would she have taken that first step?*

Your first step away from childhood. Your first step away from innocence. Your first step away from us—away from our world and into your own.

I imagined, as I watched you sleep, other first steps awaiting us in the future.

I thought of your first step up the sidewalk to school. Freshly scrubbed with shiny shoes and pigtails braided by Mom, off you'll go into the big world of pencils, chalkboards, and knowledge. Stepping proudly into the hallowed halls of chemistry, numbers, and words. What will you learn?

I thought of your first step toward friendships: When Christy or Megan or who-knows-who knocks on our door and asks, "Can Jenna come out and play?" Or when another little friend takes the place of Daddy as your buddy and Mom as your girlfriend and you ask, "Can I spend the night?"

And I thought of your first steps toward your own faith. How I pray they come. One foot carefully, but doggedly, in front of the other carrying your heart to that Roman cross, hands extended, inviting God to lead you as you continue stepping through the unpredictable fields of faith and fear.

And I thought of your first step down the aisle. Your purity, your youth, your arm entwined in mine. Your hands full of flowers. Your heart full of hopes and promises. Down the aisle we'll step, you holding my hand as you did tonight, and then, releasing my hand as you did tonight. But this time taking, not the hand of your mother, but the hand of a young man to whom I will entrust the most precious treasure I've yet received—my little girl.

So, as I held you so quietly in the darkness tonight, I felt fear. Fear that what we'd started tonight, we couldn't stop. I had a crazy yearning to push the pause button and freeze our days as they now are. You in our arms, forever giggling, kissing, and playing.

But life isn't like that. Those who love life must love it with open hands. We must release time and save only the memories. We must remember that with each first step comes a new journey of joy, surprises, and gentle whispers of God's presence.

So I'll let you walk, little angel. I'll release your hand and let you go. And I'll do my best to stay nearby. And should you fall, I'll rush to help you up. And should you stumble, I'll try to catch you. And should your steps lead you astray, I'll do my best to show you the right path.

But, Jenna, darling, I want you to know something. Should you ever grow weary of walking, or fearful of stepping into shadows, or just need to stop and see if you're aimed in the right direction, I'm here.

And, honey, you're never too old to curl up in my lap and sleep, securely knowing that any evil and pain or even hell itself would have to deal with me before it could touch my precious Jenna.

I love you,

Daddy